THE ORIGI

JELLY
ROLL
BLUES

THE ORIGINAL JELLY ROLL BLUES

THE STORY OF FERDINAND LAMOTHE, A.K.A. JELLY ROLL MORTON

THE ORIGINATOR OF JAZZ, STOMPS AND BLUES

by

William J. Schafer

Preface by Howard Mandel

FLAME TREE PUBLISHING

Publisher and Creative Director: Nick Wells
Editor: Julia Rolf
Consultant Editor: Howard Mandel
Project Editor: Polly Willis
Picture Research: Gemma Walters
Art Director: Mike Spender
Digital Design and Production: Chris Herbert

Special thanks to: Geoffrey Meadon and Claire Walker

09 11 12 10 08

1 3 5 7 9 10 8 6 4 2

This edition first published 2008 by
FLAME TREE PUBLISHING
Crabtree Hall, Crabtree Lane
Fulham, London SW6 6TY
United Kingdom

www.flametreepublishing.com

Flame Tree Publishing is part of the Foundry Creative Media Co. Ltd.

© 2008 The Foundry Creative Media Co. Ltd.

ISBN 978-1-84451-394-9

Printed in China

This book is for –

Richard and Lisse Schafer, plus Michael and Robert

Amelia and Simon Rutherford, plus William and Frederick

LIST OF ILLUSTRATIONS

■———————■

CONTENTS

PREFACE

Ferdinand Lamothe 'Jelly Roll' Morton is a far-larger-than-life-sized figure. Early in the first half of the twentieth century, in the years before the First World War, he emerged as a boastful French Creole piano prodigy – the 'Windin' Boy' from New Orleans' Storyville brothels – to tour the roughhouse territories of a fast-changing nation. Employing wit, talent, luck and sometimes the labours of significant others to support peripatetic wanderings throughout the southern Gulf Coast, Midwest and Southwest of the US, bound for Chicago, he arrived at a brand new, virtuosic yet naturally malleable and startlingly urbane sound. It was hot jazz, a transformation of American vernacular repertoire, minstrelsy, ragtime, ballads and blues with African-derived, Caribbean-steeped rhythms, European polyphony and exciting melodic strains, composed, arranged and spontaneously improvised, as exemplified by his theme song 'The Original Jelly Roll Blues'.

Jelly Roll's music announced an era of vibrancy, fluidity, inventiveness and sweeping societal change. As William J. Schafer writes in this book named after Morton's eponymous work, Jelly Roll's sound – and moreover his *style* – was almost immediately embraced as fitting the moods accompanying manifest transition. The popularity of his music grew and its influence broadened, though not always to its creator's profit; indeed, having fallen precipitously from fashion and critical favour, Morton and his music's reputation were restored only after his death in 1941. But the positive reappraisal has endured, so that now his oeuvre is recognized as among the signal achievements of modern American culture.

A founding father if not the sole 'inventor' of jazz, that most dynamic of music forms, Morton was, we learn from Schafer, both a visionary artist and a complicated man. His pride – hot jazz – remains potent, in-the-moment vivacity evoking strong emotion and capable of firing up good times. Morton was a man of many parts: a skilled vaudevillian, an inspired hitmaker, a canny bandleader, a conflicted husband and lover, a pimp, a gambler and a dandy, a relentless innovator, an exacting recording artist, a risk-taking independent entrepreneur, a raconteur of Homerian dimensions, a celebrant of the heights of life, sufferer of the depths of failure and possessor of boundless hope. Adapting advancing technologies, pursuing commercial opportunities, not always achieving his aims but inevitably engaged with life in flux, he produced in large measure the soundtrack for the Jazz Age and the Roaring Twenties, lay the basis for the Swing Era and remains resonant in much of the what has followed from then.

Besides contributing songs including 'King Porter Stomp' and 'Wolverine Blues' without recompense or attribution to the successes of Fletcher Henderson and Benny Goodman, Morton has been acknowledged by later-day jazz mavericks including Charles Mingus and Gil Evans, and such avant gardists as Ornette Coleman, Sun Ra, Henry Threadgill and Cecil Taylor. His story having been fictionalized for Broadway and Hollywood, it is hardly a stretch to mention that Morton's braggadocio and collage-like 'transformations' of well known musical tropes – foreshadowing sampling's appropriations – are echoed in the manner and methods of twenty-first-century rap and hip hop players.

Over time Morton has developed a mythic image, akin to such of his contemporaries as Mark Twain, John Philip Sousa, Enrico Caruso, Harry

Houdini, W. C. Handy, Irving Berlin, Charlie Chaplin, Ma Rainey, Bessie Smith, Bill 'Bojangles' Robinson, Bert Williams, Bricktop, Al Capone, Charlie Patton, Robert Johnson, the Carter Family, Jimmy Rogers, Paul Robeson, Al Jolson, Henry Miller, James Joyce and Duke Ellington. He contributed boldly to his own legend, as did all of the above, of course, but was unique in having dictated his story with typical lack of false modesty during an improvised oral history/performance demonstration recorded by Library of Congress folklorist Alan Lomax.

Lomax's invaluable recordings and further investigation into Morton's life and circumstances for the bedrock for all subsequent jazz studies and analysis; the issues it raises, contradictions and questions left unanswered have resulted in a stream of expansive research and enlightening criticism by authors including William Russell, Martin Williams, Laurence Gushee, Phil Patras, John Szwed and Howard Reich with William Gaines. Schafer, previously author of books on ragtime and New Orleans brass bands and a longtime contributor to the estimable journal *The Mississippi Rag*, has comprehensive knowledge of all those sources. He cites threads of their themes throughout his narrative, tying everything together with well selected facts, vivid anecdotes and his considered point of view. The organizational plan of Flame Tree Publishing's *Motivations* series prompts familiar Morton information to take fresh shape and generates original insights, but Morton really comes to life through Schafer's clear, calm, thorough telling.

Furthermore, Schafer makes Jelly's music sparkle with fresh, close attentions to some 30 years of repertoire that comprises dozens of classics – 'Tiger Rag', 'Dr Jazz', 'The Pearls' and 'Milenberg Joys' among them. The author describes Morton's canonical recordings with obvious pleasure in the task, empathy for his phraseology and admiration for his compositional accomplishments. He also illuminates the music's context, writing of Morton's receding era so as to convey significant facets and nuances of turbulent history across the decades.

For all his regard of the sheet music, piano rolls and 78 rpm shellac discs that were the media through which Jelly Roll Morton plied his art from the dawn of women's suffrage through Prohibition to the brink of the Second World War, William J. Schafer knows those artifacts are at best a distillation of the life the man practiced to perfection and of heartbreak in the course of extraordinary experience. Beyond all probability, the truth about Mr Jelly Roll trumps his legend. William J. Schafer offers clear contemplation of both aspects of man and music in *The Original Jelly Roll Blues*.

Howard Mandel
New York, 2007

PROLOGUE

'OUT VILE JELLY!'

—■—————■—

Powerful personalities are often called 'magnetic', and the analogy extends to the idea of 'polarizing' – like a magnet, these characters wield a negative and a positive pole. They attract and they repel. They are strongly loved or loathed, admired or despised, depending on how our own magnetic fields are presented to them. The man who started life around 1890 in New Orleans as Ferdinand Joseph Lamothe and ended it in Los Angeles in 1941 as Jelly Roll Morton was a remarkable case in point. He was revered, admired, emulated and despised, loathed and rejected when alive, and the paradoxical process followed him after death.

Commentators, historians and critics have read Morton's story through glasses either of rose or of bilious yellow, and some 60 years after his death – strikingly – he still attracts aspersion and ridicule as much as awe and admiration. His story is plagued with slanderous footnotes, outright lies and silly legends which obscure his major role as a pioneer of black music in the twentieth century and a major artist of popular idioms.

In the turbulent middle of *King Lear*, one of Shakespeare's blackest and most desperate tragedies, the supremely nasty Duke of Cornwall takes it on himself to blind the old, helpless and foolishly naive Duke of Gloucester. After a bout of directing tormentors in baiting and hurting the old man, Cornwall himself blinds his victim with malevolent glee, popping his eyes from the sockets like grapes (probably the basic

Elizabethan prop) and cackling, 'Out vile jelly!' For sheer mindless horror, it is a moment hard to beat, even if it derives from the climactic blinding scene in *Oedipus Rex*. The play is much about blindness, self-blindness and the failure of self-knowledge, which metaphors may apply equally to the story of Ferdinand Lamothe Morton.

Cornwall's exclamation might be the slogan and operating thesis of the detractors and enemies of Jelly Roll Morton, and their motives often seem as irrational and fathomless as Cornwall's, another curious example (along with Iago) of 'motiveless malignity'. It is hard to find another figure in the story of ragtime, blues and jazz who attracted lightning like Morton and equally hard to guess why. He was a loudmouth, to be sure, but that was part of his *schtick*, his vaudevillian persona, mostly kidding in the vein of frontier boasting and tall tales, but also a defence mechanism – in his case, the best defence being an immediate offence, with introductory phrases like 'I'm the greatest!' and 'Get away from that piano, you're hurting its feelings. Let the King take over!'. It is not hard to find parallel cases – Willy 'The Lion' Smith and other itinerant piano professors often employed a barrage of hyperbole as the opening salvo in the all-night cutting sessions that defined their roles. Mohammed Ali transformed himself from Cassius Clay to The Greatest on a similar tsunami of bragging. But Morton is the one champion boaster who gets the blame, it seems.

The testimony of Morton's sidemen and associates is almost entirely positive, admiring and even affectionate. He was able consistently to coax excellence from his musicians (sometimes they play 'over their heads' for him and never achieved such effectiveness in other settings). Even his competitors found him funny, energetic and – at most – mildly annoying in his eagerness to be known as Number One in any given situation.

But those who felt the push only from Mr Jelly Lord's negative pole often seem disproportionately damning, perhaps feeling out-talked and out-argued by the passionate Creole. Duke Ellington repeatedly went out of his way to badmouth Morton in oddly gratuitous ways. Marge Creath Singleton (Zutty Singleton's wife and trumpeter Charlie Creath's sister) had nothing but contempt and abuse for Morton, recalling him only as a braggart wastrel and a pimp. (Russell 493–96)

Morton's place (real or reputed) in the half-world of vice, specifically prostitution, seems to have shaped many responses to him. A covert trace of puritanical self-righteousness afflicts many of Morton's enemies, even though few admit so directly. Instead they make an odd, irrational leap from pimping to piano-playing and seem to imply that anyone who did one (however well) couldn't do the other at all well, the idea that Morton's ethical and legal position on (or in) the flesh industry somehow poisoned him as an artist – a purely moralistic assertion wholly indemonstrable.

Morton was not helped, in many ways, by Alan Lomax's organizing of his historic and invaluable oral autobiography, recorded in the Library of Congress in 1938. A somewhat naïve and stereotyped approach to Morton as a 'folk' musician, and Lomax's nearly prurient interest in the seamy and sensationalistic side of the New Orleans' notorious District and the jazz underworld, skewed some testimony and made Morton seem a pornographic 'party' entertainer. Morton was urged to put on record 'dirty blues' and offensive lyrics he preferred to forget, and some listeners have assumed he relished this role as a sexual titillator. To complete his important work with Lomax, he was forced to lose some of his dignity and his sense of musical and social decorum, hardly by his own choice.

His work with Lomax was groundbreaking, not only as a first oral history of a major jazz figure but as one of the first attempts to create a consistent history of jazz, from the viewpoint of a participant and eyewitness. When Morton intoned, 'Jazz began in New Orleans . . .', and launched himself on the hours of recording for Lomax, he pointed the way for all of jazz history and criticism, which in 1938 was embryonic. The scant serious writing on jazz in print was largely by enthusiastic amateurs like Hugues Panassie, who had only vague ideas of historiography or method (or of US culture) when he launched on his shapeless panegyrics to the wild, new American music that had fired European intellectuals over the past 20 years. Morton had a vision and an agenda for his history, and he commanded a remarkable panoply of facts and ideas to fill it all out. He wanted credit for African-American musicians and entertainers (with him being the prime example at hand), and he wanted to be taken seriously as an intellectual and an artist who knew the music from the inside and from the instant of its creation.

Morton's historical perspective got him labelled as an oldtimer who was no longer hip, a superannuated veteran (when in his forties!) like Sidney Bechet, James P. Johnson and others that the youngsters of the Swing Era wrote off as antique cornballs. His impromptu lectures on jazz history and the long-term context of the current music were not appreciated by the generation coming onto the jazz scene in the midst of a catastrophic Depression. They were anxious to get on with their lives and had no time to spare for a survivor from the halcyon days of ragtime, and an out-of-towner to boot, with that weird Creole accent, the flashy diamonds of the oldtime pimp and gambler, the tough attitude of the self-made pioneer.

Today, observers and contemporary artists portray Morton as a bad example, a mouthy character with a ton of braggadocio and attitude and precious little musical talent. George C. Wolfe's treatment of Morton in *Jelly's Last Jam* (1992) is a scandalous example of the practice, but it also recurred in the odd Italian romantic film *The Legend of 1900* (1998) and even colours critical discussions like those in Ken Burns' video project *Jazz* (2001), which poses Morton as a 'bad guy' in contrast to the purported saintliness of Louis Armstrong, an odious comparison of no value in understanding either of these great jazz innovators. Other Morton denigrators appear from time to time, usually armed with half-truths, outright lies or irrelevant nonsense.

But by all evidence Morton was not a liar, even if he usually coloured the truth to his own advantage. In fact, he possessed a remarkably retentive memory and a true raconteur's gift for narrative history, and many of his tales check out closely with historical facts and records, amazing in view of the circumstances of his oral biography and the sometimes offhand nature of his recollections. For instance, while he spun the complicated tale of cornet king Buddy Bolden for Alan Lomax's recording machine in 1938, he was able to recall the printed version of the little 'theme song' he attached to Bolden, published in 1904 as 'St Louis Tickle'. Morton could not remember the composer's name on the old sheet music, but he clearly identified the music itself, nearly 35 years on. (So identified with Morton's mythopoeia did the Bolden story become that Louis Armstrong, when asked once to play 'Buddy Bolden's Blues', said, 'Aw, we don't mess around with that number. Only one I ever heard do anything with it was Jell Roll.') (Russell 348)

Facts, names and places are vivid in his stories and nearly always check out on examination, erasing the idea of Morton as simply a pocket Munchausen. He had an almost pedantic dedication to the events of jazz history as he had experienced and understood it, and while an assiduous self-promoter, he was also a keen observer and often a generous commentator on musicians he knew and heard.

Morton's flamboyant Creole manner of boasting, jibing and teasing was widely misunderstood by musicians outside New Orleans, but even those he irritated valued his musical skills and insights. A young New York guitarist, Lawrence Lucie, was mentored by Morton, and he assessed his character thoughtfully:

Jelly Roll was always strict with musicians. . . . The only reason why some people would say something against him was because he was outspoken. If you weren't playing correct and he didn't think you were doing it right, Jelly would say, 'Do it this way,' and all those kind of things. And if you couldn't do it that way, he'd say, 'Well, you can't do it, so I'll get somebody else.' That's the type of guy he was. (Russell 527)

Most sidemen who worked with Morton deeply appreciated the impromptu education he gave them and were awed by his skills and advanced thinking as a player, a composer and a band leader.

Another younger man Morton brought along in his career was the fine New Orleans clarinetist Albert Nicholas, who vividly recalled a piano cutting contest in New York between Morton and Willie 'The Lion' Smith, a keyboard wizard as competitive and vociferous as Jelly Roll:

We could hear the Lion in the Rhythm Club – boomp-a-boomp-a-boom – playing solos and running all over the piano. So the guys say, 'Let's go in and hear the Lion man.' And a guy comes out and says, 'The Lion is gone today, he's playin' all around the piano.' The Lion's carrying on, and he looked up with his cigar to see Jelly was coming. And Jelly came to the door and he looked in and then finally Jelly came in. The guys were saying, 'Man, that Lion is gone.'

'Go Lion.'

'I'm in F. Now I'm in F sharp. Now I'm in C. I'm in A minor.'

And Jelly was creeping up and creeping up behind.

'Now I'm in B natural, a lot of musicians don't know this one.'

Finally Jelly came in on the left side. He was watching the Lion striding. Jelly's slick. These weren't pop tunes. This was fast fingering called stride piano – the left hand. Finally, Jelly said,

'Get up away from there, you don't know what you're doin'.'
Bam! That's what the Lion wanted, everybody fell out. Jelly
said, 'Now I'm in B natural.' That was the first time we heard
Jelly striding, because he always played with an easy tempo –
moderato. So Jelly said, 'Now I'm in this, and I'm in that key.'
This went on for about ten minutes and Jelly was really goin',
and everybody'd say, 'I didn't know Jelly could stride.' And Jelly
said, 'Man I invented all this kind of piano. Man, I invented
jazz.' (Russell 324)

This little sketch captures the essence of Morton as a musician's musician, his ardour and comic self-inflation coupled with his ability to dazzle by example, to spell out on the piano keyboard all the details of his genius as an improviser and a consummate entertainer. In the rough and tumble world of black show business, jazz and pop music, Morton was a fearless pioneer, fuelled by unshakable belief in his own vision and talent.

It is easy in retrospect to downgrade Morton and write him off as an eccentric and an unlimited egotist, but it is impossible to listen to his music, survey impartially the circumstances under which he composed and played it and to see him as an impostor, a faker or a mediocre artist. He inscribed on his piano scores and in the grooves of those old 78 rpm records a unique legacy that displays the signature of his mind and heart in every measure. Now, nearly a century from the years in which Morton believed he 'invented' jazz, it is imperative to set aside the blatant distortions in his story generated by rivals, enemies and by distant strangers with ideological missions in mind.

Morton's story is far more interesting and entertaining than the sordid anthology of lies and fables circulated since his death in 1941. And his music, reissued now in myriad recordings in every electronic format, rolls ebulliently into that future Morton dreamed it would have. In the end, those 'little black dots' on the music paper in which Morton so deeply believed, and the sounds in the air they make when translated, are the ultimate authorities that assure us of who and what Ferdinand Lamothe Morton was and what he became. All the work and sweat and agony he put into his music comes to us in posterity as the graceful, seemingly effortless, sounds of his genius, music that still retains its powers to vanquish the strident voices of earthly judges and detractors.

CHAPTER ONE

THE PERSON

■———————■

New Orleans is a hot city, and windows are wide open even at night in the big houses 'up and down the line' on Basin Street in The District. From these open windows flow sounds of revelry in full swing, endless laughter, and shouting and music of all kinds. From down the street comes the jangle of a pianola, its rhythms kinetic and compelling, and somewhere beyond that a piano played more suavely in a waltz or a sentimental ballad. Out beyond The District are taverns and dance halls where bands play, noisy little combinations that crank out every novelty tune and fragment of ragtime known.

The young man stands on the sidewalk – he would instinctively think of it as a 'banquette' – in the dark and listens to the sounds around him. The sprawling city is a whole world, an unexplored universe of wonder – songs to be learned and sung, new ways to coax magic sounds from the piano keyboard. Somewhere here, in one of the grandest houses, is the great master, Tony Jackson (1876–1921), the piano tickler or professor known to everyone here in Nighttown as 'the man of a thousand songs' and 'the world's greatest single-handed entertainer'. Jackson rules the piano world of New Orleans as a benevolent despot; a player, singer and songwriter as debonair, magnetic and as charming as the Pied Piper.

The young man doesn't rightfully belong here. He is too young, wearing borrowed long trousers, one eye cocked for the likes of 'Fast

Mail', the city policeman renowned for his blazing foot-speed and the wicked leather thong on his billy club, which he uses as a switch on kids wandering into the proscribed region. But on this night no one runs him off the banquette and back to his respectable family home Downtown.

The young man's mother has died young – at 35 – of phthisic pneumonia, according to the contemporary medical jargon, in 1906. His father is long gone, having abandoned his wife and son. His family is breaking up, and he is pulled in many directions by his interests, beliefs and loyalties. He is about to embark into a large and incomprehensible world. Years later, as he tries to write an autobiography, he says: 'In my early youth I thought New Orleans was the whole world, in spite of school teaching.' (Russell 39) Soon he will find for himself how vast and diverse the world around him is, and a restless spirit will drive him all around the US for the next 35 years.

Here on broad Basin Street are houses where Jackson worked, the glamorous mansions of Gipsy Shafer, Antonia Gonzales, Hilma Burt, Lulu White and Countess Willie Piazza; also separate, unknown worlds where wealthy white men appeared as patrons and others worked – white women

Portrait of the Artist as a Young Man: Jelly Roll Morton in his twenties.

and some faded octoroons, 'Creoles of colour' in this complex, ethnic gumbo of a city, black maids and servants, black entertainers. Once upon a time gradations of colour, caste and class were rigidly observed, with freed blacks dating back to the beginning of the eighteenth century; with quadroon and octoroon women judged as fitting mistresses for idle young white men of the uppermost classes; with fiercely black men from Africa or Haiti dancing and drumming in Congo Square to keep the lifeline to Africa, the magic homeland, intact. Also included in the cultural mix were Portuguese, Spanish, Moors, Latinos from everywhere south of the Caribbean, and many other ethnic mixes – tricolours and Cajuns and Melungeons from the deep backwoods, who looked older than time and of purely mystical origin.

The languages of the city were also mixed and mysterious – Creole French and Cajun French; half-Spanish Tex-Mexicans from out west; gumbo-mouthed Mississippians from the Gulf Coast; a smattering of educated Germans, Italians and Sicilians who knew what the Black Hand meant; Irish who had adapted to the blazing heat and smothering humidity and had settled into an offensive midden called the Irish Channel, right behind the grand houses of the Garden District. Dialects and argots abounded, today boiled down into the abrasive-accented lingo often called 'yat' (as in the phrase, 'Where yat?') and sounding like an argot from Brooklyn or the Bronx, not the deepest south. Listen to Louis Armstrong – 'woild' for 'world', 'boids' for 'birds', 'thoid' for 'third'. Georgia's great film comedian Oliver Hardy, when he made sound films, spoke the same lingo.

And the young man is not sure where he fits into this chaotic cosmos: is he merely *Creole*, a Frenchified and halfway educated youngster, whose grandparents press him to be refined, dignified and genteel? Or, given the increasing brutalities of Jim Crow segregation that grows and expands like an evil fungus year by year, is he just 'black', a 'nigger', a *negro* (with a small *n*) at best?

Tony Jackson is a dark, distinctly Negroid man, but he is a flashy dresser in a high-toned style – expensive suit, whiter-than-white shirt, silk vest, diamond studs and tie tack – that all piano professors rush to imitate. But Jackson is a genius, *sui generis*. His prodigious talents and charismatic personality put him beyond category, far above the rules of caste, class and what many call 'race'.

The young man ponders The District itself, whose history he – like everyone else in New Orleans – knows well. It was put into law, a city statute drafted by Alderman Sidney Story, who lobbied for a reserved area for 'vice' – prostitution and all its satellite industries – like the places many European cities reserved. The law was passed and subsequently enacted by the city council, coming into effect on New Year's Day of 1898. The city's population rewarded the thoughtful and diligent Sidney Story by derisively naming the section 'Storyville', an appellation that never wore off.

A section of Downtown, bounded by North Robertson and North Basin Streets and by Customhouse (later Iberville) and St Louis Streets,

New Orleans' District: Basin Street 'Down the Line', 1909. Tom Anderson's Saloon; Hilma Burt's; Diana and Norma's 'French House'; the Little Annex; Josie Arlington's; Martha Clarke's; and the grand Mahogany Hall.

was now the legitimized domain of wickedness and liberty. It drew vendors of flesh, of liquor, of gaming and of the music and hilarity that accompanied them. It drew crowds of the poor and innocent looking for ways up and out of poverty and confusion. It drew the young and curious like Ferdinand Lamothe, whose name would soon be transmogrified and garbled in various ways, who would be known as 'Windin' Boy' in The District as a youthful sexual adept, would on the stage adopt a trade name from one of his best-known tunes, 'Jelly Roll', would lift from a stepfather the name *Mouton*, anglicized soon into *Morton*, still fleeing those insistent French echoes in his past.

For the rest of his life the man we know best as Ferdinand Jelly Roll Morton would remain self-divided and uncertain about his root identity. He may have often wondered who he was, but from youth he knew *what* he was – a musician with an unquenchable appetite for finding, learning and transforming new music. To do this, he had to go on a tortuous odyssey through the underworld – the half-world of entertainment that was open to persons of colour in the United States of America in this brand new twentieth century. His nighttime venture to The District was just the first reconnaissance of a lifetime of travel, exploration and discovery. His new found land was the new world of music available under the placid surface of American gentility – the ragtime flowing from Kansas and Missouri, published by John Stilwell Stark in dignified editions, the new bits of rough blues and honky tonk brought down the river from turpentine camps by itinerant piano players who, in the common jibe of jazz musicians, 'couldn't read a note as big as a house' but who could sure read the black and white code of the piano keyboard and unravel all its hidden meanings.

Morton would later boast – no humble *confessions* for him, any more than for Casanova or Lord Byron – that he had survived as a pimp and procurer, a salesman for snake-oil remedies, a minor con artist, a skilled pool shark and (always) as an unquenchable self-promoter and fabulist, armed with a 'hard-hitting .38 Special that'll stop any living human.' (Lomax 131) He lived in a comic universe of self-inflation, Jelly Roll Land, where he was the King and the Master, who swept other players off the piano stool as he entered the barroom or dive – 'Get up off that stool, boy, you're hurtin' that piano's feelings! The king is here!' Willie 'The Lion' Smith, an alter-ego in distant Harlem, would immediately have understood Morton's roughneck humour.

⋙ ⋘

Morton had a brief, intense apprenticeship to New Orleans music and to the workings of the half-world – The Life – into which he was about to plunge. He saw and absorbed everything in The District, listened to all the ticklers, learned their tricks, and became steeped in the vices, crimes and disorder of this new life. It was a process not without cost to a young, properly reared Creole boy from the right side of town. He had to bite the bullet and take in everything of the world, even when it seemed wrong to him, when it opened a world of perversion and evil from which he was shielded in his youth.

In a fragment of autobiography Morton wrote in 1938, late in his life, he recalled the lurid corruption and decadence of The District as he first saw it in adolescence:

> *The streets were crowded with men walking in both directions; police were always in sight, never less than two abreast, this always guaranteed the safety of all concerned. Lights of all colors were glittering and glaring, music was pouring into the street from every house. Women were standing in the doorways, singing or chanting some kind of blues, some very happy, some very sad, some with desire to end it all by poison, some planning a big outing, a dance or some other kind of enjoyment. Some*

were real ladies in spite of their downfall and some were
habitual drunkards, and some were dope fiends as follows:
opium, crown, heroin, cocaine, laudanum, morphine, etc. All
these drugs could be had, some-times at the nearest pharmacy.
(Szwed, in *Complete L. of C. Recordings*, 53)

Morton's sensitivity here to the lurid scene and to the women trapped in
the flesh trade of The Life belies the reputation casually pinned on him as
a brutal womanizer and callous exploiter of working girls.

He recalled working in Emma Johnson's Circus House, a brothel
specializing in voyeuristic thrills, where elaborate pornographic dramas
unfolded, 'and the irony part of it, they always picked the youngest and
most beautiful girls to do them right before the eyes of everybody.' Morton
continued sadly, 'People are cruel, aren't they?' Then, characteristically, he
confessed his own complicity: 'A screen was put up between me and the
tricks they were doing for the guests, but I cut a slit in the screen, as I had
become a sport now, myself, and wanted to see what anybody else was
seeing.' (Lomax 127)

Once a 'sport', Morton felt committed to the half-world – in for a
penny, in for a pound. He had touched pitch and been defiled, but he was
determined to survive intact, to keep himself alive and kicking despite the
disease, ugliness and squalor of the life in which he wallowed. This moral
sense may have helped speed Morton on his way from New Orleans and
the riches to be plucked from the dungheap of The District.

Around 1907–08 he embarked on the endless peregrinations which
filled his adult life. He began, like an explorer, to probe the possibilities of
a life in music in the wide world beyond his beloved city. He tried the
North, well before the huge rush of migration there in the 1910s and
1920s: 'I went North on an excursion train in 1907, landed in Chicago and
found that nobody in town could play jazz piano.' (Lomax 130) Then he

tried the vastness of Texas, playing pool and running across the paths of reckless bad men and deciding he was not cut out to be a bigtime thug. He wandered up and down the great valley of the Mississippi River, finding little serious musical competition but learning all the roughneck piano styles and licks, shooting pool and running a few steps ahead of the local constabulary with Jack the Bear and other shady characters. Morton said Jack 'was a little bit of a guy and it seems like he must have stolen his name from some other big guy.' (Lomax 134).

In the course of these rambles he met W. C. Handy (1873–1958), at the start of his long career as a blues publisher, and Morton inserted a disrespectful little diatribe on Handy's abilities (or lack thereof) for Alan Lomax's disc recorder, to drive the points home in his ongoing debate with Handy about the 'ownership' of jazz and who 'invented' what, when and where. 'So much for Mister Handy,' Morton said to conclude that reminiscence. Lomax, the young Library of Congress folklorist and son of folklore pioneer John A. Lomax, would be a significant figure in Morton's later story. (Lomax 141)

Morton roamed across the Gulf Coast, coming into towns dead silent and appalled in the wake of lynchings. He found piano players of interest, notably one Porter King, the dedicatee of Morton's brilliant 'King Porter Stomp', which may reproduce King's riffing style. He then began to break into the world of vaudeville and tent shows – a whole cosmos of opportunities for a musician, raconteur and self-assured jack of all show-business trades. He worked with the famous Billy Kersands shows (Kersands was a black comic with a huge mouth, working in old minstrel/coon-song traditions), as well as with McCabe's Minstrels and other groups on the vaudeville circuit. In relating these years, Morton gave Lomax an edited and condensed version of the vital period in his self-prescribed apprenticeship as 'everything in the line of hilarity', probably because Lomax was not interested in or aware of their larger significance.

The experience was vital to Morton. It gave him time to organize and hone a piano style that was not just Tony-Jackson-and-water but an amalgam of all the robust, Deep South piano styles that he heard and absorbed with his sponge-like musical memory (Morton had something close to total recall for music and the people, places and things associated with it). It also made him secure that he could do whatever it took to succeed – play piano, compose, organize and lead a band, write and act in stand-up comedy, run a lowdown dive, whatever work was going. It gave him time to write and evolve his compositions – a library of effective and original piano pieces that could help him ice auditions or run off the local competition. The exercise was turning Windin' Boy, the young and fresh-faced New Orleans professor, into Jelly Roll, a grown man of obvious, considerable and impressive accomplishments.

Vaudeville, in the years when Ferdinand Joseph Lamothe entered it (to emerge a decade later as 'Jelly Roll Morton') was the primary form of live musical and dramatic entertainment for most Americans. It was available from major touring companies and minor troupes, who covered most provincial cities and towns and brought musicians, comedians, monologists, acrobats, jugglers, thespians and knockabout entertainers of every variety to the people in the years before radio and movies saturated the media market. The vaudeville stage was the goal dreamed of by young people with artistic talents, the ones who in later generations would fantasize about a life in the movies or TV, or a recording career.

The mixed media of vaudeville shaped twentieth-century popular culture in the US, and they began to transmit many varieties of African-American music from the South and elsewhere that were unknown to middle-class audiences. The remarkable Original Creole Orchestra from New Orleans toured the nation in bigtime vaudeville from 1914–18 and paved the way for the Jazz Age. The band was well-received everywhere and marked a watershed between earlier black vaudeville acts and a new kind of presentation based on the post-ragtime music of New Orleans, which would become the substance of Morton's musical career.

Morton idolized the band's powerful cornettist, Freddie Keppard, and his to-be in-laws bass player Bill and drummer Ollie 'Dink' Johnson were key members and organizers of this group. The Creole Orchestra's unique story is told in detail in Lawrence Gushee's comprehensive *Pioneers of Jazz*. Morton himself was a vaudeville-jazz pioneer. His years on the stage shaped him more profoundly than many jazz commentators have acknowledged, and he owed much of his vast and varied musical repertory and his yen for raucous comedy to the years 1907–16, when he was most involved with vaudeville.

This world of itinerant showbiz shaped Morton for the rest of his life, from his name to his lifestyle and appearance. While he approximated the flamboyant gaudiness of Tony Jackson and other high-fashion whorehouse ticklers in dress, the styles also fit the world of vaudeville. Morton relished a wardrobe of many fine suits, handmade shoes and silk shirts, as well as diamonds; these were his personal trademark, remembered by everyone who knew him in his prime – diamond stickpins, cufflinks and even diamonds set in his front teeth, the ultimate eyecatchers. His favourite phrase, 'Jelly Roll style', applied to more than the new kind of music he purveyed.

In the years between 1907 and 1917 Ferd Morton became a genuine professional musician, an artist and an entertainer in the mould of his hero Tony Jackson; however, he did it not by staying home and tending his business, but by going out into the world and taking his chances. He was a serious risk-taker in a world where risks for African-Americans could mean *life-and-death risks*. When Morton witnessed lynchings in small Gulf Coast towns, he knew that a stranger with a dark skin wandering into town might just be the next victim, and when he reminisced obsessively about packing his 'hard-hitting .38 Special', it was not boasting but a fact of everyday survival in the intimidating world that he had freely elected to explore and inhabit.

What emerges from details that Morton omitted from his condensed version of the vaudeville years is interesting, and may be one lost key to his character. In the Lomax rendering of his story (on the acetate records and in *Mister Jelly Roll*), Morton does not mention Rosa or Rose Brown, his vaudeville partner in the teens. Her presence is revealed in a publicity photo given to Floyd Levin, a jazz fan and writer who lived in California and chronicled the early jazz scene there, by Anita Johnson Gonzales (Morton?), who may or may not have been married to Morton, but who lived with him and was an important business partner in his California years (1917–23) and later. Anita knew of Rosa/Rose and her significance in Morton's life and career.

Rose Brown was a pretty young woman, light-skinned and dainty, with whom Morton teamed in vaudeville. They worked under the name of Morton & Morton, perhaps for show-biz purposes, simply for security, or because they were either married or 'married'. It is difficult to demonstrate that Ferd Morton was *ever* legally married to anyone. Perhaps he was a serial bigamist, hitching up with at least three women in his career – Rose Brown, Anita Gonzales and Mabel Bertrand. Or, in accordance with the notoriously lax mores of show business, he simply lived with all three women (and possibly more) in what satisfied everyone as 'marriage' – i.e. temporary domestic bliss, convenience and/or stability.

Given his immersion in an underworld of brothels and prostitution, and his off-and-on work as a pimp, Morton's attitude toward women was as complex and ambivalent as his attitude toward the concept of 'race'. Pimping was a way, like shooting pool or other itinerant gambling, to pick up easy money, if you knew the territory. Without venturing into two-bit psychoanalysis, it is hard to fathom his relationships with the women closest to him. Mabel Bertrand testified that he was a gentle homebody committed to his music and not highly sexed. Anita Gonzales kept him on a string and seemingly dominated him. One of his latest biographers, Phil Pastras, said of him, 'when it came to sex and his relationships with women, Morton was a deeply troubled man.' (Pastras 108) But, given the times and the mores, this may be a stretch. He had a tender side expressed in much of his music – his song lyrics and the romantic tango tunes, especially – but he was also a tough-minded businessman and survivor, and in times and places where women were commodities, business was business.

In any event, he was in public partnership of some show-biz kind with Rose Brown/'Morton', and by 1914 they billed themselves also as 'The Jelly Rolls'. This has bearing on central Morton issues or themes. Morton always said he composed the tune that became known as 'Original Jelly Roll Blues' sometime quite early – 1902, if you believe his earliest claimed birth-date (1885), or a bit later, if you accept that he was born c. 1890 (no one thinks that he composed the music as a 12-year-old). He then carried the tune with him (probably only in his head at first and then on paper) and refined it for a decade or so. It was probably unnamed or provisionally named, as many of his tunes were (see 'Pacific Rag', which he retitled 'Bert Williams' in dedicating it to the great vaudevillian, or 'Soap Suds', which he ultimately turned into the much more resonant 'Fickle Fay Creep').

Morton retailed an elaborate myth to account for his working name – 'Jelly Roll' – by attributing it to a spontaneous invention of Sandy Burns, a vaudeville colleague ('the first eccentric dancer in the United States') in these years of the 1910s (see Chapter 2). He was slightly squeamish about explicating the sexual connotations of the name (especially to the unsullied ears of young Alan Lomax and the potential ears of posterity via Lomax's acetate discs), so his 'working on the stage doing vaudeville' routine defused the name and made it just 'cute'. But the idea was always a powerful one, and when he and Rose called themselves 'The Jelly Rolls', they were capitalizing on Morton's identity and making her a part of it, as in 'Mr & Mrs Jelly Roll', or, more explicitly, something like 'two really hot performers who are sexually radioactive'.

Morton said the name of the tune was borrowed from his *nom de theatre*, but it may well have been the reverse: when he finished and named the tune, he became identified with the incipient hit. That is, he became 'Jelly Roll' just as The Rolling Stones lifted their name from a Muddy Waters tune. He was 'Mister Jelly Roll' in the sense that some film stars are permanently identified with one hit role. If this was a process occurring around 1914, then Morton jumped to make it profitable – he went to Chicago and took the score to Rossiter Music Co., who printed it in piano and band versions, an event many people then and now recognized as the first publication of a *jazz* number, as opposed to pop music, ragtime or blues scores (see Chapter 2).

It became a great hit and was played on pianos and by bands everywhere that year of 1915. When Morton called it the *original* Jelly Roll blues (Rossiter trimmed it back to 'The Jelly Roll Blues' on the sheet music), was he asserting its uniqueness and his own creativity, or had other musicians in earshot of vaudeville begun to poach it, as was common practice with uncopyrighted material? Morton conducted running battles with those he considered tune thieves and copyright pirates all his life, spending his last five years with Roy Carew setting up Tempo Music Co. in order to organize and establish his musical property. One way to clinch his rightful claim to creative genius was to name himself after his No. 1 hit tune and carry its transient fame with him throughout his life.

This idea helps to defuse some of the scorn and ridicule heaped on Morton's notorious 1938 claim to Robert Ripley, the eccentric cultural commentator and cartoonist, and *Down Beat* magazine (see Chapter 10) that 'I invented jazz in 1902 in New Orleans.' By Morton's reckoning that was not fantastic overreaching or boasting but simple fact: around 1902 he had begun work on a piece of music – half ragtime, half blues – that he would polish and finish in the next dozen years. It was then acclaimed as the 'first jazz score published'. Ergo, in 1902 Ferd Morton 'invented' jazz. In this light, the claim has as good a provenance as anyone else's and may have seemed to Morton a sober claim on what was rightfully due him: simple recognition. In the 1930s he also said that he had been fleeced by publishers, record companies and such consortiums as ASCAP (American Society of Composers, Authors and Publishers) and MCA (Music Corporation of America) of some $3 million, which also sounds far-fetched but may have been more or less accurate, counting nonextant royalties and fees which should have gone to him over some two decades of hard work creating money-making music.

The story of Morton & Morton is unclear. Impressive research has been undertaken by Lawrence Gushee and his colleagues in tracking Morton through vaudeville in the years 1908–14, by scouring show-biz columns of the nation's black community newspapers, and it is clear that Morton had a lively career with this beautiful woman, and the mystery of their relationship may explain some directions later in life (see *www.doctorjazz.freeserve.co.uk*). At some point in 1914, the act breaks up and Rose Brown/'Morton' disappears from his life, at least on public record.

There are small hints towards Rose's presence in the chapters of *Mister Jelly Roll* that deal with Morton's wandering years. Morton tells the story of a time in Texas when he bought a tailor's shop in Houston, possibly as a front for other activity:

> *I tried to organize a stock theatre in Houston, but relatives ruined it. So I took the money I had left and bought a tailor shop*

and went after the tenderloin trade, since I was a part-time piano
player in a couple of the best houses. I was sitting in my tailor
shop one day with a great big cigar in my mouth and my feet on
the desk — those days I thought in order to be a big businessman
you had to have a big desk — when Anna Mae Fritz (later in the
movies) came in with my girl friend Rosie. Anna Mae and I had
an argument and I slapped Rosie in the mouth and said I would
murder her if she didn't do like I told her. (Lomax 146)

The point to the episode in context seems to be that Morton was reaching the end of the line and losing control of himself, and this may have been the break-up of Morton & Morton — he does not otherwise mention Rose or their partnership in his long narration to Lomax.

The connection with Rose Brown is mentioned in brief notes made by Lomax or his secretary, misdated as 1905 but confirmed as a Texas story; William Russell, the longtime Morton historian, biographer and commentator, summarized these notes, saying Morton went 'back to Houston where he organized a show with Rose Brown … Their first show was in stock in San Antonio.' (Russell 52) Somehow, this pretty and elusive woman was connected with a whole vaudeville-theatrical career of Morton's, about which we know next to nothing. That he did not develop the narrative of these years for Lomax may mean that the private Ferd Morton won out over the very public Mr Jelly Lord in the conversation. Lomax may have prised pornographic blues and some too-graphic memories of brothel sex scenes from Morton, but he did not scoop this enticing mystery woman out of his heart.

As the autobiography unfolded, other secret abysses opened in Morton's story, probably the most important in his early life being his relationship with his godmother Eulalie Hecaud/Laura Hunter, the voodoo 'white witch' whose spell seemed to hang over the misfortunes that dogged him in later years. Like the melodramas concocted about mysterious Delta bluesman Robert Johnson, Morton's tale is susceptible to wide-eyed discussions of hoodoo and other mysteries of superstition. If you believe that Johnson did indeed sell his soul to the Devil at a Mississippi Delta crossroads, as his song 'Cross Road Blues' tells you, then you will believe that Morton was cursed and that various people – his agent Harrison Smith and Anita Gonzales, among others – practised black magic on him by way of powders and potions.

Morton was unashamed in talking about this half-world of magic and witchery – perhaps because it was laced with nostalgia for his childhood, when his godmother was a comforting presence, more tolerant of Morton's vitality and imagination than the rest of the straitlaced Creole family. It was also convenient to feel that the fault was indeed in the stars, not in himself; that he was not the pawn of generalized bad luck but the target of specific malevolence from powerful 'higher-ups' in the music business, from the crime connections rife around the jazz world, from inexplicable and absurd pieces of misfortune. If Morton sometimes radiated paranoia, it is no wonder. It is hard to imagine any person of colour living in his times and places who was not frequently overwhelmed with a belief that everyone was out to get him – because, given the conditions of a thoroughly Jim-Crowed society, everyone *was* in fact out to get him.

In his quieter moments, Ferd Morton recognized this mundane reality, but he constructed a world of music and fantasy to stave off the persistent bad karma that attached to all people of colour in the days of deepest segregation. When the dangerous and tragic world was too much with him, he could always sit down at the keyboard and play one of his prettiest melodies – say, 'Someday Sweetheart', 'Smilin' the Blues Away' or 'The Pearls' – to banish dull care.

CHAPTER TWO

THE MUSIC

T he single piece of music that let America know one Ferdinand Lamothe Morton had arrived was first named 'The Chicago Blues', a tribute to this new big city he planned to conquer. He started working on the music as early as 1902–05, but when he arrived in the Windy City in the mid-teens, in and out of small-time vaudeville and picking up work at the Elite No. 2 and other burgeoning Chicago nightclubs, he needed a new tune as an introduction. He polished the blues manuscript and took it downtown to Will Rossiter, the music publisher,

63rd Street and South Halstead, Chicago, in the early twentieth century.

where arranger F. Henri Klickmann (1885–1966), a master of the fast one-step ragtime in vogue, with racy compositions like 'Knockout Drops' (1911) and 'Smiles and Chuckles' (1917) to his credit, put it into shape as both a piano score and a band arrangement. This double publication heralded a new era – a fanfare announcing the Jazz Age. Commentators have often called what Morton titled 'The Original Jelly Roll Blues' the first true *jazz* publication. Rossiter's sheet music read simply 'The Jelly Roll Blues', but the top also was emblazoned with the words 'Full of Originality'.

Morton's stage name in vaudeville, he said in his mythopoeic way, derived from a moment onstage with Sandy Burns, a comic and 'the first eccentric dancer in the US', who fed Morton a line, and a new Morton persona was born:

> *One night while working ad lib on the stage, doing comedy, Sandy said to me, 'You don't know who you're talking to.' I said, 'I don't care.' Right there we had a little argument and I finally asked who was he? He said he was Sweet Papa Cream Puff, right out of the bakery shop. That seemed to produce a great big laugh and I was standing there mugging, and the thought came to me that I better say something about a bakery shop, so I said to him that he didn't know who he was talking to. He wanted to get acquainted, and I told him I was Sweet Papa Jelly Roll with stove pipes in my hips and all the women in town just dying to turn my damper down! From then on the name stuck to me.'* (Lomax 144–45)

Believe it or not! as Robert Ripley (a big player later in the Jelly Roll saga) always said. It may be as likely that Morton derived the nickname from his song title, the song that delved so far back into sexual folklore and blues mythology and that became itself famous. He was no longer 'Windin' Boy' (i.e. 'screwin' boy'), the kid professor from The District, but *Jelly Roll*, soon to be *Mr Jelly Lord*, composer of the first smash-hit jazz number.

The mythmaking tendency was part and parcel of Morton's vivid, playful and ultimately comic imagination. It is a delicious and vivid scene as he recites it, and we can smell the greasepaint, get some idea of the mangy elegance of vaudeville as it existed on most little stages in little places. We know he is reaching back into ancient blues imagery of 'jelly roll' as a sexual invocation – for the male and/or female sex organs, their sweetness, juiciness, size, etc. A jelly roll is long and phallic, but if sectioned it reveals a helix, a spiral swirl that is an ancient graffito for the vulva.

As young Morton worked through the musical resources at his command, he developed a distinctive approach to his art: his instinct was to absorb, master and then vary the music he found. Later he would call this highly personal process 'transformation', as he used the music around him – some 'found objects', such as blues themes and what musicologists call 'floating folk strains' or 'motifs' (such as the core of 'Buddy Bolden's Blues', also known as 'St Louis Tickle', by the pseudonymous 'Barney and Seymore' [Theron Bennett], or the bawdy riff 'If You Don't Shake', which appears in Robert Hoffman's 'Dixie Queen' rag [1906]),' together with some materials found in published music. His 1939 recording of Scott Joplin's 'Original Rags' (1899) is one of the best-known examples of 'transformation', but Morton at the time of his death was also working on a transformation of Tom Turpin's 'A Ragtime Nightmare' (1900); furthermore, on the recorded Library of Congress autobiography, he demonstrated the process by playing Joplin's 'Maple Leaf Rag' (1899) as written and then fully developed 'in Jelly Roll style', i.e. as what he thought of as jazz.

When Morton claimed to have 'invented jazz in 1902', this is what he meant. For him jazz was a process of alchemy, an imaginative re-rendering of music already available, as well as original composition from scratch. He was far too intelligent and shrewd to make this claim flatly and absurdly. As many musicians in his bands said, in exactly the same words, 'everything he said he could back up', and the musical examples that he left scattered across his career are the evidence showing how Morton was, in a true sense, the *inventor* – that is, *the* inventor – of jazz, as we commonly understand it in the early twenty-first century. (Which is not to claim that Morton was unique – others such as Eubie Blake, James P. Johnson and an unnamed army of black pianists on the East Coast were making the same discoveries in the years between 1900 and 1910. Like other 'inventions', jazz emerged from the *zeitgeist*, from the collective dreams of culture, just as dozens of tinkerers across America 'invented' horseless carriages and aeroplanes at about the same time in the 1890s.)

The process of invention and transformation has been a focus of swirling controversy in Morton's case for years. Like most ambitious composers and leaders of his era, he was accused of being a 'tune thief', and he countered by accusing others of the same. Morton's famous attack on W. C. Handy (in magazines that carried Robert Ripley's work) in 1938 was prompted by his sense of himself at the head of the jazz procession, and he fought with Clarence Williams, one of the most voracious music-nappers in the business, also trying to join the major music guild ASCAP (Artists, Songwriters, Composers and Publishers) and using the small orchestra-booking agency MCA (Music Corporation of America), which had represented him since the 1920s. Morton and his friend and champion Roy Carew spent years corresponding and working out legal strategies for getting Morton compensation for 30-odd years of composing, arranging, recording and publishing, for which he had little to show. He estimated the worth of his music now freely floating in the air at $3 million. He may well have been right, perhaps even erring on the side of modesty.

The charge of musical fraud or theft has dogged Morton, because he was so vociferous in claiming originality – the originality in the title of

'Original Jelly Roll Blues' – as his heraldic sign. One of the shrewdest critics, Martin Williams, tried to settle the idea in a seminal essay, 'Three-Minute Form', in the 1950s:

> *Like the question of how many of his compositions Morton stole or otherwise obtained from others (a question hardly confined to him – it might be raised about many major jazzmen), the question of how much musical knowledge he actually had and how much help he had with scoring is perpetually unresolved. One can get testimony, often from excellent jazzmen, that Morton knew little about music and played badly. One can get just as much reputable testimony that he was an excellent musician, ahead of his time in several respects, and could play extremely well. The only answer is his playing – with its faults and with its evident evolution and refinement. The answer to the complaint that Morton did not make his own orchestrations is the obvious fact that a single musical intelligence is behind them. Doc Cook, Tiny Parham, Mel Stitzel, and others have been mentioned as helpers with scoring. The answer undoubtedly is that, even if Morton needed help, the conception was nevertheless his.* (Williams 37)

The proof of Morton's single-minded genius lies in the many works that bear his unique stamp, the imprint of his mind and sensibility.

During his career he applied his method of transformation freely to musical materials that crossed his path. After his association with the New Orleans Rhythm Kings (NORK) in 1923 on an important recording session for Gennett, when he taught them the Jelly Roll way of playing his 'Milenberg Joys' (with a medium-tempo swing, not the headlong panic some Chicago bands used for the piece) and 'Mr. Jelly Lord' (*plenty sweet, plenty rhythm, plenty swing*), he borrowed one of their signature pieces, trombonist Santo Pecora's 'She's Cryin' for Me', and transformed it into 'Georgia Swing' (1928), using that term some years before Duke Ellington, Louis Armstrong and others made it the catchword of the big-band era. As blithely, Morton at the same 1928 recording session transformed the King Oliver's Creole Jazz Band 1923 hit 'Chimes Blues' (on which a young Louis Armstrong had taken his first recorded solo) into a quartet number of deep blue intensity, 'Mournful Serenade'.

On the 1938 Library of Congress autobiography recordings, Morton used an old sentimental pop song, 'My Gal Sal', as an example of his method of transformation. He took its square rhythms, swung them gently and added some jumping syncopations to make it modern and peppy, no longer corny but cool. It was much the same process that in the 1930s would be called 'swinging the classics', when applied to familiar light classical numbers or pieces by J. S. Bach.

Whether you think of Morton's reworkings as thefts, misappropriations, allusions, homages or just artistically licensed borrowings, they all reflect Morton's ability to take others' already good ideas and make them fresh, new and brilliant. They also show us how keenly Morton studied his peers and competitors, how well aware he was of musical trends and materials, and what he could make of them. He was a hustler, every day in every way, whether he was piano-playing, band-leading, pool-sharking, pimping or whatever – a step ahead of the competition and thinking of different angles and devious ways in which to sell his startling new music.

By the 1930s, when Morton – like most jazz musicians – was down and out in the deep crevasse of the Great Depression, his music had been reabsorbed and transmitted by every kind of jazz and pop musician still making music. As he cried out, 'When you play that horn, you're playing Jelly Roll!' he was not (again) merely being metaphorical or making one of his playful exaggerations. Every day, he heard his music in its original form or retransformed, adapted and repackaged by younger musicians – on the radio, on jukeboxes, in nightclubs and on theatre stages, as tangible in the air of New York City as the exhaust from buses and taxis.

The little piece that became Morton's trademark (so well-known it could be casually mentioned by Shelton Brooks in his smash hit 'The Darktown Strutter's Ball' [1918] as a *dance* tune – 'When we dance those Jelly Roll Blues') is deceptively simple, just two strains: 'The first has composed variations, and the second is designed for improvised variations.' (Dapogny 293) It displays the hallmarks of Morton's jazz composing (as distinct from ragtime writing) – breaks, a blues pattern throughout and what Morton called the 'Spanish tinge', a habañera rhythm in the left hand (bass) that runs through the second strain. Morton recorded the tune as 'Jelly Roll Blues' ('original' is gone from the title – the tune is 'the one and only' by now) first at a marathon session on 9 June 1924, as a piano solo for Gennett Records, along with other brilliant early compositions such as 'Perfect Rag' and 'Stratford Hunch', and with other 'Spanish tinge' numbers, including his own dark tango 'Mamanita' and Gene Rodemich's pretty little pop tune 'Tia Juana'.

Morton went on to record his number several more times. It was among the early Victor recordings of his consummate Victor recording group the Red Hot Peppers (December 1926), by this time reinstated as 'Original Jelly Roll Blues' and played by the full seven-piece band. The arrangement is lush and stately, with all parts clearly articulated. It is easy to see why the tune was a sensation as a new kind of pop dance music in 1915.

The band track begins with the piano arpeggios that mark the tune, followed by an echo of flourishes from Johnny St Cyr's guitar, and then the full band joins in, with the first strain melody passed back and forth between Omer Simeon's clarinet and George Mitchell's muted cornet. When the second strain is reached, drummer Andrew Hilaire pulls his castanets from his bag of tricks, and we are well and truly Spanish-tinged. After the ensemble we get a pretty Mitchell solo (repeated), a subtone meditation and some clever breaks-over-stoptime from Simeon, a set of cascading solo piano breaks and finally another headlong 4-beat ensemble that rides us out.

It is a facile and convincing performance that sounds both arranged and improvised *at one and the same moment*. Morton has found a secret in coaxing from biddable talents performances that both respect his 'little black dots' and are unleashed from score-reading stiffness or hesitation. The music seems to come from inside each player and float in the air, like the magic music that emerges from the landscape in William Shakespeare's *The Tempest*. It is easy to understand Morton's pride in the piece and his insistence that it is a patent or license that gives him primacy in the land of jazz. Such calm assurance and clarity are unimaginable in 1915, let alone 1905! Once Ludwig van Beethoven made a cocksure boast about his music that might have come from such a monumental ego as Morton's, too. He said: 'Those who hear my music truly will never again know sorrow.'

ᗡᗡᗡ   ᗡᗡᗡ

By 1923, Jelly Roll Morton had a firm idea of what he was doing – promoting and preserving the numerous piano pieces he had written over the past two decades. He had copyrighted 'Original Jelly Roll Blues' in 1915 and 'Frog-I-More Rag' in 1918, and had seen both become hits. He had seen upstart Chicago music publishers Walter and Lester Melrose appropriate his 'The Wolverines' and resell it as 'Wolverine Blues', also a big hit with major jazz groups. Now he was taking the reins and putting his name on everything he could grasp. When he went to Richmond, Indiana, in 1923 and 1924, his agenda was to persuade Gennett Records to record as much as possible of the big Morton catalogue.

First he sat in with the New Orleans Rhythm Kings on 17–18 July 1923, and they recorded six numbers with Morton at the piano: three of his compositions ('Mr Jelly Lord,' 'Milenberg Joys' and 'London [Café] Blues') and two from the NORK book ('Sobbin' Blues' and 'Clarinet Marmalade'). The records showed off both his own writing and his piano playing – he is a notable force in the numbers he plays on, compared to others the NORK made with their pianist at the time, Kyle Pierce. The band had made a hot record of 'Wolverine Blues' in March, and now the master was on hand to ensure that they got other Morton blockbusters right.

At the same time, Morton cut a series of piano solos for Gennett (which, as a subsidiary of the Starr Piano Company, was anxious to show it could cut clear, accurate records of the piano). On 17–18 July, he put on wax 'King Porter Stomp', his souvenir from the Gulf Coast odyssey; 'New Orleans (Blues) Joys', a very old tune Morton 'transformed', once just called 'Old New Orleans Blues'; 'Grandpa's Spells', his showpiece with the forearm-elbow tone clusters he would later use on 'Tiger Rag' for Alan Lomax; 'Kansas City Stomp' and 'The Pearls', written during a long musical excursion in Tia Juana in 1922; and 'Wolverine Blues [Joys]', now accommodating the Melrose brothers' title. It was a productive two-day marathon for Morton (and for Gennett!), and it set him more firmly on the path of making his music available for a wider public.

When Morton left New Orleans to make his way in the world, he was still what the multi-instrumentalist and teacher Manuel Manetta in an interview described as 'a black-key player', someone who learned fingering directly from the keyboard and used the black keys in an unorthodox way, one mark of a non-reading pianist:

> At that time, Ferdinand, he'd play everything in the key of D-flat, blues and everything, all in D-flat. He was really an ear player then. All ear players, when they'd sit down at a piano,

*they'd use the black keys because they are more apart —
separated. They wouldn't fool with the natural keys, because
they were so close, you know, and you might be hittin' two keys,
so they mostly played on the black keys, because they're further
apart.* (Russell 121)

By the time he reached Chicago, Morton had left much of his rough
apprenticeship behind and was a skilled music reader and composer. His
self-designed and self-imposed education by experience had worked.

One of his earliest pieces, 'King Porter Stomp', still shows traces of
this 'black key' practice in several versions that Morton recorded. The
sheet music, as transcribed, edited and sanitized by the Melroses, reverts to
conventional harmonizing and fingering. (Fletcher Henderson, in his
landmark swing arrangement of the tune, also removed the 'primitive'
elements from the music.)

This example may show two important steps in Morton's self-
education as he wandered the Gulf Coast and Southwest – his memory of
his own early style and his imitation of the same rough-and-ready
techniques in the music of his friend Porter King, whose playing is
memorialized in the number. While his skills at composition and notation
developed, Morton still admired the roots of his style in the fiery practices
of blues and barrelhouse players, with irresistible rhythm though
sometimes shaky techniques. 'King Porter Stomp' would go on to become
the virtual anthem of the Swing Era and the number most associated with
Morton in the popular imagination.

Morton continued working to get his music known and distributed.
The Melrose brothers were arranging for publication of piano scores and
in 1926 for some band arrangements of major works like 'Sidewalk
Blues', 'Cannon Ball Blues' and 'Black Bottom Stomp'. He was keeping
ahead of the presses, but barely, as he found recording outlets. In April

1924, he cut several small band numbers and laid down three more piano solos for the small Paramount label and the even smaller Autograph label, with limited distribution. He was still working his way through the Morton songbook, recording 'Thirty-Fifth Street Blues', 'Mamanita [sic]' and 'Frog-I-More Rag'.

Morton then returned to Gennett to pick up where he left off the year before with that label, in another marathon day recording Gene Rodemich's 'Tia Juana' (evidently a sentimental inclusion, but a very nice 'Spanish tinge' pop tango) and a slew of his own works: 'Shreveport Stomp', 'Froggie Moore' (unissued), 'Mamanita', 'Jelly Roll Blues', 'Big Foot Ham', 'Bucktown Blues', 'Tom Cat Blues', 'Stratford Hunch', 'Milenberg Joys' (unissued) and 'Perfect Rag'. Again, it was an extraordinary haul for both Morton and Gennett and indicates how determined Morton was to seize this opportunity (Gennett was a major jazz label of the time, with King Oliver's Creole Jazz Band, the NORK and other premier Chicago groups on its books). This looked like that elusive secret gateway into the bigtime that Morton had been seeking for a decade. He was hustling at top speed, or as he said, 'things was drivin' on'.

Morton next travelled on to Cincinnati, some 50 miles southeast of Richmond, to cut piano rolls for a small outfit, the Vocalstyle Piano Roll Company. Without delving into the tangled arcana of all possible piano rolls by Morton, the Vocalstyle session is notable. In another intensive session, Morton cut rolls of 13 compositions, the bulk of the large catalogue of tunes that he was carrying around and peddling. Sometime in late July, he hand-cut (i.e. played on a recording piano that punched a master roll) 'Mr Jelly Lord', 'Tin Roof Blues' (a NORK hit of two years before), 'Tom Cat Blues', 'Mamanita Blues', 'London Blues', 'King Porter Stomp', 'Shreveport Stomp', 'Stratford Hunch', 'Kansas City Stomp', 'Grandpa's Spells', 'The Pearls', 'Jelly Roll Blues' and 'New Orleans Blues'. (Copies of four of these Vocalstyle rolls advertised for sale in 1926 – 'Mamanita Blues', 'The Pearls', 'Kansas City Stomp' and 'New Orleans Blues' – have never been found.) The rolls offer fascinating comparisons with the Gennett records of the same moment – piano rolls suffered no acoustic problems and do not wear with age or playing, like shellac records. On the other hand, the mechanical process available to a small company like Vocalstyle in 1924 was not as sensitive to nuances of playing as those used by elite piano roll companies such as Aeolian or Ampico. The process tended to make keyboard styles seem uniform and slightly robotic.

The performances, however, reveal Morton as a constant improver and transformer of his own music, with the rolls varying distinctly from the Gennett disc versions. They are less pyrotechnic and more shaded toward the kind of parlour audience that bought rolls – people who were at least hypothetical pianists themselves. They represent less scintillating and more lyrically melodious renderings of the Morton repertory, the kind of music that would sound good in a nice living room with neat furnishings.

This repertory on the Vocalstyle rolls covers most of Morton's standby numbers, the music that he had been composing, playing and perfecting during his career since he fled New Orleans. It forms the core of his work, and as the Melrose scores came out, Morton used these works again on definitive recordings, this time by the biggest of bigtime record companies – venerable old Victor Records, now trying to remake itself and catch up with the Jazz Age before it got away.

❧❧❧   ☙☙☙

Jelly Roll Morton was busy enough, brash enough and experienced enough to be chosen as a flagship commander by Victor Records in the mid-1920s, when they expanded their jazz interests and tried to take a share of the 'race records' market that OKeh had largely cornered, with their competition mainly coming from smaller outfits such as the doomed Black Swan

Records, Gennett, Paramount and a few other little labels that plunged into blues, jazz and country music when none of the giants deigned to notice the raw and vital Americana blooming everywhere around them.

In the fall of 1926 Morton assembled a 'dream band' from players around Chicago to represent the authentic New Orleans jazz that he imagined, the music he heard when he closed his eyes at night and saw echelons of little black dots marching to his command. It was not a 'pure' New Orleans band – George Mitchell, the superb, lyrical cornettist, was from Louisville – but the others form a who's who of the New Orleans style: Kid Ory, the premier trombonist of his generation and leader of the fabled Ory-Oliver Brownskin Band; Omer Simeon, Morton's favourite

Morton calls his class to order. The Red Hot Peppers in their first incarnation in 1926.
L–R: Omer Simeon, Andrew Hillaire, John Lindsay, Johnny St. Cyr, Kid Ory, George Mitchell.

clarinettist, with a limpid tone, an infallible technique and a variety of highly charged hot styles; Johnny St Cyr, a longtime banjo-guitar buddy of Morton's; John Lindsay, a powerful veteran bassist (switched over from trombone); and Andrew Hilaire, a peppy and swinging drummer who was a veteran of Doc Cook's fine big bands.

At the first recording session (15 September 1926), Morton – surprisingly – used only one of his originals ('Black Bottom Stomp') and chose two hot tunes he admired and 'transformed' into Jelly Roll style: a driving stomp, 'The Chant', by Mel Stitzel (an NORK pianist-arranger) and Charles Luke's introspective 'Smoke House Blues'. The session is like a classroom demonstration of Morton's skills as a leader, arranger and organizer.

'Black Bottom Stomp' is a simple but effective two-strain tune to match the recent dance craze (a direct descendant of the Charleston), taken at a good dance tempo that floats like a riverboat on the solid rhythm of St Cyr and Lindsay, and showing the structural freedom that is characteristic of music played by jazz musicians, not strict readers. It shows off Mitchell's stylish mid-range lead playing, Simeon's low register meditations and Morton's scampering ragtime style.

Mel Stitzel's showpiece 'The Chant' is even better; beginning with fanfare-like riffs, it plunges off into jagged stop-time, singing breaks from Mitchell and a solid solo by Simeon which demonstrates why Morton admired his driving but controlled sound. St Cyr gives us minstrel-show banjo picking, and we're back to Simeon and a gorgeous Harmon-muted Mitchell solo, a brusk Ory tailgate ramble, and the disc rounds off with Jelly's stomp piano, the whole performance seamless and feeling unpremeditated. Morton, with this group of first-rate players, shows how a band can follow an arrangement – some writing, some 'head' work – and still sound as if it's 'making it up as it goes along', most people's basic idea of what jazz music is (or ought to be). Victor's multiple takes of the Red

Hot Peppers sides show how closely Morton's men followed his direction, but how fresh they kept every attempt.

Morton was a gifted leader, coaxing the best from his musicians, jollying them and keeping the explosive New Orleans tempers damped down. Omer Simeon recalled the working methods on the Red Hot Peppers sessions fondly. They began with the Melrose stock orchestrations as an 'outline': 'We used them merely as guide until we got familiar with the tunes and didn't need the music anymore. We improvised the ensembles and we would always play the solos ad lib.' Simeon summed up the format of these pioneering records:

> *Jelly would set a routine for each number, and they all had to be no more than three minutes playing time. Jelly arranged special introductions that he had in mind, and then Ory, George Mitchell, and myself got together and harmonized it and tried it out. Jelly set a routine so the order of the solos was decided. We always played an ensemble, and the melody was going at all times until probably the last chorus, the take-out chorus, you know. Then everybody would give out, but the melody dominated most of the time.* (Russell 360)

The third number, Luke's 'Smoke House Blues', is a deliberate study in the components of New Orleans jazz – ensembles that are beautifully harmonized at a slow but swinging tempo, then a series of solos, each showing off a horn: Ory's lyrical mode, Simeon in low tempo with a dash of double-timing, leading to a stark piano solo – even the rhythm accompaniment stops – broken by Morton's ecstatic shout, 'Oh! Mr Jelly!' The last ensemble leads to a series of false endings recapitulating the first solos – Ory, then Simeon, then out. It is a very simple, skeletal and quiet piece, foreshadowing what Morton would make of 'Deep Creek' three years later. Especially in contrast with 'The Chant' and 'Black Bottom

Stomp', this slow blues seems minimalist, stark and uncluttered.

Morton was back in the studio less than a week later (21 September), now with two more stellar clarinettists (Barney Bigard and Darnell Howard) and a sound-effects man, Melrose henchman/arranger Marty Bloom. Morton turned from the simplicity of the first session to a much more complex and contrived version of his music, in a vaudeville mode. He cut three originals: 'Sidewalk Blues' (he had recorded the tune in a 1924 session as 'Fishtail Blues', as part of a quintet with trumpeter Lee Collins and Roy Palmer, trombone), 'Dead Man Blues' and 'Steam Boat Stomp'.

This time around, Morton was showing off his vaudeville-comedy training in 'Sidewalk Blues' and 'Dead Man Blues', with hokum routines at the beginning and copious offstage noises like church bells and auto klaxons. Jelly Roll clearly enjoyed the funny-guy/straight-man routines and varied his lines on each take, and while modern sourpuss critics deplore the foolish and (purportedly) racist implications of such aural blackface, Morton was trying his damnedest to make truly popular jazz for Victor; the standup dialect comedy of Moran & Mack (the Two Black Crows) or of Amos & Andy (all four white comics) was wildly popular then and remained so for another two decades. He was dead right about the comic potential, but perhaps was not the person to make it work (his humour did not translate well from the piano to the stage and to recordings, although his friends said that he was an extraordinarily funny raconteur, in a wacky, Baron Munchausen vein).

Putting aside the aesthetics of melding low comedy and stately music (both tunes are in fact gloriously melodic and as eloquent as G. F. Handel anthems), Morton and the band worked hard to make them exemplary jazz. The clarinet trio in the middle of each tune is a gem of harmonizing, the ensembles are smooth and the solos at least adequate in every case. No one else could do anything like this, and no one made a version as moving and swinging as any of these by cutting out the hokum. When King Oliver cut 'Dead Man Blues' straightfacedly with his Dixie Syncopators, it is interesting but quite stiff by comparison with Morton's work. And the 'New Orleans funeral' routine in 'Dead Man Blues' brought something unique from New Orleans' jazz culture to the attention of the record-buying public. People in the following years began to notice how strange, interesting and downright eccentric New Orleans jazz musicians were – the spicy allusion in 'red hot pepper' was not just an afterthought from Morton.

'Steam Boat Stomp' drops the extra clarinets and uses only a brief comic flourish at the beginning. It is a vigorous, original piece in the same mould as 'Black Bottom Stomp', with an emphasis on the minstrel-riverboat ideas of a banjo-driven band. Morton was just about to switch St Cyr from the clanging banjo to the sweet sound of the guitar, taking advantage of the brilliant close-up recording Victor's engineers were giving him. He began to understand how to use the recording microphone as a musical instrument, as Duke Ellington would a few years later.

After these first two Red Hot Peppers sessions, Morton used this insight into the sonic possibilities of Victor's system to make his work increasingly subtle, increasingly intimate, increasingly modern – no longer New Orleans jazz as it was but the new jazz of the immediate present, going on to wax in Victor's Webster Hotel studios in the modern, streamlined city of Chicago. In those microphones and cutting lathes, Morton had found new partners in the jazz enterprise, and he moved quickly in order to take every advantage of them, as if he foresaw the lean days that were coming when the huge bubble of the 1920s New Age burst on cold old Wall Street.

For the third Red Hot Peppers session (16 December 1926) Morton brought in a pair of violinists (J. Wright Smith and Clarence Black) to inject the appropriate sweetenings into 'Someday Sweetheart', a tune that

Morton had worked out with the Spikes brothers – black musicians and publishers from his Los Angeles excursion – and one that he hoped would become a big pop hit. It was widely recorded by jazz groups and became a standard, but as usual little direct cash flowed to Jelly Roll from the tangled copyright. His recording is definitive – a romantic, ballad-like flow with the two violins carrying the lilting melody and Simeon again rising to the occasion with a gorgeous, brooding solo on the bass clarinet, a surprise sprung on him by Morton, who had a calm assurance that the New Orleans reedman could do absolutely anything with this untried instrument:

> On 'Someday Sweetheart' I took a solo chorus on bass clarinet. Jelly wanted it and Melrose rented one somewhere. Took a little time to get familiar with it and I didn't like it too much. Jelly was always fond of effects and wanted to be different. He was always trying to find something different, and whatever he wanted, we would have to do. He was fussy on introductions and endings and he always wanted the ensemble his way but he never interfered with the solo work. (Hodes and Hansen 93)

On this occasion Morton got from Simeon a striking and unique entry into the sweepstakes for great jazz solos, anticipating the emotional depths he would wring from young Paul Barnes on 'Deep Creek' a couple of years in the future.

The third session also included 'Grandpa's Spells', one of the Morton piano showpiece numbers (everyone remembered how he used his elbow and forearm to produce 'tone clusters' such as the kind Modernist composers, especially Henry Cowell and Charles Ives, were exploring – a trick he explained when he played 'Tiger Rag' for Alan Lomax in the Library of Congress). It is lively stomp (someone said that Morton's grandpa must be an amazingly vivacious old coot!) with an infectious, rhythmic drive that recalls both late ragtime and early one-step jazz.

Take 1 begins with St Cyr now on guitar, floating the whole band on brilliant picking and chords. After an ensemble Simeon enters with witty chalumeau-register noodling over St Cyr's Spanish guitar, then Ory plays a terse solo against John Lindsay's driving 4/4 bass line. We return to Simeon on the next strain, fluent middle-range and lower-register playing with Morton dancing in and out for piano breaks. The tune ends with a bright guitar lick. Morton has discovered how to make the Red Hot Peppers a true chamber-jazz group, with everyone playing comfortably in *p–mf* range, in the middle registers – no strain, no gut-busting fireworks, but a sound like Creole songsters on a New Orleans veranda with their guitars. On Take 2 of 'Grandpa's Spells', they follow Morton's outline 'routine' again, but all the soloists relax and become more ambitious and exhibitionistic. The music goes very well until St Cyr garbles the guitar exit. Take 3, an even better effort, was released by Victor.

Next the band tackles Morton's signature, 'Original Jelly Roll Blues'. It is handled with aplomb, Hilaire's pit-band experience making him a master of the 'Spanish tinge' that flavours everything here, castanets and all. It is the opposite end of the spectrum from 'Grandpa's Spells', a mid-tempo dance tune that may indeed invite you to 'dance off both your shoes', but in a very polite, cotillion-style way. No gaudy, exhibitionistic Charleston, Mess Around or Lindy Hop here.

Then the band makes another surprise turn, picking up Joe Oliver's 'Dr Jazz', a signature tune for the trumpeter but waxed in a fairly tame version by Oliver's Dixie Syncopators. Morton twists its tail and drives it home by singing the tune in a sandpaper-coarse vaudeville shout, which erupts like a sincere cry for help in the middle of the take:

> *Hello, Central, give me Dr Jazz!*
> *He's got what I need, I'll say he has ...*

It's clear that the real Dr Jazz is sitting behind Victor's microphone, and the world suddenly learns that Morton can sing, too! The tune begins with an *fff* ensemble accent, topped by choked cymbal, and then plunges into a descending Simeon solo break – and then we're off with an ensemble led by Mitchell's incisive, Harmon-muted lead that twists and wriggles like a seductive chant.

When we reach Simeon's solo chorus, which turns out to be one vastly sustained note over the vamping rhythm section and Morton's dancing piano, it builds an agonizing suspense – *can he really hold it for that long? what will happen next?* Then Simeon repeats the trick, and the long note slides us into Jelly's voice, which cracks like a whip as he enters on '*Ahhh*, Hello Central – !' The whole band churns away over Hilaire's pounding woodblocks, pauses to quote one of the famous cornet breaks from Oliver's old Creole Jazz Band (the 1923 Gennett recording of 'Snake Rag') and exits, full speed ahead.

Simeon recalled how the sustained note arose: 'Jelly was sure full of ideas and he used them. I remember on "Dr Jazz", the long note I played wasn't in the stock arrangement. Jelly liked it and had Melrose put it in the orchestration.' (Hodes and Hansen 93) It was all grist for the mill – Morton trusted his picked men for their insights and extemporaneous inventions, and he was shrewd enough to hoard any gems that might be lying around. His gift, always, was to hear and recognize good music, wherever it came from, and to know how to use it, reshape it, elaborate and improve it. No mean talent!

The final side on this session is 'Cannon Ball Blues', co-credited to Morton, Charlie Rider and Marty Bloom. It sounds like pure Morton, and the recording is far more interesting than the score. Take 1 gives us the band opening the three-strain blues, going straight to a fine Mitchell solo and a very vigorous shouting Ory chorus, then a Simeon chorus against choked cymbal punctuation. Next Morton and St Cyr duet playfully, almost in the mode of a 'chase chorus' or 'trading fours', like the routines that Bix Beiderbecke and Frank Trumbauer invented a bit later. The end is a careful, solid ensemble with great dignity. Take 2 is at a considerably lower tempo, to sound more 'bluesy', perhaps, but it only seems sluggish and anemic by comparison – luckily Take 1 was issued by Victor.

The last Chicago Red Hot Peppers sessions – and the culmination of Morton's great experiment – took place on two days in June 1927, no longer at the Webster Hotel studios but now at Victor's Oak Street location. Morton assembled another New Orleans-focused band, now using Mitchell again, with Johnny Dodds (clarinet) and his brother Warren 'Baby' Dodds (drums), both veterans of the Ory-Oliver band, riverboats and other New Orleans venues. Bud Scott, Morton's favourite guitarist (he said he dropped all thoughts of playing guitar himself when he heard Scott play), was another New Orleanian. Others were veterans of the vital Chicago jazz scene: Gerald Reeves (trombone), who led an excellent band with his equally skilled trumpeter brother Reuben, Paul 'Stump' Evans, a saxophonist (alto in this instance) who had played with Oliver's Creole Jazz Band, and Quinn Wilson, a young tuba player who would go on to have a fine career as a bassist with Earl Hines, among others. Also in the studio on the first date was Lew LeMar, an iron-lunged sound-effects specialist with a grab-bag of vocal tricks.

The session began with two tunes employing LeMar for hokum interjections (the usual quasi-vaudeville), 'Hyena Stomp' and 'Billy Goat Stomp', pieces obviously renamed to suit LeMar's dubious talents. On the first he injects wild laughter (like the ever-popular 'laughing records' issued for decades, probably the best-known a British disc called 'The Laughing Policeman' by Charles Penrose [a.k.a. Charles Jolly] in 1922 – for inscrutable reasons, large numbers of people liked to gather around the gramophone and be tickled into uncontrollable laughter by such stimuli).

On 'Billy Goat Stomp' he repeats but this varies the sound to not very lifelike nanny-goat outbursts. Again, jazz purists and pickle-sucking commentators have tut-tutted over Morton's 'bad taste' and abysmal crudity, but pop music is pop music is pop music, and you get it with a lot more than just warts and all!

In any event, both tunes are extraordinarily beautiful compositions, among Morton's very best, which may have seemed too tame or effete for jazz public consumption. 'Hyena Stomp' is a simple tune with complex development (Morton chose it as exemplary of his writing and played a beautiful solo version on the Library of Congress sessions). After LeMar's hokum dialogue and a small sample of his laughing repertory over the band playing softly, the band enters, rising to full volume for a Johnny Dodds low-register solo, followed by jagged bicycle-pump trombone breaks from Reeves and then a spirited ensemble, which gives over to LeMar's laughter (against interesting clarinet breaks). Then Evans enters with a snappy, slap-tongued solo, leading to a neat Morton solo and back to romping ensembles that trail off in LeMar's madhouse giggle. This was Take 2, the issued take, but Take 3 is as interesting – with Morton, Johnny Dodds and Evans in even better form. The final out-chorus is wildly driving, as if the band hoped to blast LeMar and his loony guffawing into oblivion.

On 'Billy Goat Stomp', we get similar routines. It has only two strains, but it is a chain of virtuoso breaks from everyone and very hot, with much energy and dense ensembles packed with spirited counterpoint from the four horns. Bud Scott takes a jumping knife-blade solo that recalls Lonnie Johnson's best work, Baby Dodds constructs a pulsating cymbal solo and Morton plays a solo without rhythm, as if baiting LeMar. Johnny Dodds goes into his best muttering and meditative low-register mode for a solo finale – no big-band out-chorus. Take 1 was issued, but Take 3 is even better in terms of solo vitality and sheer drive, with the last ensemble exploding then shading down to Dodds' last quiet notes and LeMar's final bleat.

'Wild Man Blues' is an important tune, because it had just been taken up by Louis Armstrong and reworked into a personal statement, in two contexts – with his own Hot Seven (May 1927) and with a Johnny Dodds band including Roy Palmer and Earl Hines (April 1927). Morton got into the sweepstakes to be sure that he had a 'cover' of his own tune! It begins with a brief snatch of hokum (cage-rattling and a cry from Morton of 'Get away from there, boy, before the Wild Man gets you!') but settles into a driving slow blues. Mitchell gives a long, sincere solo, followed by Paul Evans stating the pretty melody without much adornment. Morton and Johnny Dodds trade blues bars, including some scatty double-timing, then we get a contorted Evans break, and a return to Dodds's low-register clarinet, with Evans inserting double-timed tongue-twisters, some more rococo breaks and end.

This 'Wild Man Blues' is much more ornate and fussier than the intense and stark version that Armstrong crafted in both of his recordings, one of his finest shapings of the blues, and full of his characteristic rips, growls and flourishes. Armstrong's 'Wild Man' is not a carnival freak but something human and infinitely strange trapped inside the trumpeter, a profound blues voice struggling to rise out of him. Especially on the Hot Seven version, Armstrong uses twisted, tumbling breaks to heighten the feeling, but otherwise he hews to a singing, lyrical line, as if he were not playing but singing or chanting the tune. Morton's arrangement is more formal and stately, an elegant, loping blues at medium tempo, not so much lowdown as highbrow, after Morton's uncouth introduction.

The next number waxed was 'Jungle Blues', a distinctive piece of exotica in a mock-Ellingtonian vein, which begins with an ensemble and passes to an open-horn Mitchell solo with punctuations from Baby Dodds's Chinese cymbal. Then Stump Evans makes a parallel solo before a return to the ensemble, on a chugging rhythm dictated by Quinn Wilson's moaning tuba and Dodds's cymbal. Johnny Dodds gives a writhing clarinet lament, after which we go to ensemble and then to Morton's piano, which is immediately echoed by a plaintive guitar solo from St Cyr. It is a simple, low-down blues, ending with a jolting gong crash like the brazen voice of Fu Manchu. It is an effective piece, and interesting enough for Benny Goodman to record just before he got fully into the King of Swing business (on the disc, Goodman played both clarinet and *cornet*).

Almost a week later, Morton was back at Victor's Oak Street recording lab with the same band. They cut two band tunes – 'Beale Street Blues' and 'The Pearls' – and two with a trio (Morton and the Dodds brothers) – 'Wolverine Blues' and 'Mr Jelly Lord'. These were some of the most polished performances that Morton elicited from his Chicago sidemen.

'Beale Street Blues' Take 1 is amusing – almost a parody or burlesque of W. C. Handy's standard blues, converted into something like a street march. It begins with a march beat, a Gerald Reeves fanfare, then an Evans solo, set against swirling background riffs and melodic figures. The main melody is given by George Mitchell in one of his patented Harmon-muted utterances. Stump Evans duets with St Cyr's guitar, and Johnny Dodds then solos to lead in Morton's piano. In the background, like a ticking clock, Baby Dodds uses his 'swats' (Morton's term for brushes) on the back beats. The ensemble marches on out and up the street to Evans's saucy slap-tonguing. On Take 2, the solo routines are sharpened and clearer (Take 1 was Victor's choice to issue).

In 'The Pearls', one of Morton's favourite tunes (he recorded it over and over, and taught it to protégées such as Mary Lou Williams and Bertha Gonsoulin), the same big-throated, march-like rhythm prevails, making the tune much less delicate and evocative than in Morton's caressing keyboard treatments. Paul Evans solos well, and he also duets fluently with Johnny Dodds, carrying the melodic second strain. Then Mitchell and Dodds reprise the duet, leading to very articulate trumpet breaks and the basic walking rhythm which concludes. The two tunes are like distorted mirror images – lyrical numbers that are turned into (first) a steady march and (second) a relaxed saunter, but they are both more like Promenades than Foxtrots. It is an odd and whimsical idea that only Morton would have attempted.

The two trio sides are among the best of the chamber jazz that Morton had created in several years. 'Wolverine Blues' is a spectacular Morton solo, a breakneck bit of fast, finger-busting ragtime that mutates halfway through, when Johnny Dodds sneaks in after two strains. It is hard to imagine anything topping Morton's solo effort until Dodds's low-register voice creeps in after a fanfare, with brother Baby tapping out figures, first on the cymbal and then afterbeats with brushes on the snare drum, and finally with a precise tom-tom figure (the same running beat he used on the cymbal) that pushes both piano and clarinet headlong to the end. Morton is as assertive and dominating here as he ever got on record, and his fingering is crystal clear. (Incidentally, Benny Goodman, who made a mint with his own chamber jazz trios, quartets and quintets at the apogee of the swing craze, was running in parallel with Morton in the Chicago recording studios of Vocalion, on 13 June 1928, at the age of 17, cutting two fine trio numbers with Morton's associate from NORK days, Mel Stizel, on piano: 'That's a Plenty' and 'Clarinetitis'.)

'Mr Jelly Lord', a Morton theme song, is presented as a stately narrative without words (he wrote humorously eccentric, self-praising verses which he sang on the Library of Congress discs), Morton playing with Baby Dodds swatting away, then Johnny Dodds again edging into the conversation in his lowest voice. Morton solos with sprinkled arpeggios, and Johnny Dodds's clarinet re-emerges momentarily, hushing to let the piano finish the strain. In the next chorus Dodds takes fluid breaks and the three voices rise to a courtly conclusion. It is a fitting sign-off for the Chicago Red Hot Peppers, an amazing first chapter in Morton's Victor work. Using two slightly different versions of the platonic ideal of New Orleans bands, Morton presented his songbook and also used work by other composers to demonstrate the basic vocabulary and design of jazz, as he understood it. It is like a manifesto in sound, an accomplishment never really challenged, even by Chicago masters such as Tiny Parham and Jabbo Smith, who also made remarkable and highly individualistic small-band sides around the same time. Morton scaled Parnassus while the others were still gazing up at the peaks.

⟫⟫ ⟪⟪

The jazz centre of gravity was shifting from Chicago to New York, as the Harlem Renaissance heated up and more and more music venues opened for African-Americans, from nightclubs (white audiences only) like the Cotton Club to big dance palaces like the Rosemont Ballroom or the Savoy Ballroom, to Broadway musicals with black casts, such as *Shuffle Along* (1922), Lew Leslie's annual revue series of *Blackbirds*, or *Hot Chocolates* (1927), which featured both Louis Armstrong and Fats Waller, among other luminaries. Opportunities bloomed everywhere, and the city housed a large cadre of experienced younger musicians, as well as New Orleans veterans. Morton went to New York City in 1928, further swelling this arts migration.

Morton travelled hopefully, as always, and took part in a couple of ineffectual recording sessions for Columbia and Gennett – the first with a band led by Johnny Dunn, the self-regarding trumpeter who had been an early rage in New York (four tunes issued, two of them by Morton), the second a session accompanying singer Frances Hereford, which came to naught. Dunn was a self-appointed trumpet king with an old-fashioned doo-whacka-doo style (think Henry 'Hot Lips' Busse or Clyde McCoy), long displaced by Oliver, Armstrong and other stars. Dunn had been a significant jazz figure, and his current band included ace New York sidemen such as Garvin Bushell, a multi-reed master, and Herb Fleming, a fine trombonist.

Dunn has been described as an early blues promoter:

> *Dunn was the first jazz celebrity, in the modern sense, to record, and although his name is almost forgotten now, he was one of the biggest names in the Negro entertainment world throughout most of the 1920s. . . . Dunn, on blues after blues, featured himself. His tone was thin and hard, and his technique was limited, but he could play more blues than anyone in New York. He was the first real blues man to record, even doing solo sides, with just rhythm accompaniment* (Charters and Kunstadt, 86)

Morton, however, had little good to say about Dunn. Dunn had a gimmicky approach that excited fans, using a fanfare or 'Aida' trumpet (Morton called it a 'coach horn'), which was about six feet long, for high visual impact.

The band cut four sides in March 1928, including one Dunn trumpet speciality ('Sergeant Dunn's Bugle Call') and two Morton standards – 'Ham and Eggs' and the catchy 'Buffalo Blues' (a.k.a. 'Mister Joe'). Morton then returned to Victor in New York, creating a new and modern eastern edition of the Red Hot Peppers, one which emerged from his original conception of the band but took new directions, dictated by the talent at hand and the new currents in jazz that Jelly Roll charted in the east.

The 1928 model band that Morton developed included Ward Pinkett (trumpet), a sturdy and assertive lead player; Geechie Fields (trombone), a distinctive blues specialist with a range of muted growls second only to Ellington's 'Tricky' Sam Nanton; Omer Simeon (clarinet), Morton's good right hand; Lee Blair (banjo), an able young player and the Benford brothers

– Tommy (drums) and Bill (tuba), skilled and biddable young musicians. Morton sat down to teach them about jazz, Jelly Roll and the American Way, and to score new numbers – he had almost reached the bottom of his old music satchel and had new ideas galore ready to translate into working scores.

On 11 June he took the band into Leiderkranz Hall, a Victor venue with great natural acoustics. They cut six numbers, half new and half familiar Jelly classics. The group's sound was wholly new, even with the highly characteristic Simeon and Morton styles in the mix.

They began with a 'transformation', a judicious borrowing, 'Georgia Swing' – from trombonist Santo Pecora's 'She's Crying for Me', recorded by the NORK; Morton makes it a solid riff tune, a textbook demonstration of the term 'swing' as it was becoming current (popularized as much by Louis Armstrong as anyone else). It opens with a cymbal rhythm and a cry from the band, then the melody is played by the ensemble, followed by its conversion to an ensemble riff. Simeon takes a tumbling solo, like a conversation with himself, while Morton churns along behind him through a series of kinetic ragtime variations. Pinkett follows with a solo, then Fields with his muted trombone. Morton goes into a solo (backed by Tommy Benford's swats), and then the horns come back in with a rocking riff and the band rolls out. It is a kind of perpetuum mobile and a study, in the European sense of '*étude*' – a little lesson: 'this is how you build up a real head of steam with a seven-piece band.'

The second number was a classic Morton piano piece, 'Kansas City Stomp', named for a Mexican-border (Tia Juana) bar, he said, and one of his most sparkling and pianistic stomps. His band version is equally facile, using the ensemble to spell out the elegant melodies of the three strains. He retained the rounded structure of the piece, coming back to the first strain to close out. It begins with a klaxon-like call by each of the three horns, then goes into an ensemble first strain, a Simeon solo and Morton playing the second strain solo, then back to the first strain (ensemble), a Blair banjo solo, and a short tuba solo from Bill Benford, which is traded back and forth with a muted Ward Pinkett to tie up the third strain. The ending is a tricky stop-and-go effect by Simeon and Tommy Benford that recalls the klaxon at the beginning. For a piece so strongly associated with Morton's solo stomp piano style, it becomes in his orchestrating a very solid group effort, showing off Morton's incomparable skill at turning 'pianistic' numbers into band tunes, and vice versa.

The third number cut was 'Shoeshiner's Drag', an alternative title for Morton's old 'London [Café] Blues', a standby that Morton cut for Gennett with the NORK the same year and with his own Natty Dominique/Zue Robertson band in 1923 for OKeh, and which had also been cut by King Oliver's Creole Jazz Band, again in 1923 for OKeh. It is a pleasant blues, a good dance tune. It begins with a catchy little fanfare and flourish, a call-and-response figure like those frequently used by ragtime master James Scott (Morton arranged and recorded his 'Climax Rag' in 1939) and settles into two simple strains of sustained, long-tone blues melodies. Each of the horns has a solo swipe at them, then the ensemble plays the second strain as a solid, gently swinging refrain, returning to the little fanfare-break idea that opened the tune. Victor advertised the record heavily as a 'slow drag' dance number, which seems exactly right. The new Red Hot Peppers play it fluently and forcefully. This edition of Morton's band is less exuberant and surprising than the New Orleans men in Chicago, but it is also self-contained and precise in its voice, not at all like what people thought of as small-group black jazz, but as expressive and soulful as anything on record.

The fourth tune was a new one, 'Boogaboo', evidently named for the 'spooky' piano quavers and whoopee whistle that open it. A slightly hokey atmospheric number like Morton's 'Fickle Fay Creep', the New Orleans Owls's 'White Ghost Shivers' or a novelty pop tune recorded by several jazz groups in 1929, 'Mysterious Mose', it resolves into a lyrical slow blues that makes great use of Bill Benford's sustained tuba tones, along with more tremolo effects. It chugs along on Tommy Benford's brush and choked cymbal backbeats, with delicate solos by Simeon, Pinkett and Fields, who mutes his trombone to a hoarse whisper. The middle section is an organ-point chorus of piano over tuba and band chords, then back to a louder ensemble, ending on a last shrill from the whoopee whistle. It is an odd piece – similar to some of Ellington's creepy tone poems or the movie-palace orientalia of Tiny Parham (see 'Bombay' or 'Golden Lily') – and a new direction in pop jazz for Morton.

For the fifth side recorded that day, Morton created a trio with himself, Simeon and Tommy Benford, recapitulating his earlier forays into chamber jazz, this time bringing out one of his fiercest finger-busters, 'Shreveport Stomp'. The number was a pianistic showpiece of fleet runs and cascading figures, and Morton confidently called on Simeon to play these finger-twisters as tongue-twisters, which he did with insouciance. It includes a second strain of fourteen bars in odd chord progressions that show no sign of fazing the clarinettist. (Dapogny 113–14) Benford provided solid brush rhythms, and the three men cooked up an astonishing etouffe from the fast, one-step rhythms and ragtime format. It is still rare for clarinettists to try matching Simeon's fluid grace on the number.

The last side was a quartet, and another 'transformation' by Morton – 'Mournful Serenade', which adds trombonist Fields to the clarinet, piano and drums combo in a reworking of the venerable 1923 King Oliver hit 'Chimes Blues'. With his borrowings, Morton extended his ongoing lectures on jazz from the present into history itself, as if he were saying, 'Listen – here's how it *should* have been done!' to Oliver (or to Louis Armstrong, who, as we have seen, cut his first solo on 'Chimes Blues').

It is taken at a slow, relaxed tempo, opening with Morton and

Benford, the basic tune of the first strain stated. Simeon enters with a meditative solo in the middle register, followed by Fields's growling, which leads to the second (or 'chimes') strain, which Morton and Benford play, utterly simply. Then they replay it with jagged syncopation. As they return to the first strain and smooth it out, they float on pretty organ chords from Simeon and Fields, then comes an ensemble with Morton playing stately, sweeping runs in the background. It is clearly the same piece as Oliver's 'Chimes Blues' but also totally different – brought down a notch in rhythmic intensity and elevated in emotion, as if the four men were trying to plumb the depths of the simple format and find something under the slightly banal gimmick of a piano mimicking bells. Whatever was there, under that surface, they found it and brought it to light, without drama or excess. Like many Morton pieces, it is surprisingly understated and minimalist, an exercise in decorum and modesty.

The session was good, in the light of history. At the time it did not cause much of a ripple in the tide of music recorded, touted and sold in New York and in the 'race' market. Competition in the city was fierce, and even if it was a wide-open emporium for African-American music, it was also a Tower of Babel, with a thousand new singers and bands recording, broadcasting and playing onstage every day, and lone voices were indistinguishable in the deafening clash of languages, cultures, ideas and schemes. Everyone was hustling, the stock market was soaring to stratospheric heights. Lucky Lindy had promised a new era of rapid transportation, the nation was awash in beer and booze despite the lip-served pieties of Prohibition, and everyone was stretching to grab the brass ring and ride the carousel on to paradise. Or as F. Scott Fitzgerald had put it in a little book that hadn't sold well a couple of years before, everyone was hypnotized by the little green light at the end of the dock, the light promising everything to anyone who wished on it.

After this session, Morton's fortunes slid another notch downward. Morton had conquered Chicago, but New York was a tougher town, a colder venue, and he had few connections and entrees in the Big Apple. He scrambled for work around New York, just as he had worked in and around Chicago, especially in southern Wisconsin's resort regions, with pickup bands, borrowed bands – aggregations he could cobble together to read his scores in a dance hall or nightclub. He also assembled pickup groups for recording in Camden, New Jersey, 9–11 July 1929 – *not* the 'Red Hot Peppers' but 'Jelly Roll Morton and his Orchestra', a generic title. Some groups gave the sessions valiant tries, but none were outstanding.

They read interesting scores – the music that Morton was imagining for biggish dance bands of the day – ten or twelve parts, intricate section writing, riffs, call-and-response licks, the whole works. He cut imaginative big band numbers such as 'Burning the Iceberg' (in part a rip-roaring, big-band 'transformation' of Artie Matthews' old reliable 'Weary Blues'), 'Tank Town Bump' and 'New Orleans Bump' (he was forever trying to find catchy new dance ideas – a 'bump' was something he dreamed up in the years after the Charleston and before the hot jive of swing), as well as 'Red Hot Pepper' and 'Deep Creek'. On this session, Morton included as clarinettist George Baquet, one of the grand old men of jazz and a veteran of the fabled Original Creole Orchestra that toured vaudeville in 1914–18; his vigorous ragtime-like playing flavours the otherwise modern big band in an odd and somewhat endearing way, like a musical footnote from yesteryear.

Returning to the title of Jelly Roll Morton and his Red Hot Peppers, Morton went back to New York City on 13 November 1929 and fronted six of Luis Russell's fine players on a session that produced numbers including 'Sweet Peter', 'Jersey Joe' and 'Mississippi Mildred' (people's names seemed a saleable motif at that moment). He then was hired by the hyperactive contortionist and 'gaspipe' clarinet-tooter Wilton Crawley to record his rackety playing on four fairly good tunes that Crawley had written, using excellent musicians from Luis Russell's and Duke Ellington's bands. The results are amazing and quite listenable, if you can adjust to the caterwauling sound that Crawley often emits.

Amidst these sessions, Morton recorded some brilliant solo sides; on 8 July 1929 he cut four of his best piano pieces – 'Pep', 'Seattle Hunch', 'Frances' (censored down from 'Fat Fanny') and 'Freakish'. They reveal him at his best, playing vigorously and incisively, with every atom of his earlier self-confidence and *joie de vivre*. If he couldn't hold a band together the way he used to, he could still command a piano to do anything he asked.

He began to pull himself back to the heights around the time America woke up to realize how disastrous the October stock market crash had been. On 17 December 1929, he took a trio into Victor's 46th Street studio, using himself and two New Orleans buddies – Barney Bigard (clarinet) and Zutty Singleton (drums) – for a brilliant set of sparkling miniatures. The tunes were lyrical little pop tunes that Morton's sometime agent Harrison Smith would later claim were written by an obscure and self-effacing genius, Ben Garrison, who also just happened to be managed and published by Smith. However, Smith's claim is dubious, since some tunes he claimed Morton swiped from Garrison were ones Morton recorded years before Garrison purportedly wrote them. It seems a naked scam by Smith to hijack the Jelly Roll music, using Ben Garrison as his stalking horse. (Russell 511)

In any event, the music on the session comprised exceptionally sunny and swinging little numbers that gave Bigard great scope for the lyrical style he honed so well with Duke Ellington and allowed Singleton to stretch out on the drums (resulting in much more variety than the simple brush offbeats that Morton had demanded from earlier drummers). The numbers were 'Smilin' the Blues Away', 'Turtle Twist', 'My Little Dixie Home' and 'That's Like It Ought to Be'. If they were not as widely sold and distributed as the band numbers, it is a shame, for the music is some of the most limpid and accessible of all Morton's work. None of the pieces is complex, most are structured like pop songs, and all display memorable melodic invention, with the three New Orleanians in close synchronization. Singleton, who could be a problematic sideman if crossed and was capable of out-blasting all comers, is subtle and sympathetic throughout, obviously listening closely to both the clarinet and the piano.

In a few months, Morton reassembled the Red Hot Peppers, a Ward Pinkett-led band with Wilbur De Paris (trombone), Bernard Addison (guitar), Billy Taylor (tuba) and Cozy Cole (drums), along with Ernie Bullock (clarinet) and an unknown second trumpet. On 5 March 1930 they cut three numbers – 'Each Day', 'If Someone Would Only Love Me' (a gorgeous slow ballad by Morton), 'That'll Never Do' and 'I'm Looking for a Bluebird'. On 'If Someone Would Only Love Me', Morton repeated the trick from 'Someday Sweetheart', using bass clarinet again for an effective solo. All these band numbers are as light and pop-flavoured as the trio sides – Morton, with his distinctive gift for catchy and lyrical tunes, was making a desperate bid to enter the pop songwriting market in a big way. But unfortunately it was too little too late, with the Depression crashing down like an avalanche.

Morton reconvened a Red Hot Peppers band on 19 March 1930, with Pinkett (his most dependable lead since George Mitchell) and Bubber Miley, Ellington's distinctively voiced, trick-mute artist, on trumpets; De Paris again on trombone; an unknown (and fairly uncertain) clarinettist; Addison's guitar and the Benford brothers once more on tuba (Bill) and drums (Tom). They cut two moderately satisfying sides: 'Little Lawrence', a perky stomp that is more freewheeling than the pop jazz Morton had recently pushed, and the aptly titled and superb 'Harmony Blues', an exercise in close ensemble arrangement which the little band executes with aplomb. Both Pinkett and Miley acquit themselves well on solos on 'Little Lawrence'. 'Harmony Blues' features a meditative Morton solo followed by a good one from Pinkett. But the band itself is the star here, playing sweetly and solidly. Bernard Addison gives out a strong solo, with plangent picking reminiscent of Eddie Lang.

The next day the band reassembled, having moved from the 46th Street studio to a Victor laboratory on 44th Street, with (possibly) a different clarinettist and an unknown banjo sitting in. They cut two characteristic Morton numbers, 'Fussy Mabel' (a somewhat backhanded tribute to Morton's current wife Mabel Bertrand) and 'Ponchatrain' [sic]. The sides are less disciplined, with another brief bass clarinet trick on 'Fussy Mabel'. 'Ponchatrain' is a marching blues with a band sound a little like some of McKinney's Cotton Pickers' funkier numbers. It is simple and restrained to the point of dullness, especially given the weak reed playing and indifferent solos by De Paris and Miley. McKinney's excellent group would have played it better.

After these routine-to-mediocre sessions, Morton tried another variation by melding some original New York Red Hot Peppers with the most recent players he had coached; on 2 June 1930 he recorded three numbers with a quasi-big band – Pinkett on trumpet; Geechie Fields, trombone; an unknown clarinettist; Walter and Joe Thomas on saxes; Lee Blair, banjo; Billy Taylor, tuba; and Cozy Cole, drums. It is a throwback group, sounding somewhat archaic or lost in a time warp, not quite a real hot dance band and not fleet enough to deal with Morton's hottest jazz. They waxed 'Oil Well' (a sardonic jab at Morton's bigmouthed manager Harrison Smith, who dabbled in stock), 'Load of Coal' (featuring, obviously, Cozy Cole), 'Crazy Chords' and 'Primrose Stomp'. (Wright 79)

The first tune is a confused effort, with the saxes fogging the ensembles and featuring undistinguished soloing. 'Load of Coal' gets off better, because Pinkett attacks the melody at once and incisively. Walter 'Foots' Thomas gives out a lush, convincing alto solo, leading to a kinetic Morton solo (with Taylor's tuba), which whips the band along to reach Cozy Cole's frisky, cymbal-pummelling solo and a brisk ensemble out-chorus. 'Crazy Chords' is interesting, because it is one of Morton's rare forays into odd harmonies and sounds, something that fascinated him but which at the time must have seemed outré and dangerously noncommercial. He recorded 'Freakish' as a piano solo attempt at 'crazy chording' and this number as a band effort, but we know that in cutting and bragging contests, he could resort to 'advanced' musical thinking and make many strange chord changes work well. 'Crazy Chords' is interesting but not particularly swinging or energetic. 'Primrose Stomp' is a much more solid and well-crafted dance tune, a medium-tempo swinger that gives solo space to everyone and is well played all around. It makes the rest of the session seem anemic by comparison.

After a hiatus during which Morton recorded with Wilton Crawley, he went back to the drawing board and convened a superb version of the original New York Red Hot Peppers on 14 July 1930. It drew on Pinkett (trumpet), Geechie Fields (trombone), Albert Nicholas (clarinet), Howard Hill (guitar), Tommy Benford (drums) and Pete Biggs (tuba). Morton, after a devastating clarinet drought, was blessed with Nicholas, a superb and consistent New Orleans reedman nearly as clever and capable as Omer Simeon and with a distinctive signature tone. The band immediately clicked, playing as if they had been together for years. Their output was as solid and brilliant as the first version of the New York recording units.

On this session, the band recorded 'Low Gravy', a lively stomp with fluid lines and lots of opportunities for clever breaks and solos; 'Strokin'

Away', another subtle and swinging tune; 'Blue Blood Blues', which gave Nicholas a chance to show his powers as a blues specialist with a beautiful, lower register style; and 'Mushmouth Shuffle', a medium-tempo tune with *dancehall* written all over it. The group seems very self-assured on the recordings and used a low number of takes, so well were they co-ordinating themselves and following Morton's scores. And even the writing seems better than the earlier sessions, as if he had been holding these aces up his sleeve until he found men worthy of waxing the music for Victor.

Morton capitalized on his fortune by trying again on 9 October 1930, with a hybrid of the recent bands – Pinkett and Fields, an unknown clarinet (the bane of his life seemed to be retaining a New Orleans reedman for two successive sessions!), Bernard Addison's guitar, Billy Taylor's tuba and Bill Beason on drums. They cut two tracks – the swan songs of the Red Hot Peppers, it turns out – 'Gambling Jack' and 'Fickle Fay Creep' (a.k.a. 'Soap Suds', as recorded years before by one of his pickup bands). Both tunes are almost up to the standards of the last session, and 'Fickle Fay Creep' is an especially attractive Morton composition in the 'Boogaboo' or shakes-and-shivers vein of minor-key gothic.

Clearly, Morton was on a roll and gaining control over the quality and consistency of his New York recording bands at this date, but the deepening Depression made Victor reluctant to back anything but sure-fire winners (such as Duke Ellington, Fats Waller or Louis Armstrong) rather than historic long-shots like Morton. His recording career went on ice until the late 1930s, when Alan Lomax worked him through the Library of Congress sessions, when Victor would again take a flier with the old professor, and the small General Records label would make both solo and band albums in tribute to his long career and his sudden stature as a jazz treasure and historical monument (all this for a man in his early 50s!). He had enjoyed flush times and good times, so in 1930 Morton battened down the hatches and tried to keep himself afloat and intact until a rainbow followed the deluge.

As Morton hunkered down in obscurity at the depth of the Depression, his sidemen and companions fared no better. Most scuffled in music, but many abandoned their horns for the duration: Kid Ory raised chickens in Los Angeles; Johnny St Cyr fell back on his profession as a plasterer; George Mitchell worked as a bank messenger. A few found refuge in big swing bands, dance bands, dime-a-dance-hall groups – whatever makeshift musical work drifted in the aftermath of the economic tsunami. A few great musicians stayed atop the wave; Louis Armstrong kept an ace band at work through the period and employed as many New Orleans men as he could haul aboard. But at the same time, a towering jazz genius such as Sidney Bechet, back in the US from France, was reduced to running a tailor's shop with his musical partner Tommy Ladnier, a gifted trumpet stylist (Jelly Roll would later seek out Bechet for some of his last sessions). Clarence Williams, once atop the profession as a musician, entrepreneur and publisher, sold his stock and opened a junque shoppe. It was that kind of time in America.

CHAPTER THREE

THE SOUND

■———————■

A question always atop the consciousness of Jelly Roll Morton was 'what is jazz?' The answer was obvious to most people: jazz is rowdy, loud, fast, hot, bawdy, extroverted, frenetic music. It was the heartbeat and soul of the New Age of the 1920s, the hectic era that inherited Cubism, Futurism and every kind of Modernism, which F. Scott Fitzgerald was quick to dub the Jazz Age.

But jazz can also be meditative, quiet, cool, aloof, restrained, elegant, mysterious and ineluctable. It is often just – *beautiful*.

By 1938, when Morton spoke his story to Alan Lomax and his acetate-disc recorder at the Library of Congress, the pianist had worked out a comprehensive aesthetic, which he described eloquently:

> *A lot of people have a wrong conception of jazz. Somehow it got into the dictionary that jazz was considered a lot of blatant noises and discordant tones, something that would be even harmful to the ears ... Jazz music is to be played sweet, soft, plenty rhythm. When you have your plenty rhythm with your plenty swing, it becomes beautiful.*

He went on explaining his jazz theory and stated another prime Morton principle: 'Always have a melody going some kind of way against a background of perfect harmony with plenty of riffs. A riff is something that gives an orchestra a great background and is the main idea in playing jazz. No jazz piano player can really play good jazz unless they try to give an imitation of a band....' (Lomax 63–64)

By the mid-1920s, Morton was a veteran of recording sessions of all sorts: solo recordings, recordings with scratch pick-up bands and ultimately the biggest of the bigtime – a contract with Victor Records, the oldest prestige outfit, whose Red Seal records had delivered stellar performers such as Enrico Caruso, Madame Schumann-Heink and John Philip Sousa's band into millions of American homes. Victor was shifting from the old acoustic recording technology, with its giant metal horns into which musicians poured their souls, to the miracle of electric recording – now small, sensitive microphones could be positioned unobtrusively to capture every tone, timbre and nuance of dynamics, bringing to the discs an astounding clarity and lifelikeness.

In 1926 Morton became a flagbearer for Victor, their house bandleader (under the cognomen Red Hot Peppers) for *race records* – the trade term recently adopted for jazz and blues played by black musicians and aimed at black consumers. The production masters of his Victor discs were all meticulously labelled either 'race' or 'colored', maintaining the sanitary boundaries of segregation even for the nation's ears.

Morton had scaled a pinnacle, and he produced for Victor a stream of masterworks demonstrating the full range of New Orleans jazz as he had heard, absorbed and transformed it for two decades. He rounded up the acme of veteran musicians and set them about unfolding the portfolio of Morton tunes and arrangements which formed his wish book. The records were stunningly well-recorded by Victor's engineers, and Morton found that he could communicate the delicate inner voices of his music as well as the brazen surfaces – passages of intricate guitar-piano duetting occur, for example, on many of the first Red Hot Peppers sides, and you can clearly hear the full drum kit (no longer just clattering wood blocks and clunky choked cymbal accents), the urgent plangency of the string bass, the woody throatiness of a blues clarinet in the chalumeau register.

And Morton matched his music to the perfection of Victor's engineering, inserting passages that would have been impossible with the old acoustic horns. Thinking as quickly as ever and summoning his full creativity, he tried to seize this supreme opportunity to show the world – at last! – that 'the king was in town' and everyone could sit back and listen to the master at work. In addition to his own work, Morton appropriated brilliant music from his peers and made some tunes so much his own that they are forever identified as Morton's – Charles Luke's mournful 'Smoke

Taking a break in a recording session, Camden, N. J., 1929. L-R: Morton, Benny Alexander, George Baquet, William Laws, Joe Thomas, Henry Prather (sousaphone), Charlie Irvis.

House Blues', Mel Stitzel's quintessentially jazzy 'The Chant', the polished 'Cannon Ball Blues' of Morton, Marty Bloom and Charlie Rider, all among the first Red Hot Pepper Victor discs.

⤞⤞⤞   ⤝⤝⤝

But – *beauty?* An instance of Morton's work that illustrates his aesthetic credo occurred later, after the great Red Hot Peppers recordings of 1926–27 in Chicago. Still recording for Victor, but also scuffling to put together hot dance bands for work around New York, Morton went into Victor's West 46th Street studio on 6 December 1928, with a band like those he had fronted around Chicago and New York – three brass, three reeds, four rhythm. The musicians were sound and capable professionals but not much more, no great New Orleans stars to solo. A few future mini-stars were on hand – Russell Procope (alto sax and clarinet), later with John Kirby's powerhouse 'biggest little band in the world'; Lee Blair (guitar), a stalwart with the De Paris brothers' neo-New Orleans band in the 1950s; and Manzie Johnson (drums), a steady all-rounder with a long career.

The band cut four sides that day, but two masters were rejected and destroyed by Victor. The survivors were the extroverted swinger 'Red Hot Pepper' and a haunting, meditative blues, 'Deep Creek'.

'Deep Creek' is a study in slowly rising sublimity, an exquisitely slow blues – almost static in passages – and drenched with melancholia, the deepest kind of lyrical blues ('blues without words', like Schumann's 'songs without words'), as its title implies. It defines a subterranean stream of feeling that ripples for three-and-a-half minutes and then disappears into silence. The tune itself is imbued with profound silences – pauses and gaps in the texture that are as significant as the musical sound itself. As visual art – drawings and paintings – can be defined by 'positive and negative' space, what is inside the outline and what is outside the outline, so 'Deep Creek' defines itself by the way it fills silence and silence fills it.

This provisional version of the Red Hot Peppers reads Morton's 'little black dots' attentively and even works up impressive swing, energy and cohesion on the free-wheeling 'Red Hot Pepper', foreshadowing the Swing Era and its riffing, shouting styles. It is a satisfying dance number, celebrating the hyperactive routines that flowed from the Charleston and Black Bottom. It is the music for which jitterbugs were born.

'Red Hot Pepper' is no more than on a par with the contemporary records by Fletcher Henderson, McKinney's Cotton Pickers and other standard hot dance bands. It is less skilled, driving and exuberant than work by many 'territory' bands, such as the Missourians or Bennie Moten's orchestra. What it does show is how well Morton could drill a band of unknown sidemen into a semblance of a good hot dance orchestra, all on short notice.

On 'Deep Creek', however, these semi-anonymous musicians delve way into themselves and use Morton's score – here just a sketch or 'head' arrangement – to drag out profound feelings, interjected into a solemn hush. The side begins with a simple, repeated, fanfare-like figure that is punctuated by a choked cymbal and ends in a brief cymbal solo, a sound like an usher clapping gloved hands to quiet a room.

The music then unfolds very slowly, with a stately trumpet solo (probably Edwin Swayzee), then a clever restatement by trombonist William Kato. This leads up to a stunningly beautiful soprano sax solo by Paul Barnes, the most elaborate variation on the very simple blues threnody. Morton (accompanied by Johnson's brushes and William Moore's tuba) adds a sparse and eloquent piano solo, with a brief passage of double-timing that is almost shocking given the solemn pace. The clarinet (Russell Procope) follows, again quite starkly. The effect is of a chain of subdued elegies, pronounced in a muffled room.

A tumbling ensemble re-declares the theme, with choked cymbal punctuation throughout, and the music subdues into silence. In some three-

and-a-half minutes, Morton has etched into the master disc a powerful hymn to melancholia, won by sheer understatement and control. It is a feat of jazz Minimalism, akin to country blues picked out of a few spare notes on a few chords: more silence than sound, architectonics of thin air.

Underscoring the wonder of 'Deep Creek' is the soprano sax solo by Paul 'Polo' Barnes (1902–81), a journeyman New Orleans reedman who later returned home for the era of 'kitty halls' and became a familiar figure in revived oldtimer bands of the 1960s. He was an amiable, not especially striking player. His minutes of enduring fame and glory came before Victor's microphones in 1928.

Consider Barnes' instrument on 'Deep Creek' – the cranky, difficult soprano sax, only thoroughly tamed by the genius Sidney Bechet and a crucifixion to most reed players asked to double on it. Johnny Hodges (a Bechet student) and Charlie Barnet used it effectively, and many jazz revivalists tried to follow Bechet's tortuous path – his sky route through operatic lushness and rococo fantasy. But Barnes, for Morton, played it as simply and plaintively as a bugle – recalling 'Taps' or 'Lights Out', the American equivalents of the sweet and sad 'The Last Post' played nightly by the British army.

The soprano sax's one true early master, Bechet, is paralleled by the 'owner' of the unlikely and ungainly C-melody sax, Frank Trumbauer, the only player who ever got much out of it but mooing vacuity. In the 1920s, the role of the saxophone was only slowly becoming defined by these men and a handful of others – Coleman Hawkins, Jimmy Dorsey, Don Redman, Paul 'Stump' Evans. The brontosaurian bass sax was mainly the province of the multi-instrumental genius Adrian Rollini and a scattering of others willing to deal with its cavernous sound. There was no handy textbook to guide reedmen in jazz bands, but on this one day, Paul Barnes made the little saxophone his own passport to destiny.

Barnes, like a nameless poet ('Anon.') from an ancient anthology of troubadour songs, uses an approach diametric from Bechet's – not grandiloquent and imperious chanting (how Bechet hated it when trumpet players jibed him about his 'fish horn'!) but simple plainsong, a thread of melody without ornament or tricks, other than a trace of slap-tonguing at the end. 'Deep Creek', rising to and falling away from his solo, is one of Morton's great achievements, thrown out (evidently) as an impromptu idea in a workaday recording session. It was just one of many beautiful aces from Morton's sleeve, from the inexhaustible font of invention he could summon and which rarely failed him, as a pianist, a composer, a leader.

Barnes spoke of Morton's methods: 'He'd never tell a man how to play a solo, unless you asked him for suggestions; he wanted everybody to play from the heart, the way they wanted to.' He recalled the work on the 1928 Red Hot Peppers date: 'We had no music for "Deep Creek". Jelly just made it up when we recorded it, played it on the piano, and let us listen at it; then we played it. We never had to do our numbers no more than about once.' The Red Hot Peppers made three takes of 'Deep Creek' for the Victor engineers that day, and Take 3 was issued.

Barnes was familiar with Morton's exuberant braggadocio, his playful *amour propre*: 'Jelly Roll's Creole manner of joking was often misunderstood by musicians up north. If you understood him, you'd laugh; if not, you'd think he was self-conceited. But that would be the wrong idea about him. He never meant any harm, and he was very jolly and liked to joke and kid the fellows in the band ...' (Russell 463)

So a small but precious, subtle work of art, an impromptu number Morton created to fill out a recording session was completed, produced, pressed and distributed by Victor to its public – the 'race records' market at which they aimed this music. 'Deep Creek' made no more immediate impression on the general public than Morton's other recordings of the era. Years later, after Morton's death in 1941, they would be discovered by collectors, journalists, musicologists and scholars, would be praised and damned, analyzed and argued over endlessly. Like all works of unselfconscious art, 'Deep Creek' exists aloof and alone as its own justification, beyond our cares and anxieties. It illustrates the timelessness and inscrutability of pure musical beauty.

One of Morton's associates at the time (1927) was Karl Kramer, a publicity agent for the newly formed MCA (Music Corporation of America), a booking agency for bands working out of Chicago. The corporation would go on to become a major powerhouse in radio and film music, and one of the corporate enemies that Morton battled in the 1930s as he tried to bootstrap himself back up to prosperity. Kramer was an articulate and observant young man, and 40 years later he set down a memoir which comments on Morton as a musician and bandleader – his idiosyncrasies and foibles, and his strengths as a performing artist. Kramer was enough of a parlour pianist to appreciate Morton's scores and his style of playing, especially the sheer beauty and elegance of the music most people of the time would have dismissed as barbaric trash:

> There were two . . . aspects of Morton's music which many critics have neglected. The first was the tremendous 'cleanliness' of his playing, both as a soloist and with his orchestra. I hesitate to apply the word 'dainty' to music of such vigor, but it comes close to conveying the extreme gracefulness of that fusion and confusion which so many mistake for hot jazz. Morton was as classical in his field as Mozart to his. Many of his phrases are intellectually, rather than emotionally, musical. Perhaps that is why Jelly's music has weathered so well, and why it sounds just as fresh today as it did thirty some years ago.

The second item that has been overlooked was the tremendous tempo of Morton's stomp playing. We don't have anything like it today, and haven't had since the Thirties. The Morton one-step beat was a product of the early 1900s and wasn't his alone, but was popular wherever dance music was played. The original one-step as introduced by the Castles about 1912, was played at just about the same speedy tempo as Jelly's stomps in 1927. (Russell 406)

The case of 'Deep Creek', when added to the list of major accomplishments by the smaller Red Hot Peppers bands of 1926–27 in Chicago and 1928 in New York, helps to illuminate the mixture of planning and improvisation, of preparation and opportunism, that was Morton's operating agenda. For Morton, at the peak of his powers as a musician, 'the readiness was all' – his years of wandering, of grabbing at local jobs and smalltime vaudeville, his chance connections with the New Orleans Rhythm Kings and King Oliver, his uncanny knack for making a grand slam home run from what should have been a foul ball, all led to the triumphs of his recordings. Which were, of course, triumphs of the heart and soul, not of the wallet.

Morton had no backers like Ellington's Cotton Club connections, which took him to national radio network hookups and enduring success; no consigliore like Armstrong's agent Joe Glaser, who could make sure his man got square treatment – or else! – and who also led Armstrong to international tours, recording contracts and a steadfast band that carried him straight over the abyss of the Depression. Morton's connections with MCA and a useful friendship with Roy Carew were thin reeds in the storm of the times, not enough to ensure him material success, stability, a solid place on which to stand so that he, like Archimedes, could wield a lever to shift the world.

❧❧❧ ❧❧❧

Among all his accomplishments, Jelly Roll Morton was a recording pioneer. The phonograph industry had been well established as a modern and developing technology since the turn of the century, but Morton connected with it when momentous changes were occurring. In 1887, Emil Berliner developed a machine that played disc records to replace Edison's original cumbersome cylinder machine, and by 1895 this mechanism was refined and marketed under the general name of 'gramophone' (later 'phonograph', except in Britain). A thriving industry produced simple, relatively inexpensive machines and made records for them to play in the home.

By the teens of the next century, a revolution in media was well underway. In that age of trusts and cartels, the phonograph (or gramophone) industry had followed the familiar path, with the manufacture of phonographs and phonograph records in the hands of the first exploiters of Berliner's invention:

> In 1912 there had been only three manufacturers [of talking machines] in the business – Victor, Columbia, and Edison. In 1914 six new companies invaded the field; 1915 saw eighteen more newcomers; and in 1916 there were forty-six. . . . The dance craze had started the spectacular climb of the phonograph economy, and it was accelerated by a general upturn in business conditions when the country as a whole began to prosper from the effects of a great war in Europe. (Gelatt 190)

Phonographs demanded recordings, and many manufacturers of machines also produced records to play on them – like Gennett Records in Richmond, Indiana, a subsidiary of the Starr Piano Company (which had at hand all the machinery and methodology to make phonographs and their fancy wooden cabinets). Gennett was one of the small companies that went to court and broke the stranglehold of patents by Victor and the other giants, and by 1920 the floodgates of recording were open across the country. (Kennedy 27) A small, improvised recording studio in a valley of the Whitewater River and across the noisy Chesapeake and Ohio freight tracks stood waiting for some wandering genius to cross the threshold.

Jelly Roll Morton, too, had benefited from the 'dance craze'. By the time he reached Richmond and the gimcrack Gennett recording studios in 1923, they were deep into cutting discs by folk, popular and jazz musicians, and he had a whole folio of his original piano and band works tucked under his arm. It was a union presided over by the smiling fates. Gennett wanted to make piano recordings to show that its new technology could capture and reproduce the elusive and diverse sounds of the instrument, and Morton was as anxious to demonstrate how the piano could also show the range and subtleties of his brand of jazz. The match was perfect, and in 1923–24, Morton cut a series of solo piano records for Gennett, records that demonstrated the full range of jazz piano as well as the full range of the Starr piano and Gennett's recording technology.

While in Richmond in 1923, his course intersected that of the New Orleans Rhythm Kings, a crew of rollicking white musicians down from

King Oliver's Creole Jazz Band in California, 1922. L–R: Tubby Hall, Honore Dutrey, Joe 'King' Oliver, Lil Hardin, Paul 'Stump' Evans, Johnny Dodds, Jimmy Palao, Ed Montudie Garland.

a long stand in Chicago, who knew of Morton's youthful reputation as 'Windin' Boy' and his work with all manner of New Orleans musicians. By one of those freak accidents, they all made history by integrating Gennett's old warehouse recording studio for a session by the NORK with Jelly Roll at the piano. The wily Creole was at the helm of a rowdy bunch of youngsters, whose ideal was the King Oliver Creole Jazz Band, not the ragged-but-white Original Dixieland Jazz Band. The young men wanted to play bluer than blue and blacker than black, and Morton was more than willing to inject his red hot Creole ideas into their little outfit.

Cornettist Paul Mares idolized Joe Oliver and tried all his mute tricks and blue smears, trombonist George Brunis was a skilled tailgate artist from a vast family of jazz musicians, and clarinettist Leon Roppolo was a brooding Sicilian (soon to lose his mind and then his life following bouts with marijuana, finally throwing his instrument into Lake Pontchartrain) with a dark, sombre tone and exceptional swing, one of the first fluent jazz clarinet soloists on record. The NORK swelled and shrank as it recorded, sometimes a fleet little quintet, sometimes a fairly cumbersome hot dance band with three saxes as well as the cornet-trombone-clarinet front line. On the dates with Morton (17–18 July 1923) they were in their elephantine mode, although Gennett's fairly foggy recording does not give it much depth or sonic perspective.

Mares recalled the eagerness with which the young New Orleanians began their recording career in 1922:

> We were so anxious to record that we took the first offer to come along and beat out all the rest of the bands. We could have made a fortune with that band if we had played our cards right, but we didn't. We rushed into everything like we did that recording deal. Actually, the band was playing good music. We had only two tempos, slow drag and the two-four one-step. We did our

best to copy the colored music we'd heard at home. We did the
best we could, but naturally we couldn't play real colored style.

(Shapiro and Hentoff 123)

Morton's forceful presence on that one session gave the NORK the newest version of 'real colored style' available.

For Morton was on the verge of pulling his own career together. He was knocking around the country, stopping off at recording studios when he could cobble together a little band to play his music, sometimes striking gold as he did in Chicago in June of 1923, when he scraped together a band that included trumpet master Tommy Ladnier and Roy Palmer, Morton's favourite trombonist. Another good group in October 1923 included the elusively lyrical trumpeter Natty Dominique and veteran trombonist Zue Robertson. A little 'Steamboat Four' or 'Stomps Kings' group in April of 1924 included raucous clarinettist Boyd Senter (of 'Senterpedes' fame) and several kazooists, and was highly makeshift. Such impromptu minstrelsy paid off when Morton found congenial soloists such as King Oliver (two sides in December 1924) and the lively white clarinettist Volly de Faut (two sides in May 1925). He was perfecting a new kind of chamber jazz – his powerful piano coupled with one or two skilled solo horns and drums.

In the next jazz generation, Benny Goodman became renowned for his trio, quartet and quintet groups, which made him piles of money. But Jelly Roll was there *fustest with the mostest*, like old foxy General Nathan Bedford Forrest. If he didn't have a band at hand, he could mould one out of materials available locally and through his sheer genius and energy create something like genuine hot jazz. He wrung very good solo music from Joe Oliver (duets) and from de Faut (a trio), keeping them going with his piano by staying out of their way when necessary. His object was not to show himself off but to make music that was true collective improvisation, two or three players merged into one super-instrument. His years of wandering and practicing as a musical bricoleur, cobbling up new and original music out of found objects, was about to end as he made a stand in Chicago and put on to record the definitive anthology of New Orleans jazz.

⟫⟫⟫   ⟪⟪⟪

The ideal that Morton had shaped in his mind was one of great purity — a small band of New Orleans players steeped in the tradition but capable of some note-reading and willing to listen to a persuasive leader. He had spent years in tacking together makeshift bands from whatever aggregation of locals he could hire, with or without jazz experience. His persistent stock comment in describing his travels for Alan Lomax was, 'Arrived in 19XX at YYY City, found that nobody there could play any jazz.' This at first seems to be one of his self-important put-downs of others on the early scene, but is probably a small cry of anguish from a man eager to get a band together and play some really hot music, right from his suitcase full of scores. His hit-or-miss band recordings prior to the Red Hot Peppers sessions are notably uneven, with decent jazz musicians mixed together with those clueless or talentless, or both.

Morton had a special yen for superb clarinettists, and through most of his career he chased them without consistent results. When he did get an Omer Simeon, a Johnny Dodds, an Albert Nicholas or a Barney Bigard, he made very good use of them. He also liked to lean on a guitarist equally skilled at rhythm and solo work. He was lucky enough to bag Johnny St Cyr and Bud Scott, but when they were not on hand he cultivated and taught young men of promise, including Lee Blair, Bernard Addison and Lawrence Lucie. He liked trumpet men who played an unadorned lead in the middle range and in middle dynamics, and his two most consistent players — George Mitchell and Ward Pinkett — reflect this aesthetic. (He admired some virtuoso cornet and trumpet men, mainly Freddie Keppard, but his distance from Louis Armstrong may reflect his distrust of those he judged flamboyant or self-serving.) Morton stated his preference for Roy Palmer as a trombonist, but used the familiar sound of Kid Ory and the very odd style of Geechie Fields, so a whole range of sound on this instrument – from conventional to bizarre – seemed to satisfy him. His rhythm sections varied a great deal, with the banjo sometimes prominent and brass bass as often used as string bass. He was fussy about drumming and insisted on the use of brushes (he said he 'invented' them, too!) to simplify and mute some drummers. On many recordings, Morton's piano solos are recorded without the full rhythm section, sometimes as true solos – some of this dictated by microphone techniques, some probably requested by Morton.

Duke Ellington is usually described as the composer-leader who 'discovered that the microphone is a musical instrument', but from the moment Morton began hearing the playbacks of Victor's electrical process, he had the same insight, making arrangements that separated instruments, allowed them to jump forward sonically in breaks and solos and otherwise manipulating the perspective of his band's sound. The technique is most striking on the sides of the second Red Hot Peppers sessions, where Johnny St Cyr is given a duet role with Morton, and we suddenly know what a well-recorded jazz guitar sounds like and how seraphically it blends with the piano. These details were not accidental and reflect Morton's compulsive drive to take control of his music and get it right. He was a music perfectionist (many sidemen remark on this quality), but he did not drive his men or radiate anxiety about their work. He knew that quality emerges when artists are relaxed: when they are unselfconsciously enjoying themselves, the music is bound to be pleasing and memorable.

Other sonic trademarks occur, not as vivid and quirky as those Ellington created over the years with his band, but still interesting and revealing. His sessions often used brass mutes and 'freak' effects supplied ad lib by his players: George Mitchell used a Harmon mute much of the time, and Geechie Fields used a variety of mutes and trick effects to choke down his trombone sound. Both their brass parts were thus reduced to the same level of volume and timbre as the reeds, guitar, piano, etc. This creates an intimacy of sound surprising in what most people then (and now!) believe to be a raucous and uncontrolled music. Morton was quite serious in his little sermonette on jazz being *plenty sweet, plenty rhythm, plenty swing*, and he found ways to build those ineffable qualities into his recordings.

The other way we know Morton was consciously trying to bring down the noise threshold and establish control in jazz was in his repeated experiments with chamber jazz. From the beginning of his recording career, Morton was as happy to play with one, two or three others as with an orthodox 'full band'. While that six- or seven-piece band was an ideal for New Orleans jazz, Morton also knew that one or two of the right players could wring great music from small resources, that 'any number can play'. In fact, prior to 1917 and the emergence of recorded jazz with its 'Dixieland' format of cornet, trombone, clarinet plus rhythm, smaller groups were probably a norm in the music, often using instruments like violin, guitar, even flute. (Gushee, 61-62)

He had the delicate ear and touch for accompanying a single cornet or clarinet, for playing lightly yet forcefully with one horn and one rhythm. These practices obviously existed anywhere that musicians had to assemble groups on an ad hoc basis, but Morton used them in the recording studio, where the close-up sound of even acoustic recording techniques could help a jazzman clarify his style and ideas, allow him to whisper and not shout, to come down to a lyrical level of directness. His trios and quartets, even the duets with King Oliver, were revolutionary in redefining jazz, rejecting the received idea that only one particular kind of group using a certain number of instruments could produce swinging, moving and imaginative music in the robust vein of New Orleans jazz.

But Morton was an innovator on so many levels that it is hard to enumerate them. Balancing his gift of the gab and his ability to sell himself, he also possessed the canniness to assess, nurture and use musical talents as he found them. Without the luxury of building and sustaining a band like an Ellington or a Basie, he had to become a talent scout and a leader who could cajole the best from players who were often only mediocre or uncertain in technique. His session players are uniform in agreeing that Morton was a master at putting a band together and getting its maximum effort on to wax. Even when they were aesthetically and stylistically at odds with Morton (for example, Sidney De Paris on the 1939 Victor sessions), he coaxed passable work from them and let them turn their egos loose. As a band pianist, he was alert to the musicians around him and used his piano part as a goad, a cushion, a lifeline, to keep ensembles going and to present a beautiful background for soloists. His version of the NORK's 'She's Cryin' for Me', which he retitled 'Georgia Swing', is a textbook example of the band pianist as rhythm master, as gyroscope, as genial accompanist – his work in the background charges and channels the group's energy and spirit to justify the title. It is one of the swingingest three minutes of 1920s jazz, mainly because of Morton's foundation role.

It is easy to use the periscope of hindsight to assert that Morton oversold himself and his role in jazz history, but in the late 1930s nothing in the way of 'jazz history' or 'jazz criticism' existed, apart from ephemeral journalism. In many ways, Morton's self-awareness in the Library of Congress memoir is the basic starting-point for later jazz enquiries. Morton related ragtime, blues and jazz as musical forms and genres, told the story of Buddy Bolden and other pioneer musicians, laid out the quasi-legendary role of New Orleans in African-American musical heritage and gave copious examples to illustrate all his ideas. At a time when no one took either jazz or African-American culture seriously, Morton made a comprehensive and dignified start on his people's story. While he was shrewd enough to look after Mrs Morton's son Ferd first, he also had his mind and his eye on the many musicians and characters who people his recitations, and he left them engraved on our consciousness more vividly than all the later textbooks and romances about the music could do.

CHAPTER FOUR

PERFORMANCE

■————————■

The most important performance of Morton's life was semi-private and had an extended run in Washington, D.C.. Morton performed at his favourite place, the rightful throne of Mr Jelly Lord – behind the keyboard of a grand piano. It was a one-man duet performance – Jelly Roll talking and singing, accompanied by the incomparable piano of Jelly Roll. Like an ancient bard, he meditated, chanted and chatted his way through a lengthy heroic autobiography, to a bemused audience of one or two and a pair of whirring portable disc recorders, cutting large aluminum-and-acetate records. The series of recordings changed Morton's life and legacy and altered jazz history.

The project was conceived in 1938 by Alan Lomax, the young Folk Music Curator at the Library of Congress, who knew that Morton was living and playing in Washington and thought him a likely source of amusing anecdotes and folklore – another of the antique musicians that Lomax had learned to interview and record in his apprenticeship with his distinguished father John A. Lomax (1867–1948), the virtual inventor of modern American folk-music collecting and analysis. The elder Lomax had established the Archive of American Folk Music at the Library of Congress towards the end of a long, fruitful career as a song-finder, heralded by his landmark collection *Cowboy Songs and Other Frontier Ballads* (1910), the work that put the 'western' into 'country and western' and, along with early cowboy films and Owen Wister's novel *The Virginian* (1902), made the cowboy a primal figure in America's popular mythology.

Young Alan joined his father in 1933, aged 17, accompanying him in rugged automobile odysseys across America, especially in the South and West, lugging a barely portable disc-recording machine to document the work songs, blues, shouts and hollers of rural workers, cowboys, prison and chain-gang inmates, itinerant wanderers of the Depression and others who had their own songs, stories and culture to share. John Lomax reports the labour that he and his son invested in the work:

> ... *we also carried a 350-pound recording machine – a cumbersome pile of wire and iron and steel – built into the rear of the Ford, two batteries weighing seventy-five pounds each, a microphone, a complicated machine of delicate adjustments, coils of wire, numerous gadgets, besides scores of blank aluminum and celluloid discs, and, finally, a multitude of extra parts* ... (J. Lomax 111)

So, for Alan Lomax, the work with Morton in the comfort and quiet of the Library of Congress itself must have been a blessed relief from roughing it in the field.

Lomax provided Morton with the stage he needed to tell his story to the world, and Morton, ever the showman, sat down at the piano in staid Coolidge Auditorium on 23 May 1938, and in collaboration with the folklorist invented a form for his tale. Starting at the beginning of America and the beginning of his family he spun out a mesmerizing tale, his mellifluous voice drifting over a series of soft arpeggios, chords and broken melodies on the piano, like a bard from ancient days reciting the florid and heroic saga of the demigods. For weeks he cut discs and reminisced about a remarkable life in music, recounting stories far richer than anything Lomax might have anticipated.

The staid façade of the Library of Congress, Washington, D.C..

Over his career, especially in his younger years, when he wandered the South and Southwest in the company of indelible characters including Jack the Bear and Game Kid ('he was ragged as a pet pig'), riding boxcars and hiking down Mississippi dirt highways, selling phony medicines door-to-door, jumping into gambling games such as Tonk or the Georgia Skin Game, shooting pool or shooting craps, Morton played in every imaginable venue before every imaginable audience. In the whorehouse days in The District he was sometimes placed behind a screen as he played, to shield the delicate clientele from the sight of a working Creole musician. Then there were bucket shops so low their only purpose was to make you as drunk as possible as quickly and as cheaply as possible, like the rancid eighteenth-century London dives in William Hogarth's 'Gin Lane' – *drunk for a quarter, dead drunk for four bits*.

He worked in slightly upscale honky tonks, where women performed backwoods can-cans (without benefit of undergarments), such as the 'Ham Kick', in which they tried to punt a smoked ham dangling from the ceiling, giving bystanders glimpses of their celestial attractions (although said bystanders were probably far too blasted on rotgut to recognize them). He played in small-town vaudeville theatres, rackety barroom/brothel palaces, and struggling nightclubs such as Chicago's Elite No. 2. On the West Coast in the early 1920s, with his partner/wife Anita Johnson Gonzales, he even tried his hand at running dives, managing declining dumps with names like 'The Jupiter'.

With his bands Morton had played dance halls, lakeside pavilions, amusement parks, bigger vaudeville theatres, speakeasies. He was ready for anything in the line of hilarity, and when this Lomax fellow, an amiable white boy with a soft southern drawl, met Morton, heard him play at yet another smoky dive in Washington and suggested he could tell all he knew about music to the Library of Congress's recording machine, it was another star-crossed conjunction in Morton's rollercoaster career. Lomax may have thought that he would pick up a few new blues numbers, fresh anecdotes about life in music from a veteran African-American performer and other odds and ends for the vast files of musical anthropology that he and his father were busy filling in the Library of Congress. What he got was a seemingly endless font of fact, fiction, poetry, rumination, opinion and observation, all told in a matter-of-fact way but imbued with the zest of romance and mythology. Morton was his Hesiod, unreeling the tale of the genesis of the gods, the genealogy of jazz, against a seamless tapestry of his own and others' music – everything that he had heard, learned and tucked away in over 30 years of hard work as Mr Jelly Lord.

Throughout May and June and concluding with a session in December of 1938, Lomax and Morton cut the big acetate discs on the Library of Congress recorders to capture Morton's speaking, singing and playing. The scene is thus described in the latest release of the fabled sessions, remastered and released in 2005 by Rounder Records:

Alan Lomax's recording sessions with Jelly Roll Morton were held at the Coolidge Auditorium of the Library of Congress, known for its fine acoustics. The project commenced on May 21, 1938, continued through June 12, and ended in a final session on December 14, 1938. Jelly Roll played a Steinway Concert Grand and Alan Lomax, then the Library's Head of the Archive of Folk Song, sat across from him running two battery-operated Presto disc-recording machines.... The sessions produced nine hours of music and narrative on 54 twelve-inch discs (AFS discs 1638–88 and 2487–89). The first 51 of these were acetate and recorded at 78 rpm. The final three, recorded in December, were double-sided lacquer-covered aluminum discs recorded at 33 $^{1}/_{3}$ rpm ...

(notes to Complete L. of C. Recordings, 43)

His narrative was interwoven into a new art form: part ballad, part historical lecture and musical analysis, part adventure yarn and romance, starring Ferd Morton in all the parts; an Everyman like the universal hero of James Joyce's *Finnegans Wake* (which Joyce was completing at the same time Morton spoke into Lomax's microphone), Humphrey Chimpden Earwicker, whose name is also Here Comes Everybody. Morton was at his best in the chamber music hall, playing with great certainty and finesse, delving into ancient memories for names and places and being surprisingly accurate when Lomax insistently drove him into deeper and deeper recesses of the past.

Lomax's reedy southern drawl is heard often on the recordings, interjecting queries or commenting on the narrative. While he was experienced in interviewing folk musicians and prided himself on understanding southern and rural blacks, he was unprepared for a sensibility as expansive, subtle and profound as Morton's. (Lomax dubbed him a 'Creole Benvenuto Cellini' in the introduction to his book derived from the recordings, *Mister Jelly Roll* [xiii].) Lomax at times is insensitive and treats Morton as a minstrel figure, but Morton patiently deals with this young white fellow (all people of colour in the south then knew how to deal calmly with the free-floating racism as palpable in Washington – a mossy southern town under all the white marble – as anywhere). He had learned the hard lesson that the grandfather on his dying bed teaches the young narrator of Ralph Ellison's *Invisible Man*:

> *'I have been a traitor all my born days, a spy in the enemy's country ever since I gave up my gun back in the Reconstruction. Live with your head in the lion's mouth. I want you to overcome 'em with yeses, undermine 'em with grins, agree 'em to death and destruction, let 'em swoller you till they vomit or bust wide open.... Learn it to the younguns,' he whispered fiercely; then he died.* (Ellison 16)

Morton was ambivalent on what some call 'race', because his family, his culture, his city was also ambivalent on the whole cloudy notion. The 'segregation racket' that followed the end of Reconstruction was only catching up to New Orleans when Morton was a young man, poisoning life in what had been an 'open city' during the race wars of the years after the Surrender. Morton thought of himself as French, as Creole, as a citizen of the world in the grand old eighteenth century sense. He didn't think of himself as poor, black and victimized – that was far below his dignity. He was brought up better.

In the Preface to the second edition of *Mister Jelly Roll*, which Lomax wrote in 1972, he talked about his motives in his field recording project, which included his sessions with Jelly Roll Morton. Lomax had a specific ideological or didactic aim for his work:

> *... I dreamed of recording an oral portrait of the American working class – the mule skinners, the truckers, the sandhogs, the lonesome housewives – turning over the mike to them,*

letting them have their say for a change, reversing the direction
of our so-called 'communication' system, which really has only
one direction: from the establishment down.

He characterized the idealized speech that he sought for this project: 'The people I met at the end of the line (urban and rural) spoke sentences that wound across the page like rivers or mountain ranges. Jelly Roll spoke like that.' But Morton hardly fit into any of the categories of 'working class' Americans that Lomax listed, unless you assume all people of colour were *ipso facto* of that social stratum at the time.

Interestingly, Lomax noted how Morton himself had a plan for the organization and direction of his narrative, how much control he exerted on the project: 'He had thought out and organized his story before he came to the Library. Listening to him was like being present at the birth of the new music that has since become the first international music.' (ix–x) Morton had developed a plan for the narrative, and he already began to mine his ideas for publicity purposes, as he was interviewed for a *Down Beat* magazine article by Sidney Martin in June 1938. (Complete L. of C. Recordings 10)

The whole vast Library of Congress project is more of a collaboration, more shaped by Morton's own agenda and ideas, than is usually acknowledged. Morton had in mind a series of ideological, a

esthetic and highly personal points that he desperately wanted to see preserved and disseminated, in this case by the august powers of the nation's library and archives, the very incarnation of Posterity. He is in many ways the genuine author of the work, while Lomax is a capable amanuensis and assistant to the Creole genius.

In any event, Morton handled Lomax smoothly on what quickly became his own greatest show on earth – another act in the ongoing Jelly Roll pageant, in which he could depict the invention of jazz and his role in the creation; explain how 'Tiger Rag' sprang from an old French quadrille he happened to transform, describe the street bands, Mardi Gras, the Indians and other byways of New Orleans' florid and fascinating culture, as he recalled it and could illustrate from the keyboard. No one had ever quite attempted what Morton did, when Lomax handed him the golden key to immortality by way of the big Coolidge Auditorium Steinway.

On the many sides released commercially from the Library of Congress archives (the recordings filled a dozen LPs and seven discs on the 2005 CD edition: roughly nine hours of music and talk), Morton is effortlessly amusing and sharply focused on his task. At Lomax's persistent prurient prodding, he delves into the seamier sides of his adventures, but when he has his own way, he is slyly comic, highly descriptive and very persuasive in describing his past and trying to show the grandeur of his career. It is for him, clearly, a redemptive effort – a chance literally to put the record straight, like Marcel Proust's attempts to chase down, retrieve and possess lost time. It seems, at first, wholly quixotic, a Romantic's last stab at self-anointment, but then the realization comes that Morton knows exactly what to do with a recorder and a microphone, that he is a professional – a master of this trade, like Tony Jackson, with 'a thousand tunes' at hand, each one freighted with stories.

But his approach to music had always been mixed and complex. He was a musical perfectionist, determined to get it right and force his players to read his scores as needed, but he was also a genial and laid-back entertainer, aware of his audiences and eager to get a laugh, to dazzle and awe his listeners. He was clearly an artist and felt he should be so regarded, but he was also embedded in a popular culture that could be crude, crass and simple-minded as well as subtle, insightful and infinitely touching. His bad vaudeville jokes were the other side of the coin from his tender, lullaby-like melodies; the deep-sprung blues; the pure, abandoned vitality of his stomps. (Morton coined the word 'joys' to describe what he thought of as unbuttoned anti-blues, and one of his early tango-inflected tunes could be played either as 'New Orleans Blues' or 'New Orleans Joys' – while 'Milenberg Joys' was a one-way barrelhouse number.)

On the long series of big acetate records, Morton unleashed a torrent of small anecdotes and details – recollections of individual musicians or minor events in his wanderings – but, as the weeks rolled on, he also developed major themes to define himself and his experience. They would help him to shape his immediate career, as he recalled them and used them in the commercial recordings that he made from 1938 to 1941. The grand exercise of recalling and narrating his life story served to aim him towards a future that he wanted to shape and control. The chaos of the Depression and the loss of his steady work in music had shaken him, and Lomax's sessions became a lifeline into the past and then into a possible future. Clearly, as Morton delved into the vivid memories of the past 40 years, he began to see how his past might predicate the present and future – the key to capturing lost time lay in the ability to remember it clearly and in microscopic detail. 'Recollection' for Morton seems to have been more literal than for most people.

The long recital at Coolidge Auditorium was also a time for Morton to sift his life and career and make sense of them. The autobiography is like an extended excursion into the blues, and the brilliant commentator on African-American music and culture Albert Murray has insights into how the blues can function as catharsis and recall:

> The blues ballad is a good example of what the blues are about. Almost always relating a story of frustration, it could hardly be described as a device for avoiding the unpleasant facts of Negro life in America. On the contrary, it is a very specific and highly effective vehicle, the obvious purpose of which is to make Negroes acknowledge the essentially tenuous nature of all human existence. (Murray 88)

He also points out that it is not just self-expression that the blues bring, but a way to measure and make sense of life:

> *As an art form, the blues idiom by its very nature goes beyond the objective of making human life bearable physically or psychologically. The most elementary and hence the least dispensable objective of all serious artistic expression, whether aboriginal or sophisticated, is to make human existence meaningful.* (Murray 89)

Lomax's sessions with the piano and the recording machine were vehicles for Morton to review and assess a long career, interwoven with frustration and triumph, and in his last years put it into perspective. It launched him on his last recording campaigns and his last run at the bigtime.

Some major themes or tales that Morton wove as he spoke and played were: 1) the true origins of jazz with African-American musicians in New Orleans; 2) the sheer diversity of brilliant music available in his youth, including the legions of good-to-great pianists Morton praised unstintingly (such as Sammy Davis, Albert Carroll, Tony Jackson, Porter King and many others); 3) the folkways and manners of Creole New Orleans, including hoodoo and other extravagant beliefs; 4) the marching bands and traditions of brass band playing, and the social aid and pleasure clubs and fraternal organizations that used them for funerals and other occasions; 5) the Mardi Gras Indians, the neighbourhood gangs and other groups that dominated the annual holidays; 6) the ambience and mores of the sporting world and the characters who represented it; 7) disquisitions on individual jazz and ragtime piano players, with extensive samples of their styles and techniques; 8) the 'Spanish tinge' and its role in jazz, with Morton's own works as examples; 9) theories on sources of New Orleans jazz, including dances (quadrilles), the French Opera and other influences, with musical examples; and 10) life on the road in the segregated Deep South and its picaresque implications.

The most famous example of Morton's interweaving of cultural history and jazz history was his well-shaped narrative of the 'invention' of an ancient jazz standard, 'Tiger Rag', which Morton claimed to have fabricated from bits of old quadrilles and finished off with the 'tiger sound' that typified it. The story is a *tour de force* of integrating narrative and music and of *ex post facto* definition. Morton begins with 'Tiger Rag' as it was made universally familiar by the Original Dixieland Jazz Band's 1918 Victor recording, a 'jazz classic' that anyone in 1938 would instantly recognize. With this model in mind, Morton does a fanciful job of 'deconstructing' the music, taking it strain by strain (it is a fairly complicated five-part ragtime structure) and playing each one in its original form, then reassembling it as a whole, in swinging 'Jelly Roll style'.

He begins the sequence with a key idea – 'Jazz started in New Orleans'. The demonstration is to show the primacy of that place, and in that place the primacy of Ferd Morton, present at the birth, the Socratic midwife. The music 'happened to be transformed from an old quadrille that was in many different tempos.'

Morton then plays the introduction – 'meaning that everyone was supposed to get their partners.' It is the familiar four-bar phrase (a kind of riff, repeated) that opens the ODJB record. He then describes a dance hall and people rushing to assemble for the quadrille. Then, Morton says, the band repeats the intro.

'The next strain would be a waltz strain, I believe,' Morton intones. He plays what is recognizable as the ODJB first strain but in a very simple 3/4 time pattern. (Someone once said it sounded like his Aunt Tilly practicing at the parlour piano.) Then, 'they had another strain that came right beside it'; Morton plays a fractured rhythm which he explains as 'mazurka time' – again, the second ODJB theme in the upside-down waltz (3/4) rhythm, which is the Polish mazurka. It is, again, a skeletal version of piano dance music.

'And of course they had another strain that was in a different tempo,' Morton says – and he plays the halting stop-time riff most familiar as 'Tiger Rag' to most people, the one New Orleans players called the 'Jack Carey' strain (named for the trombonist-bandleader and brother of cornettist Thomas 'Papa Mutt' Carey). The chant 'Play, Jack Car-ey!' 'Play, Jack Car-ey!' fits the pattern and was purportedly called out by fans of the trombonist when his band played ballyhoo jobs on the streets. Morton informs Lomax that the theme is in 2/4 time.

'Of course they had another one,' he continues, playing the 2/4 'rideout' or final strain in ODJB style. 'It happened to be transformed' – Morton says, using his important key word – 'by your performer at the present time. "Tiger Rag" for your approval.' He then reassembles the strains in order, in a driving 4/4 stomp tempo. But before he launches, he answers Lomax's query about the name – 'I also named it, from the way I make the tiger with my elbow.'

Then we follow Morton through a brilliant performance that leaves tenuous theory behind and unwraps his best jazz piano style. When he gets to the 'Jack Carey' strain he unleashes the forearm-elbow tone clusters of the 'tiger' and for good measure shouts 'Hold that tiger!' The performance is like some long-distance response to the famous frenzied performances of the tune by Louis Armstrong in the late 1920s and early 1930s, as if Morton wanted to prove absolutely that he could 'make the piano sound like a band' and swing such a blazing showpiece, in the way of being 'the world's greatest single-handed entertainer'. When he concludes, he says emphatically, 'That was many years before the Dixieland had ever started, when I played the "Tiger Rag."'

It is, of course, a direct takeoff from the ODJB standard but Morton is making a fine point: that black musicians were there first, that what may have been copyrighted and advertised as original music by such johnny-come-latelies as the ODJB was as old as time and generated from the deep African-American-Creole history of New Orleans. It is a myth in the most important sense of the word – a genesis story that encapsulates and illustrates a transcendent reality which cannot be 'proven' by factual history or analysis, but which makes a way of belief possible.

Morton would have known about the recent revival of the Original Dixieland Jazz Band in 1936 as a result of the newsreel feature *The March of Time*, which gathered the oldtimers together to film them in a recreated Victor acoustic recording session. They made new recordings in the original style and with a big swing band and became, momentarily, a pop sensation. If they can come back from the dead, Morton must have felt, then I too can be reborn – and I've got more imagination and originality to sell than those boys ever did! His stint at the Library of Congress could at last reassert the claims of African-American creators on their music.

To show the tendency of his thought, when Morton continues immediately after the dazzling exhibition of 'Tiger Rag', he says, 'Of course we had lots of other good numbers, for instance "That's a-Plenty". No, we won't say that, we'll say "Panama".' It is a revealing bit of mind-changing in the context: 'That's a-Plenty' was a piano rag (1914) by white Lew Pollack, adapted by and closely associated with the white New Orleans Rhythm Kings (collaborators of old [1923], at the beginning of Morton's career on records), while 'Panama' was originally a popular tango by African-American William H. Tyers, a colleague of the great black exemplar James Reese Europe, adapted and played by black New Orleans musicians. Normally colour-blind, Morton wants to keep this bit of history as black as he can make it, for ideological reasons. This segment of his epic narrative aims to show that people of colour in New Orleans, like Creole Ferd Morton, were the 'only true begetters' of jazz, that he was on hand at the inception, that the intellectual property of the music should have his name firmly emblazoned on it.

Probably the segment of Morton's story best known after the 'Tiger Rag' vignette is his extended discussion-demonstration of the brass bands and their social functions. While many people knew street bands were important in New Orleans jazz history, few had heard or seen them. None was recorded until the 1940s, after the peak of their initial popularity and efficacy. So Morton's one-man-band show was a valuable bit of jazz education, leading to future research and discussion of the diverse roots of the music.

His discussion of the marching bands is almost a meditation. It does not star Jelly Roll Morton but the collective musicians of New Orleans, so it lacks the egocentric edge of other Morton tales and is steeped in nostalgic details such as the 'ham sandwiches slathered all over with mustard' served at funeral suppers (as good a detail as Hamlet's 'funeral-baked meats' any day!) or the well-armed 'second lines' who escorted the bands from one district to another in the contentious city. He is quite good at painting a lively word-picture, and his piano underlining is superb. He renders bits of the musical ritual as well as one player could – the funeral dirge (an old spiritual, 'Flee as a Bird to the Mountain') read off the band cards and played in easy whole notes by the brass band musicians; the return march (an impudent rendering of the old English tall-tale folk tune 'The Derby Ram', now known as 'Oh, Didn't He Ramble?' and a backhanded tribute to the dead man's hedonistic life). Morton sings the words to deliver the colourful zest that funerals meant in the New Orleans of his memory, ending with another beautiful capstone phrase: 'That was always the end of a perfect death!'

He contrasted the work of the street band musicians, who were paid little ('two dollars or two dollars and a half'), with the big money flowing to the professors – the piano players who cleaned up on salaries and tips.

He is patting himself on the back, but he also radiates simple nostalgic envy for those players in the bands who had only companionship, simple music and a bit of fun as their goals. In some ways, the bandsmen had it lucky, while the ticklers had to work a tedious and sometimes indecent, disgusting grind in order to accumulate their larger heaps of spondulicks.

Morton would mine this segment of the Library of Congress narrative for recordings in the following years: 'Oh, Didn't He Ramble?' and 'High Society' (another glittering street march) with the 1939 Victor band, 'Panama' with his Hot Seven and Henry 'Red' Allen's assured trumpet lead (his father, Henry Allen, Sr., had been one of the most esteemed New Orleans brass band masters, with a longstanding group from Algiers). The memory session helped to firm up in Morton's mind an agenda which meant revisiting the past as well as exploiting the present with his pop tunes and jump-swing numbers for the hepcats. He tried to use the material that Lomax helped him plumb to lever himself from the dead-end realities of the present. Memory also distracted him from the helplessness and paranoia that sometimes afflicted him, and which prompted the ranting about his lost three million dollars and the sharks who had so thoroughly robbed him of his own work and property. It was almost like 'talk therapy', this pleasant work at the keyboard of the Coolidge Auditorium grand piano.

৩৩৩ ୧୧୧

In 1938, no one had ever done what Morton attempted for Lomax – assemble a systematic and self-consistent story of jazz from its origins to the present. Books on jazz were nearly nonexistent, aside from blundering journalism like Henry O. Osgood's early *So This Is Jazz* (1926), the misguided long-distance critical works of Hugues Panassie (*Le Jazz Hot* [1934] and *The Real Jazz* [1942]) and the about-to-be-born *Jazzmen*, the first serious and solidly founded work on America's most remarkable

Morton in the midst of the Victor recording sessions of 1939.

music. A few shrewd observers such as composers Virgil Thomson and Deems Taylor, and cultural commentators Otis Ferguson and Roger Pryor Dodge wrote insightful pieces lost in the columns of popular magazines; Marshall Stearns began what he called a 'history of swing music' for *Down Beat* magazine; and other collector-critics such as John Hammond scribbled for tiny fanzines with obsessively detailed commentary on jazz records and their arcana. But there were no big models for Morton to follow, no accepted template in the culture. He became the Homer of jazz, singing his expansive tales of *The Iliad* (an invading army of New Orleans jazzmen against the world, in a 10-year campaign) and *The Odyssey* (the chartless wanderings of Odysseus F. Morton over the known world). In many ways, modern jazz history follows Morton's outline, if only unconsciously, with certain elements still *de rigueur*: the whorehouse professors, the street bands, the 'jazz funerals', the primacy of New Orleans musicians over all followers. It was Morton who painted the big mural that allowed fans, journalists and academics to fill in the details and vignettes of the narrative.

In laying out his epic, Morton also became the first influential historiographer of jazz, especially in telling the Buddy Bolden story. Like Hesiod, he contrived a tale that explained the genesis of the gods of jazz – in this case, black gods who were the true begetters of the new music, and with whom young Ferdinand Lamothe rubbed elbows in the dives and on the streets of The District. Morton described Buddy Bolden as the *ur*-trumpeter of a genre known (largely through the huge example of Louis Armstrong) as Gabriel's music. Morton talked about Bolden as a larger-than-life tough guy and musical genius, who blew louder than anyone else, so that he 'blew his brains out through the trumpet', who 'drank all the whiskey he could find' and went crazy from his excesses – musical, gustatory and sexual.

Morton's recitation, over the piano strains of the tune he identified as Bolden's signature – an ancient ragtime ditty known up and down the Mississippi Valley, and published by the mysterious team of Barney and Seymore (actually Kansas ragtime writer and publisher Theron Bennett) in 1904 as 'St Louis Tickle'. Morton called it 'Buddy Bolden's Blues' and gave it raunchy words – 'Funky butt, funky butt, take it away!' – evocative of the dance hall where Bolden often played, the Union Sons Hall, also known as 'Funky Butt Hall', presumably because of its overpowering reek.

After Morton's bravura recitation of 1938, the Bolden legend was enlarged by William Geary 'Bunk' Johnson, a sweet-toned and loudmouthed trumpeter who claimed to have played with Bolden's band and thus wedged himself into the earliest chapters of jazz history. The pioneering critical anthology *Jazzmen*, edited by Charles Edward Smith and Frederic Ramsey, Jr., appeared in 1939, putting Johnson's brags and much other dubious Boldeniana into print. Morton had launched a whole chapter of early jazz studies, ultimately revised and verified in 1978 by Donald M Marquis, whose work lays out the bare bones of Bolden's life and career (Marquis 1–9). Morton had pegged down jazz history to its first voice, a powerful and mysterious black man from New Orleans who struggled his way up from nothing and nowhere – a heroic figure rather like that of one F. Lamothe, 'your entertainer at the present time'.

That Morton had the vision and capacity to create this strange new kind of musical autobiography is rarely discussed. It sounds so natural, spontaneous and well-crafted as to be more a 'fireside chat' than an academic disquisition or a didactic discourse. Morton is whimsical and sometimes 'comic' in the old cornball mode, but he is most often *descriptive*: he remembers names, places, details and the way things looked, sounded, smelled, tasted decades before. He had a prose-poetry gift – to evoke the past in simple terms and highly concentrated doses. This talent must have been part of his gift as a composer, but in most such artists it is never called into play. Morton must surely have wanted to be about his own business – creating and making music, entertaining audiences – but the Depression and the eclipse of his fortunes threw him back on his own resources, which Alan Lomax had the mother-wit to exploit when he switched on his disc recorder.

The act of performance that Morton undertook was daunting, and he must have been anxious to keep the flow going and convince this young fellow Lomax to help with the campaign to rehabilitate the King of Jazz. But part of the charm of the narrative is that Morton, even when most blatantly self-promoting and ambitious in his talk, is often a seemingly objective voice, the solemn tones of History or Truth. He hailed from a city whose commonest streets are named after classical sub-deities and demigods such as Clio and Terpsichore, and something of this Olympian perspective is reflected in his measured cadences. He wants to create a sweep of history, from the beginning of America into the modern age, and he tries to summon the gravitas and dignity to make the tale of Ferdinand L. Morton something more than an individual tragicomedy. Sometimes this sounds slightly ludicrous, but most often Morton is convincingly authoritative in his delivery. No other jazzman has left such a legacy, and no modern jazz documentary film can touch the simple grandeur of those crackly old acetate discs left on deposit forever at America's public library.

CHAPTER FIVE

AUDIENCE

■————————■

Ferdinand Morton's music was initially and through most of his career presented to black listeners – dancers, barroom habitués, vaudeville and medicine show crowds, night-clubbers. Like all early jazz, it was highly functional music imbedded in a practical-minded, working-class culture. As a solo pianist, Morton would have played mostly in brothels and drinking emporiums. As a bandsman in New Orleans, he worked with brass bands on the street ('I would play trombone, sometimes bass drum, or sometimes the snares', *Mister Jelly Roll* 123), providing ceremonial music for funerals and meetings of fraternal orders (i.e. cornerstone-layings for the Masons) or 'social aid and pleasure clubs' – basically burial insurance societies. They played for picnics, excursions and lawn parties, as did other jazz and ragtime combinations – small dance bands; string bands of guitars, mandolins and banjos; vocal quartets of ambitious teenagers on the roam (both Morton and Louis Armstrong were alumni of these extemporaneous buskers). On the streets hokum bands of homemade instruments – jugs, washboards, kazoos – played for passers-by.

Music kept New Orleans alive – it was the lifeblood of the city, dispensed by everyone from the French Opera to the waffle man or fish vendor with his tin bugle, or the Razzy Dazzy Spasm Band playing for pennies on a street corner. Music at the turn of the century in New Orleans was a part of social life – played by part-timers who had manual labour for income – rather than a business. The idea of 'professionalism' was farfetched, although musicians were proud of their learning and 'efficiency' as players and strove to get as much helpful education in technique and music-reading as could be garnered. But it was a city of 'big ears', as jazz musicians say: everyone listened, grabbed music out of the air, repeated it, embellished it, personalized it, claimed it as their own.

Morton was no different from others in this regard, but he had a more tenacious memory for music, a voracious appetite for playing and a powerful ambition to rise out of his 'place' in the world – in a family mixed of genteel, Frenchified folk aspiring to what there was of a Creole middle class, and working-class African-Americans, who were versed in the manual arts but still attracted to music and culture. No one in this hermetic world could imagine being a 'superstar', known around the world, franchised as an industry and groomed to be famous (not talented, imaginative or capable – just *famous*). That world in its barest infancy was a generation away. Morton would see the modern alchemy of fame at work with Louis Armstrong, one of the first great pop megastars, and would always be puzzled by the complex industrial-technological processes at work. He was born into a world without radio, and when movies and the phonograph were barely invented, when player pianos were the zenith of mechanical media.

He certainly wanted his share of fame, honour and glory, but all he had to work with was his brain, his ears and his hands. There were no corporate sponsors, no international media complexes, no worldwide, instantaneous communication. Society moved at the pace of a walking man (or horse), not at the speed of light. No wonder Morton, until he was largely grown, assumed New Orleans was in fact the whole world. It was enough for him, as Dublin was enough for young James Joyce; a self-sufficient microcosm that might as well have been the entire known universe.

ᗔᗔᗔ   ᗕᗕᗕ

Morton grew up into a new era, the shining promise of the twentieth century, heralded by World's Fairs in Chicago (1893, a year late in commemorating the four-hundredth anniversary of Columbus' first voyage) and St Louis (1904, a year late in commemorating the centennial of the Louisiana Purchase). At first he was bounded by the old musical culture – pianos and basic instruments that would have been as familiar to Beethoven as to him. But change was occurring: a genuine recording industry was evolving, with a demand for discs to carry music all around the world, into every kind of home. A decade later, radio would follow the same trajectory, and music could then be broadcast into homes high and low across the country. Morton, as always, was vividly aware of the latest trends, and in 1936, two years before his great venture with Lomax, 'he was on radio station WOL in Washington where he hosted a program called *The History of Jazz*. Morton undoubtedly was seeking to promote his own music, but at the same time the program created what just may have been the first radio show on jazz in the United States.' (Szwed, in *Complete L. of C. Recordings*, 5) Now such a phrase as 'The History of Jazz' seems commonplace, but in 1936 it was revolutionary.

Musicians were becoming more than local heroes – they were absorbed by mechanisms they could not see or understand. By the year of Morton's death (1941) rudimentary television broadcasts were made, and people pondered how to create calculating machines to communicate with each other and even do something along the lines of *thinking*. The new century was well-defined in the title of a James P. Johnson tune – 'You've Got to Be Modernistic' (1929).

Morton became one of the early itinerant jazz recording stars: wandering into studios wherever he found them on his travels; making deals to record as a solo act, as an accompanist for singers, with all kinds of small groups; and casually breaking down barriers of race, as he did with the NORK, with white Chicago clarinettist Volly de Faut, with others. Morton was determinedly unaware of 'colour' in an increasingly racist culture, cutting brilliant piano solos for Gennett, the company that was the custom recording company for the Indiana Ku Klux Klan, the most vicious of the whole racist mob in the 1920s (Kennedy 37). He was a pragmatist and an unashamed opportunist, ready to find a job he could handle, ready to seize a musical group and shape it into a bona fide Jelly Roll combo, ready to dispense the full-service musical gospel of F. Morton.

After the initial explosive entry of 'jass' or jazz into the American consciousness in 1917–18 with the Original Dixieland Jazz Band recordings, there was a scramble to label any vaguely lively music as jazz; then a period of searching for authentic purveyors of the style; then a few years while the nascent recording industry decided 'jass' was a fad, a fancy that would fade, like the recent brief enthusiasms for Hawaiian music, the

tango, oriental foxtrots. But it didn't fade, it gestated, while hundreds of young people learned (from records) how to play it and began to organize into bands and combos and finally into a vital culture.

By the early 1920s the purportedly deceased jazz was revived in new, exciting

Mamie Smith, vaudeville blues shouter, whose smash-hit 'Crazy Blues' recording of 1921 kicked off the 'classic blues' mania of the era.

incarnations – a 'blues craze' erupted in 1921, when Mamie Smith, a vaudeville shouter, recorded 'Crazy Blues' for OKeh. She was promoted to the record company by the energetic and ambitious African-American hustler Perry Bradford, who foresaw a big market among black people for music by their own. The label had hired ace songwriter-publisher-promoter-pianist-bandleader Clarence Williams (1893–1965) to head its new 'race' division (in parallel with its division that was scouting and defining backwoods artists in what would soon be known as 'hillbilly', then 'country', then 'country and western'), headed by the genius field scout Ralph S. Peer. OKeh was almost as foresighted as Gennett in its emphasis, and other recording companies fell in line, establishing 'race' sub-labels and categories to tap a subterranean market for African-Americans.

Actually, jazz was moving in so many directions, and so many new audiences and subcultures were responding to it, that this industry strategy was only partially effective. Young men on both sides of the apartheid line were absorbing the music on record and finding ways to re-invent it, of which Morton would have approved. Both Bix Beiderbecke, a young white high-school student, and Louis Armstrong, already apprenticed to Joe 'King' Oliver, polished their jazz cornet styles by playing along with the ODJB records. Armstrong retained a lifelong affinity for 'Tiger Rag', and Bix later revisited and rejigged the frantic ODJB one-step ragtime style into a cool and relaxed parlour jazz on numbers such as 'Ostrich Walk' and 'Clarinet Marmalade,' as well as recording ODJB standards like 'Tiger Rag' and 'Lazy Daddy'.

The 'blues craze' stimulated searches for talent, especially among female singers in what was then dubbed 'classic blues', a style evolved for the vaudeville stage and removed from the folksiness of down-home country blues. It was actually a branch of pop music, and the developing market for slightly laundered and regularized music was collected and published by entrepreneurs such as W. C. Handy, Clarence Williams and Spencer Williams, a trend which led Harry H. Pace (a former W. C. Handy partner) to set up a daring enterprise – a black-owned, black-run recording company, Black Swan Records. They pushed genteel art music and promoted blues singers or would-be blues singers, including the young Ethel Waters and Trixie Smith. The enterprise struggled along, but Black Swan had sung its last by mid-1923, downed by the fierce competition in the young industry. (Foreman 74–81)

In addition to the 'blues craze', recording companies began to attend again to jazz, among their entries into the burgeoning dance music market. Any band or combo considered to be new, peppy and in vogue was pushed out the door as 'jazz'. Bands such as Art Hickman's San Francisco dance group were hits, and a young violinist from Denver named Paul Whiteman thought he could crack this jazz puzzle and cash in, too. So the larger labels promoted dance bands as jazz, and smaller labels like Gennett found offshoots of the hot dance trend – small bands to be sold as 'real' jazz like the ODJB, which was now fading off the scene. A skillful society bandleader such as Sam Lanin could organize dozens of recording jobs for quintets of dance band players and sell them under names like Bailey's Lucky Seven or Ladd's Black Aces (there was no 'Bailey' and no one in the fictitious 'Ladd' band was even remotely 'black'!). These little potboiler groups made surprisingly lively and competent pop jazz – the ODJB with the wrinkles smoothed out and their wacky surrealism suppressed. (Gracyk 220–23)

These groups banked on the cachet of 'black' for promotion but their records sold as much to white college students and jellybeans as to a black audience. Odd things were happening to American culture, down in the depths of popular music, jazz and blues. It was *good* to be black on some levels – to be free, happy, sexy, in touch with the primitive Old Adam under the skin, liberated from care and convention. On the other hand it was *bad* to be black as everyone had been drilled since the Civil War – to be poor, shiftless, invincibly ignorant, dirty, smelly and hopeless. How could this schismatic contradiction be swallowed by a whole culture? A new wave of African-American music was beginning to teach America exactly how.

Other fads and fancies of the early 1920s shaped the music. A fad for even more sensuous new dances struck like an invisible plague (the brilliant poet-novelist-visionary Ishmael Reed develops this trope in his amazing allegorical rendering of jazz history, *Mumbo Jumbo* [1972]) – the 'shimmy craze' sparked by vamping females such as Gilda Gray and Bee Palmer, remembered mostly now in the Spencer Williams hit 'Shim-Me-Sha-Wabble' of 1923, or in his publication of a ditty called 'Get Off Katie's Head' by young Louis Armstrong, appropriated and re-titled 'I Wish I Could Shimmy Like My Sister Kate', also 1923. Blues singing led also to 'torch singing' and a whole sub-industry of female crooners like Ruth Etting, Carol Kane and Helen Morgan. Other components of a definable 'jazz mainstream' were congealing across the US, where wandering minstrels like Morton carried them.

The oddly missing ingredient in all of this music was authentic black New Orleans jazz – *where was it?* It was heard in Chicago, on the West Coast, in New York City, still in New Orleans and its environs, but it did not appear on those shellac discs that were revamping the world's listening, singing and dancing habits. In 1922, a tiny West Coast label, Nordskog, recorded a band led by Edward 'Kid' Ory, the great New Orleans trombonist, who had led the Brownskin Band in co-operation with Joe 'King' Oliver for several years before both men left the Crescent City for greener pastures. Ory would become the trombonist on the first great Red Hot Peppers sessions in 1926 and would star with Louis Armstrong's Hot

Fives, with the New Orleans Wanderers and Bootblacks and with King Oliver's big Dixie Syncopators. But in 1921 he was out west fronting an excellent band of veteran New Orleans musicians, including Mutt Carey (cornet) and Morton's brother-in-law Dink Johnson (clarinet), as well as Ed 'Montudie' Garland, who worked with Ory throughout his long career.

The records were produced by two ambitious African-American musical entrepreneurs in Los Angeles, Benjamin 'Reb' and John Spikes. Somewhere in the process, legal wrangling developed between Ory, the Spikes brothers and Arne Nordskog, the record manufacturer, and the discs ended up being called either 'The Seven Pods of Pepper' or 'Ory's Sunshine Orchestra', with the Spikes' Sunshine label glued over Nordskog's original one. The records sold poorly on the West Coast and elsewhere. They did contain authentic New Orleans style music, as in 'Ory's Creole Trombone' and 'Society Blues', both instrumentals, and in accompaniments for several blues singers. (Levin 14–24)

After this came a slight pause, then Gennett recorded the New Orleans Rhythm Kings in 1922 and 1923, cutting records by a white New Orleans band playing in a style close to the music of King Oliver and other great black musicians that they had heard and admired while growing up. Jelly Roll Morton, as we have seen, helped to lift their careers when he sat in for the 1923 NORK sides. Gennett then tapped more of the Chicago scene and brought King Oliver's great Creole Jazz Band to Richmond in 1923 for music straight from the original source. It was now possible to find on record samples of the jazz that lay behind the pale imitators of the ODJB, itself to some extent an imitation of the African-American sound basic in New Orleans.

Morton added to this trove with the large series (13 sides in 1923–24) of original piano jazz numbers he cut for Gennett. Other musicians were found and documented, also – New York blacks Fats Waller and James

Sidney Bechet, Emperor of the Soprano Sax, at the height of his fame and glory, 1949.

P. Johnson, for example, and the OKeh sessions with Sidney Bechet and Louis Armstrong in 1923–24. Black music was bursting the floodgates and reaching a large listening public – mostly 'race' audiences – and records were preserving precious moments in a music evolving and mutating with astonishing speed.

As Morton became a Gennett recording artist, in the company of the NORK and Oliver's Creole Jazz Band, the breadth and depth of African-American music was becoming obvious, and the potential seemed unlimited. After classic blues singers were waxed, then country blues were tapped by portable recording laboratories in the hinterlands. And the constant, swelling migration from the South to northern cities brought more and more 'new' music to light, so that 'race' records seemed a cornucopia, a bottomless supply of imaginative and energetic music. White musicians learned from increased contacts with black counterparts, and commercial possibilities for hot dance bands, jazz singers and jazz dance seemed exactly parallel to the ever-expanding economy and prosperity of the US, a crystal bubble that could never burst, that only grew larger and more glistening.

⟫⟫⟫   ⟪⟪⟪

The first audiences for Morton's music after he left New Orleans around 1907 were in bars and brothels, tumbledown joints he found across the South. But within a few years, he was also meeting audiences in the vaudeville revues and tent shows which carried him. At this point, some public record of his work as an entertainer begins to appear. Black community newspapers of the era (1910–15) were important sources of information for African-Americans, who were systematically excluded from white newspapers, excepting some large city papers that might run a column headed 'Of Interest to Our Colored Readers'. Most often this 'news' was simply a gazette of comings and goings by 'acceptable' middle-class black families.

Papers such as the *Chicago Defender* and the *Indianapolis Freeman* were important organizations with professional standards and aims and a large readership. They reported the 'unreportable' news of the day vital to African-Americans (lynchings and other crimes the white press chose to censor or ignore), but they also ran social and community information, paying close attention to black entertainment. They ran columns with perfunctory reviews but which (more importantly) listed when and where various acts and shows appeared. In columns covering black vaudeville, Morton's name begins appearing regularly as he (literally) gets his act together and becomes a known quantity as an actor-comedian-musician.

When he and Rose Brown solidified their routine into 'The Jelly Rolls', they were routinely tracked in many papers.

The reportage was more or less free advertising or 'puff pieces' describing the acts and praising them in conventionalized terms. It is impossible to know if they indicate real success or fame, but they show that Morton was making enough of an impression to deserve coverage. The *Indianapolis Freeman* ('An Illustrated Colored Newspaper') for 13 June 1914, ran one of these promotional reviews:

MORTON & MORTON

Comedy, Music, Dancing

Ferd and Rose Morton are an interesting pair who do a number of good talking stunts. Miss Morton is a wide awake performer, helping out the fun all the way through. She puts over the 'Blues' to the satisfaction of the audiences who for some reason take very kindly to that kind of singing. Her voice is of good quality.

This is interesting for the emphasis on Rose and the absence of comment on Ferd Morton. But the review then covered Jelly Roll separately:

FERD MORTON

As New Orleans Jelly Roll

Mr Morton, 'Jelly Roll', is a slight reminder of 'String Beans'. He does a pianologue in good style. He plays a good piano, classics and rags with equal ease. His one hand stunt, left hand alone, playing a classic selection, is a good one. They do an amusing comedy bit, singing 'That Ain't Got 'Em'. This is sung by both of them in a duo style. They make a hit with this, which is Morton's own composition. In fact, he composes most of his own song and arranges his other work. As a comedian Morton is grotesque in his makeup and sustains himself nicely through the work. They are a clever pair, giving a pleasing show.

This indicates a high level of vaudeville craft, but it is hard to tell where criticism ends and promotion begins. At least it shows that the act was big enough to merit this dual coverage. (Russell 476)

This indicates two possibilities about 'Morton & Morton – the Jelly Rolls': the little domestic-comedy idea (dainty, pretty woman and loutish, tramp-like man) may have been original and intriguing, like a forecast of domestic-duo comedy radio acts two decades later – Burns and Allen, the Bickersons, the Halls of Ivy, etc. Or else the striking tramp get-up Morton designed (pre-Charlie Chaplin and before such famous 'tramp-clown' circus acts as Emmett Kelly's) was original enough to be memorable. The photographs of Morton in his rig are odd and faintly disturbing – he wears badly misfitting 'work clothes' of different kinds, including oversize gloves and a porkpie hat, and assumes a posture like a broken marionette. The publicity photo with Rose Brown is especially notable – she is pale and sylphlike in a white gown, and he (heavily blacked up) looms over her like the monster Caliban contemplating Miranda in *The Tempest*. (Russell 476–77)

We have Morton's scant narrative about his vaudeville career, but the tireless William Russell found and interviewed some colleagues to verify Morton's remembrances. Among them were Billy and Mary McBride, well known in black vaudeville for half a century (1908–59) as Mack & Mack, or under the rubric Mack's Merry Makers. They habitually recruited New Orleans jazz musicians (including future stars and big names like Kid Ory, Mutt Carey and Johnny Dodds) for their shows, and also recorded some of their bands in the 1920s. They recalled Morton clearly at the very beginning of his vaudeville years. Billy McBride said: '... sometimes [Morton] happened to be in the neighborhood and we went up and down the Gulf Coast. Jelly Roll was not a regular member of the band that played for the show. He had what he called a specialty act, but he played solos in the pit (where the piano was located) and the band gave him background music.' He remembered Morton singing 'Windin' Boy Blues'. Mary McBride recalled Morton teaching her original songs and blues and that he 'played by ear'. She called him a 'fine fellow' and a 'fine musician'. (Russell 343–44)

Morton also worked with a smalltime vaudevillian, Will Benbow, and in this small troupe, *c.* 1910, he may have found the basic model for his act – Butler May, a.k.a. String Beans, a well-remembered comic and bluesman of the era. When the *Indianapolis Freeman* review (see p. 121) called Morton 'a slight reminder of String Beans', it is a gentle footnote on his sources. The connection called forth one of those odd Dickensian coincidences that intersperse Morton's career: in 1917 his future wife Mabel Bertrand and her vaudeville partner Billy Arnte wrote an obituary for the *Indianapolis Freeman* on String Beans, a decade before Mabel ran across Jelly Roll Morton (who must clearly have reminded her of the vaudeville years and their common backgrounds). (Gushee, 'Afterword' in *Mister Jelly Roll*, 2005 edn., 338)

Other Morton sightings appear in Russell's scrapbook. Reb Spikes, the Los Angeles musical entrepreneur, opened his interview by saying: 'Jelly Roll was doing a blackface comedy act with his wife when I first met him down in Oklahoma in 1911, I think it was. He wasn't with Anita, Dink Johnson's sister, back then.' The 'wife' here must be Rosa Brown. Anita Gonzales was his West Coast 'wife', 1917–23, and Mabel Bertrand his New York City 'wife', 1927–41. Spikes then says he got Morton a job with 'McCabe's Troubadors' in Kansas in 1912, with Morton playing the piano, but he 'brought his wife with him'. Presumably, Morton took either single jobs or bookings for Morton & Morton, when available. (Russell 550)

On the West Coast after 1917, Morton also hooked up with vaudevillians and theatrical stars-to-be like Shep Allen (1891–?) and Ada 'Bricktop' Smith (1894–1983), the latter of whom became internationally famous as a Paris cabaret-keeper and entertainer through the 1920s and

1930s. (Lomax referred to her only as 'Bright Red' in *Mister Jelly Roll*.) Cole Porter wrote 'Miss Otis Regrets' for her; she was instrumental in starting the careers of Josephine Baker and Duke Ellington; and she and Morton had a long, ambiguous relationship. She worked at the Cadillac Café with Morton and his band, and may have also worked in shows with him. If so, he was travelling in high-octane company out west as early as 1918. (Russell 453–55)

Shep Allen was a successful black show business entrepreneur (he owned or managed a string of theatres and nightclubs around Chicago from 1912 through the 1920s, including the Pekin Theatre, the Deluxe Café and the Sunset Café). Allen knew Morton when he and Tony Jackson were both playing at the Elite No. 1 nightclub in Chicago, *c*. 1915. Allen reconnected with Morton when he took a top-flight vocal trio of future black stars – the Panama Trio, with Florence Mills, Ada 'Bricktop' Smith and Cora Green – to California in 1917, with Morton as their piano accompanist. Allen said of Morton: 'Jelly was a king in those days. There was no one better, and he wrote a lot of hits.' (Russell 391–92)

As indistinct as the history of Morton in vaudeville may be, clearly he had found another string for his bow – he no longer was just the wandering bordello tickler, but made extensive connections in show business and learned everything he could about the complex craft. Reb Spikes recalled one of Morton's keystone character traits – his unquenchable eagerness to do and try everything at hand – from the stint with McCabe's Troubadors around 1912:

> *We had a little girl playing the piano. She could read the music so she could play all the songs and things for the show. But after they heard Jelly play, they wanted him to play the overture. So, we persuaded Jelly – at least he wanted to – he'd go out and play the overture. Oh, he'd wear them out. He was great, you know;*

he'd play, he'd run the people crazy. He wasn't paid to play the
overture. Then he'd come up to do his blackface comedy act on
the stage, and the girl would take over the piano for the show.
Yes, Jelly could read music in those days. (Russell 550)

Morton often boasted of his ability to dazzle rivals (he recites a long narrative about all the St Louis ragtime players and composers he bested) with his 'sight-reading' of hoary warhorses like von Suppe's *Poet and Peasant Overture*, which may well have been learned in exactly these circumstances.

Vaudeville and nightclub acts gave Morton a sure foothold in bigtime black entertainment before the 1920s. By the time he returned from his western wanderings, he was ready to strike out on his own and use his experience to make the single act of Jelly Roll Morton, composer, player, bandleader, a sure-fire national hit. His background and show-business sensibility differed from the average New Orleans jazz musician's curriculum vitae. He was an off-the-shelf 'single-handed entertainer' with the commanding manner of a born leader and with a satchel full of highly original blues, stomps and songs ready to take the Roaring Twenties by storm.

❧❧❧ ❧❧❧

Those who heard Jelly Roll Morton in his earliest incarnation as a wandering minstrel were impressed by him and left vivid recollections of both his larger-than-life persona and his musical skills. He had grown up very fast in New Orleans, and a decade on the road with vaudeville and in every kind of dive, bordello and dance hall sharpened him as an entertainer and as an entrepreneur. While his footloose life barred him from putting down roots in a complex black community like those of New Orleans, Chicago or New York, he was in contact with the musical and show-business currents of the era. He met rival pianists and composers, but he also met black celebrities such as Bert Williams and Bill 'Bojangles'

Robinson, and he worked with future stars like 'Bricktop' Smith before she attained international star status. He knew the rough world of serious big-money gambling and recalled notorious bad men he met on the road. He was 'acquainted with the night', but he also saw black artists making the big time and reaching a pinnacle of fame and respect in a society generally loaded against them.

His music, his monologues, his memories were important bequests to American cultural history. In basic ways, all his contributions are unique and individualized, but in other ways, his voice is that of his culture and his era. The paradox of his inventiveness is that voices of both the individual and the group emerge in crystal clarity from his music.

CHAPTER SIX

THE BUSINESS

■———————■

Jelly Roll Morton lived a dense, complex life, and his part in the business end of popular music and culture was as convoluted as the rest of his career. If Silent Cal Coolidge was right in asserting that 'The business of America is business', Morton was a stalwart American by any measure.

No recourse existed for a musician like Morton when it came to preserving and distributing his work – no 'instant print' facilities for 'desktop publishing' music manuscripts, no pocket-sized digital recorders to capture performances and burn them onto CDs from a computer. The mechanism of music reproduction was huge and ungainly, and *no* private person could use it at a whim. Ditto for the emerging mass media such as radio and movies – they were large-scale, industrial operations, from which individual producers were barred. It was as practical to think about building an ocean liner in your basement as to dream of putting out your own records or films, or (even) sheet music. So the venture with Roy Carew to create and develop Tempo Music Corp was a pioneer venture, and still one more way in which Morton was years ahead of his culture.

It is interesting to speculate on how Morton would have adapted to and used today's music technology and culture: the instantaneity and ease of recording, distributing and controlling the media might have appealed to him, and he certainly was a 'mixed-media' artist from the beginning, with his vaudeville skills, his composing and arranging talents, and his penchant for storytelling and dramatization. It is not hard to imagine a 'Doctor Jelly' dominating the hip-hop culture, or a modernized Morton on TV and in films – media big enough to capture and hold his wide-screen, Technicolor flamboyance. He certainly would have been able to make his fortune, given the legal protections and corporate welfare of the modern entertainment culture.

He did maintain his 'sidelines', especially in the early years – pool-sharking, a line of prostitutes (called his 'Pacific Coast Line' when he was in California), boxing promotion, a few small scams – to tide himself over the lean times, but unlike most of the musicians he knew in New Orleans, he was not a working man or tradesman (many were cigar-makers or other cottage craftsmen, many were driven in bad years to the toughest manual work, like stevedoring on the docks or other brutal day labour). Morton disdained this life for a trickier, riskier existence as a self-made man, a one-man corporation – Jelly Roll, Inc..

Johnny St Cyr, the superb banjoist and guitarist who starred on the early Red Hot Peppers records and was a charter member of Louis Armstrong's Hot Five and Seven bands, carried a business card in later life that read only 'Plasterer * General Jobbing'. (Russell 128) One of Morton's cards from the 1930s reads '"Jelly Roll" Morton (Originator of Jazz) * Staff Writer * Tempo Music' (Russell 237), although his more flamboyant business card and letterhead read:

Originator of JAZZ-STOMP-SWING

VICTOR ARTIST World's Greatest Hot Tune Writer

JELLY ROLL MORTON'S ORCHESTRA

But most musicians in the early years of the teens and even during the exuberant twenties and especially during the Depression were in the same boat with Johnny St Cyr, eking out a living at a 'day job' and occasionally playing music for nickels and dimes, if they were lucky. (Russell 281)

Many musicians who stayed in or returned to New Orleans in the 1930s played at dime-a-dance joints, which meant grinding eight-hour shifts of playing two or three choruses of a number, pausing to let the girls grab a new customer then plunging on, without a break, into another abbreviated pop tune. It was at its best a soul-detroying proposition, only marginally better than hoisting boxes and bales on the waterfront as a day-labouring stevedore. The bad times rapidly aged and killed most of the first generation of jazzmen, and Morton struggled not to become a victim, until his health and heart wore out on him, too. He was in his early 50s when he died in 1941, but the jitterbugs thought of him and his contemporaries as 'old men', fossils from the dawn of time.

By the mid-1920s, Jelly Roll Morton was at the top of his game; he had recorded a stunning anthology of original piano pieces, cut some on piano rolls, made a splash in Chicago's booming entertainment world and then cut an unparalleled series of recordings with the most accomplished New Orleans jazz band assembled. How did this achievement look in the context of his times?

In light of the lofty artistic ideals and ambitions of the burgeoning Harlem Renaissance, unfurling half a continent away, Morton was only a rough-edged smalltime vaudevillian, with a whiff of the bordello in his past. Measured against other jazz musicians in Chicago and New York, however, he was a proven master with two decades' craft and expertise stored in his mind and fingers.

Louis Armstrong's star was just ascending. Sidney Bechet, the master of New Orleans reed styles and consummate soloist, was restless, junketing back and forth to Europe, with no steady base of operations. Bessie Smith, Ma Rainey and a legion of blues divas brought their

Ma Rainey, Queen Mother of the Blues, in 1923. L–R: Gabriel Washington, Al Wynn, Dave Nelson, Rainey, Eddie Pollack, Thomas A. ('Georgia Tom') Dorsey.

vaudeville-honed works to popular music and drew admiration from the literati of the Harlem Renaissance. Fletcher Henderson's big band was at the apex of its success in New York's big dance palaces, and Duke Ellington was assembling an orchestra that would go on to play and record over five decades.

As the Red Hot Peppers recorded for Victor, from 1926 to 1930, they presented the music of the immediate past, the high New Orleans jazz style that had coalesced in the late nineteen-teens and transferred itself to the West Coast and Chicago just after the First World War. Ellington, meanwhile, was creating the music of the immediate future, born from East Coast jazz, show music and modern dance band styles, and catalyzed by Ellington's composing genius.

It is interesting to speculate, in the manner of alternative-history buffs, what might have happened if Ellington's public career had been snuffed out by the Depression in 1930, like Morton's. What would jazz and jazz history look like in such a parallel universe? Whose status would loom largest in retrospect? Ellington's opus would lack all the big extended works, the suites and tone poems, all the experimental works from the 'Blanton band' of the late 1930s, all the resurgent revisions of the 1950s and 1960s. No *Time* magazine cover, no TV coverage, no widely known public persona for this Duke. Would his unique orchestra, deceased in 1930, be regarded as just another average 1920s hot dance band, ranked with McKinney's Cotton Pickers, Fletcher Henderson, Jean Goldkette and Paul Whiteman?

In the fragile ecosystem of fame, sheer longevity and persistence often trump youthful genius, and one tragic aspect of Morton's amazing career was that at age 40 he lost the spotlight and was thwarted from developing the satchel full of scores and musical ideas that he had carried since Teddy Roosevelt was in the White House. The hopeful coda in Morton's life was, of course, the astonishing self-resurrection of 1938–40 and its cornucopia of stories, theories and sterling musical performances that document and justify his imperishable genius.

By the late 1930s, Morton was in partnership with Roy Carew (1884–1967), a white enthusiast for the old music who had lived in New Orleans from 1904–19, witnessing the heyday of early jazz, The District and the unique ambience of the goodtime city. He and Morton shared memories and Carew, a financial expert who worked for the Internal Revenue Service, helped Morton to set up Tempo Music Publishing, Inc., which would protect Morton's scores, recordings and arrangements, the large and diverse body of work he had completed over the years. It worked co-operatively with Clarence Williams' well-established publishing business in New York, and Carew was diligent in sorting Morton's tangled affairs and finding what he owned, what was owed to him and how he might still exploit the treasure of his talents. (Russell 157–305)

Carew had met, interviewed and documented the careers of other musicians, such as pioneer ragtimer S. Brunson 'Brun' Campbell (1884–1952), who claimed to be Scott Joplin's star pupil. Carew remembered and revered Tony Jackson, as did Morton, and he had good insights into the worth of the music – financial, aesthetic and social. He was calm and methodical, in contrast to Morton's mercurial temperament, which led to tirades about the $3 million that music business predators had lifted from him over the decades. Bottled resentment led Morton to send one circus-like rhodomontade to Robert S Ripley, blasting W. C. Handy and the others that Morton viewed as mere scavengers in the great river of African-American music, while he was a creator and developer of the music, an imaginative force from the fonts of art. Carew spent much time putting the brakes on Morton's bitterness and anger over the way in which history had passed him by, keeping him focused on working and creating. Carew was in some ways an ideal amanuensis for the temperamental Creole.

But this was at the end of Morton's working life, when the task was archival more than anything else. Carew hoped to get Morton back on his feet financially, ready to create new music, playing and band-leading, as the US seemed to head out of the Depression. But Morton had been prodigal with his own gifts, a minnow in an ocean of carnivores, the big time of the pop music business, where 'every man's hand was raised against every other man'. The raw Hobbesian State of Nature, with the working life for an entertainer 'solitary, poor, nasty, brutish and short', as the old philosopher had predicted. The struggle started when Morton made his first brilliant moves to establish himself as a known artist, to break out of his gypsy existence and put himself onto the stage of the Jazz Age where fortune and fame could be seized by the bold.

Howard Reich and William Gaines made a thorough study of Morton's business affairs and mapped his career in as much detail as existing documentation and testimony afforded, in their book *Jelly's Blues*. Morton made his Gennett sessions with the NORK and also cut his string of Gennett solo sides just after he met the Melrose brothers – Walter and Lester – in Chicago, where they ran a music shop on South Cottage Grove Avenue, in the burgeoning entertainment district of the South Side. The Melrose brothers were cornfed hustlers from Kentucky out to wring fame and fortune from Jazz Age Chicago at the moment when everyone was getting rich by speculating in something – stocks, shares, futures, who knew what? They began to speculate in the new black music that was making Chicago hot and jazzy, that was part of the touted cultural renaissance of the Windy City that included architecture (Louis Sullivan, Frank Lloyd Wright and the architectural 'prairie school'), literature (Hemingway, Carl Sandburg, James T. Farrell and many others) and the manifold forms of Prohibition-breaking that proved so lucrative to Dion O'Banion, Al Capone and legions of gangsters who became the city's international trademark.

The Melrose brothers, casting around for get-rich-quick gimmicks, in 1923 acquired the copyright to Morton's brilliant 'The Wolverines' from their West Coast counterparts the Spikes brothers, because it was being played to great acclaim by King Oliver at the Lincoln Gardens in Chicago. They tinkered the name into 'Wolverine Blues' to make sure every rube knew it was jazzy and bluesy, and not some University of Michigan marching song. Then the NORK and King Oliver recorded it for Gennett. The clumsy hit-making apparatus of the early 1920s lumbered into action.

Then Jelly Roll hit town, went down to the Melrose music shop and saw a big banner plugging his tune. He was pulled ambivalently between irritation at the blatant pick-pocketing and pride in his own powers. He may have been robbed, but he still knew it was *his* music that was selling, regardless of who plugged it and played it. He talked with these two seemingly naïve entrepreneurs and decided he could handle them. He got them to add his name to their copyright, top billing over Reb and John Spikes. *But he got no financial share in the copyright*! The Melrose brothers may have seemed amiable, easy-going southern boys used to dealing with 'darkies', but when it came to dollars and cents, they were no fools. (Reich and Haines 80–84)

From this point on, Morton was fair game for the Melroses. He was willing to let them take the risk of publishing, printing and selling his music, assuming that profits flowing from it would be equitably divided and he would take away the artist's (or lion's) share. He was one big meal ticket for the Melroses, who had little musical talent themselves and had only begun to make contacts with Chicago musicians who might stable themselves under the Melrose banner. They

> ... *were discovering that when Morton had strolled into the store on that lucky day in May, he carried with him a seemingly bottomless satchel of composed music ready for the selling. In just the first months of their collaboration with Morton, in 1923, the Melrose lads published 'Grandpa's Spells', 'Kansas City Stomp', 'London Blues', 'Mr Jelly Lord', and 'The Pearls', as well as the already released 'Wolverine Blues' – in effect, the first great canon of jazz compositions. (Reich and Haines 87)*

The Melrose brothers were classical capitalistic parasites to delight the hearts of Marx and Engels – they did nothing except pass their hands over their 'product' and thereby collected *everything* from the sales. Whether they rewarded Morton *anything* for his work was at their discretion, and soon they decided to dispense with the goose – they collected the big, golden eggs and could sell and resell them magically, forever.

A music industry paper, *The Music Trades*, testified at the time to how the Melrose efforts paid off in publicity, fame and (for them) a steady cash flow of hard currency:

> *The unprecedented demand for 'Kansas City Stomp', by 'Jelly Roll' Morton, published by the Melrose Bros., has caused the firm to bring all the hits of this popular rag writer into one folio, soon to be placed on the market. The demand for the Gennett Records of all Mr Morton's hits has exceeded the supply of these popular records. They are, it is reported, among the best selling numbers of the Gennett list. 'Jelly Roll' Morton will be remembered as the man who wrote 'Wolverine Blues', 'Grandpa's Spells', 'London Blues', 'New Orleans Blues', 'Chicago Breakdown', 'Stratford Rag' [sic], 'Shreveport Blues' [sic], and the popular 'Kansas City Stomp'. Especially does the last number seem destined to be a popular and standard rag. People hearing it buy it, and after playing it for some time lay it aside, only to come back to it later. 'Grandpa's Spells', 'The Pearls', Chicago Breakdown' and 'Stratford Rag' [sic] ... if there is such a thing as standard rags, these numbers, by their popularity, can be said to be in that class.*
>
> (quoted in Reich and Gaines 94)

This is half puff piece and half reportage, but it testifies that Morton was for a moment a hot property in the pop music business and good copy for a trade paper, even if he himself saw little money from this selling spree.

In the next years, as Morton completed his trifecta of solo recording, publishing and recording the Red Hot Peppers with Victor, the Melrose brothers continued to represent him, collecting fees and royalties, cutting themselves in on his copyrights and otherwise sucking his life blood while he was busy at work. The brothers were about to give Morton the heave-ho, but they squeezed every cent from him beforehand:

... there was the payment due Morton for the Victor recording sessions. Though the discs had been commercial hits, Melrose had paid Morton simply a flat fee for the sessions, with no artist royalties. The contract for Morton's great Red Hot Peppers dates, in fact, was between Melrose Brothers Music of Chicago and the Victor Talking Machine Company of New York, and it provided for all money to be paid to Melrose, none to Morton. This was a routine arrangement for black artists who – unlike their white counterparts – did not make contracts directly with record companies and were not paid by them. It was the white impresarios who cut the deals with the white labels, so that operators like Melrose were in position to deny black artists their royalties. (Reich and Gaines 127)

Louis Armstrong as a young virtuoso, laughing in the face of the Depression.

Only the topmost echelons of black jazz musicians reached a financial stability that let them weather the Depression and even live in some luxury. At this same time Louis Armstrong was suffering managerial blues, until Joe Glaser, a hoodlum-connected manager, took over his case and set him up as a long-running, self-contained corporation. Duke Ellington had the same luck with the underworld figures who put him into the Cotton Club, got him national radio airtime and set him on the road to permanent stability.

While blue-nosed critics and commentators sometimes expiate righteously on Morton's low-down life, his association with pimping and gambling and small-time con games, they rarely acknowledge the bigger crime connections that floated jazz in the Roaring Twenties, even though taletellers like Eddie Condon, Mezz Mezzrow and others left long narratives of the high life in the speakeasies and the omnipresence of gangsters all along the borders of the music business. But contemplating 'legit' operators with the ethics, principles and practices of Walter and Lester Melrose, who needed genuine thugs and *mafiosi*, anyhow?

It is impossible to know exactly how much the Melroses milked from him (Morton always claimed *somebody* owed him $3 million) and how much Morton lost (in more ways than one) by their association, but they ended up as successful 'businessmen' and Morton ended a near-pauper, his heart and health broken after a decade of scuffling through the end of the good times. He was famous, and he made the Melroses famous, but he got little financial security or social stability from the work he did, still living nomadically, always hustling, unable to hoard time and energy to see where that fabled bigtime money might be, until Roy Carew came along at the very end and tried to untangle the vast, woven web of financial might-have-beens.

The Melrose brothers are, in the end, no better and no worse than most of the half-hand bigshots who crowded into the bull markets of the 1920s, this one the market for music and for the humans who made it. When Morton finally objected to the piracy the Melroses practiced on him, the brothers cut him loose. He was old hat by now, in the fast-moving world of pop music, and nothing stinks more than yesterday's success. The Melroses had other targets on their radar screens:

> ... Morton was dealing with a man who had become one of the craftiest finaglers in the already corrupt world of music publishing, grabbing rights and royalties from other publishers as adroitly as he did from his songwriters. A year earlier, for instance, on January 12, 1926, the copyright on Scott Joplin's 'Maple Leaf Rag' ran out, inspiring Melrose to file his own copyright on the tune before Stark & Sons of St Louis had gotten around to renewing theirs. (Reich and Haines 128)

Morton was too innocent, too self-involved, too busy with the rightful work of creating and playing his music to exist in such an atmosphere. He was left with bitterness and a belief that everyone was out to get him (more or less true!) and very little money coming in after decades of flat-out work.

At the beginning of the twenty-first century, it is difficult to realize how naked and unassisted were the great innovators in America's popular music. No apparatus of promotion, advertising, manufacture and distribution for their wares existed, and no legal protection for the intellectual property was anything but rudimentary. The tradition of copyright protection for artists dates back to the early eighteenth century, when the engraver, painter and social satirist William Hogarth, more or less single-handedly made the British government consider and develop laws that let artists hold and profit from their own works. The development of such laws was important early in US history, mostly focused on the patent process – to encourage American inventors and tinkerers to add to their stock of new technology (and, by extension, their wealth). Other workers with their brains and imaginations – writers, artists, musicians, etc. – were admitted to the big tent of patent and copyright protection in the early nineteenth century. But it was a process not well understood by itinerant and lower class workers. It was simple for sharpers to bone up on the laws and to fleece creators of new music by taking the onerous business of legal protection off their hands.

The most common practice of agents and publishers of vernacular music was to add to the original scores – usually a matter of writing lyrics, no matter how inane, for an instrumental piece – and thereby claim co-authorship. Morton was the victim of this ploy from both the Spike brothers in California ('Someday Sweetheart') and the Melrose brothers in Chicago (dozens of Morton's best numbers), all of whom effectively horned in and took some or all publication royalties through this ruse. Morton was savvy enough to understand the practice and to try deflecting it by rewriting his works in other forms. He also knew that big fish must eat little fish, so he joined the culture by appropriating as his own 'floating folk strains' and antique blues melodies ('Alabama Bound', 'Don't You Leave Me Here', 'Tee-Nah-Nah' and others), getting *his* name on their copyrights.

For songwriters and practicing jazzmen on the road and off the precincts of Tin Pan Alley, it was difficult to compete in a marketplace skewed in favour of those who held the means of production – music publishers, agents, recording executives, promoters, etc. Even an assertive, stubborn worker like Jelly Roll Morton could not stand up to large corporations and manufacturers.

Morton was quintessentially a man of his times, the kind of musician nurtured by the novel heat of ragtime and the emerging emotional cortex of the blues, able to cope with a show business whose models were George M. Cohan, Irving Berlin and other self-made, first-generation immigrants. Morton lived the version of the American Dream open to people of colour – he could attend and even participate in the Big Show, but he could only enter by the side entrance, conspicuously signposted COLORED ONLY.

CHAPTER SEVEN

RELATIONSHIPS

■————————■

The primal relationships that shaped Morton were with his family. As Tolstoy told us, 'Happy families are all alike', and Morton's family was of the other, interesting, kind, the family tangled in its own connections, contradictions, beliefs and demands. His mother Louise Morton was recalled as 'so fair she could always pass', and his father Ed Lamothe is barely described in Morton's recollections. (Lomax 8) He passed out of the scene early, and Louise married one Willie Mouton, a working class man. Later Morton anglicized his name to Morton as part of his early effort toward 'Americanization', losing the oddities and affectations of the shabby-genteel Creoles. Louise and Ed had their son and two daughters – Amede Eugenie and Frances (called Mimi) – and lived in a bustling household that included a grandmother, Laura Peche, an uncle, Auguste ('Gus') Monette, and aunt, Elena Peche. Hovering over the family was Morton's godmother Eulalie Echo (Hecaud), also known as Laura Hunter, a voodoo queen who served the ladies of The District with pills, potions, spells and magic of all sorts. It was, you see, no ordinary 'happy family'.

The family home was at 1443 Frenchman Street, a respectable spot in the Seventh Ward. The family was steadfast in its pretensions to gentility and social cachet, respectful of education, including proper musical training, and Morton was encouraged to be a cultured youth. His idea of culture was not that of faded Downtown families, however, and the family wanted no part in him becoming a professional musician, a footloose scamp no better than a bum. He knew by his teenage years about The District and the new kinds of raucous music played and sung there. He came to prefer Uptown and his godmother Eulalie (called 'Lalee' by young Morton), and lived with her as he worked his way into the unmapped musical cosmos of The District. He was about to plunge straight from Family Life directly into The Life.

The complexity of culture and identity in New Orleans was shaped by consciousness of caste, class and family connections. The ancient category of 'Creoles' was as vexing as all the nuances and gradations of colour-consciousness under Jim Crow would ever become. Peculiar to the Crescent City was the social idea of 'Creoleness', a concept hard to define or even illustrate but known intimately by everyone in the city. In 1877, the keen-eyed writer Lafcadio Hearn tried to pin it down and explain it to those beyond the magic circle of New Orleans:

> *The common error of interpreting the word 'Creole' as signifying mulatto, quadroon or octoroon of Louisiana, and particularly of New Orleans, is far from being a local one, and dates back through centuries. It is not even confined to the uncultivated classes of the population of the Northern States, but flourishes, curiously enough, even in the South ... Strangest of all, it actually lives in New Orleans, where the word Creole is a term of proud honor among the aristocracies of the South. There are numbers in this cosmopolitan city who have some vague idea that the more lightly-tinted half-breeds are rightfully called Creoles.*

Hearn goes on to trace this idea in various ways, including one crude notion that 'the Creoles of New Orleans are "nothing more'n dammed niggers who jabber French"' or that 'a Creole means a New Orleans Frenchman and nothing else.' Hearn ends by defining Creoles as ethnic mixes of many cultures from Mediterranean to Scandinavian. (Hearn 30–31)

Morton (as a Lamothe of the Peches, Monettes and Hecauds) was more precisely describable in the lexicon of racial parsing as a 'Creole of Color', which may have meant little more than a 'dammed nigger who jabbers French' by the time of his boyhood. He was caught in a stroboscopic light that analyzed every tint and hue of skin colour and tried to assign it a slot in the hierarchy of society. To flee this fate was to reject his family, which ultimately he did, although he never shed the hold their memory exerted on him, a constant sense of paradise lost, innocence shattered. The family was part of the rosy memories of New Orleans and boyhood, and generated a sweet, impotent nostalgia.

Morton's family formed him as a person, not as an artist. As he gravitated toward music and the cultures that nourished it in New Orleans – from the French Opera to street bands to blues musicians to

New Orleans' Canal Street around the turn of the twentieth century. Note the electric sign advertising the French Opera, a longtime Vieux Carré institution lovingly remembered by Jelly Roll Morton.

itinerants in saloons, brothels and on the streets – he was at odds with the family's values and self-definitions. Stubbornly, with the will of a young man who has discovered a deep love that will last him for his lifetime, he tried to determine what it might mean to be a 'Creole of Color' and a working musician. How could he live and find a living using his strong innate musical gift and uncanny ear for the many kinds of music that burst from the scene around him?

The one complex relationship that shaped Jelly Roll Morton as an artist and entertainer was his ambivalent but powerful worship of Tony Jackson, a mentor and model but also a flawed surrogate for father and family. It is unclear how well Morton knew Jackson personally, but he certainly had a connection that was part adulation and envy for Jackson's genius, part admiration of Jackson as a figure of fashion and what Morton usually called 'notoriety', and part a wish for a father or big brother in music to guide the young man through the perils of The District and the vastly uncertain music business.

Since only sketchy details are known of Jackson's life and career, we get no direct insight into parallels with Morton, but he idolized Jackson and hoped to live up to his standards of excellence, as evidenced by his many laudatory descriptions of Jackson as 'the greatest single-handed entertainer in the world' and other encomia (Lomax 43–44). However, one powerful contradiction affected the relationship and made it paradoxical and ironic: Jackson was an open homosexual amidst the big business of heterosexual promotion and sales that defined The District and dominated the whole genre of pop music, with its conventional romanticism and sentimentality.

Morton focused on this disturbing X-factor when he dictated his autobiography to the Library of Congress recorder. In a forced offhand comment and a bad joke, Morton said, 'Tony happened to be one of those gentlemens that a lot of people call them lady or sissy – I suppose he was either a ferry or a steamboat, one or the other, probably you would say a ferry because that's what you pay a nickel for – and that was the cause of him going to Chicago about 1906. He liked the freedom there.' (Lomax 45) This was a gigantic issue in Morton's world of macho men and women who were commodities, a creature who was unmanly and used by men for sexual purposes was as mythological as a hippogriff. And probably as puzzling and unsettling, to a young man who could plainly see how talented and impressive Jackson was as a piano player and a singer. With his queer sensibility, Jackson dressed as splendidly as a rising courtier attending to the Sun King, so his fashion sense was stunningly cool.

Jackson was everything a model should be for Morton except for the hugely important idea of manliness and masculine control. How to surmount this problem?

First, the idea of imitating Jackson in everything but his sexual orientation was easy – Jackson was famous and unmistakable, an icon in New Orleans around 1900. New Orleans jazz historian Al Rose quotes Ricard Alexis, a bass and trumpet player, who said the ideal was, 'If you can't play like Tony Jackson, look like him.' Jackson's dress sense and personal style were not identified only as homosexual but as *flamboyant*, as *gaudy* – like the rest of The District. The parlour piano player fitted right into a world of crinolines and silk underwear, feathers and silk stockings in every rococo pattern. He was more of the furniture of sex and hilarity that made a trip to Lulu White's an excursion into a delicious, exotic world, like a flying-carpet jaunt to the harems of the Orient.

Rose has a caustic response to the remainder of Alexis's Tony Jackson memory, which included the characterization of the entertainer as 'Happy-go-lucky! Not a care in the world!' Rose editorialized bitterly:

Oh, to be an epileptic, alcoholic, homosexual Negro genius in the

Deep South of the United States of America! How could you
have a care? Anyone would be happy, naturally, being among
the piano virtuosi of his era, permitted to play only in saloons and
whorehouses for pimps and prostitutes and their customers. How
could anyone be anything but 'happy-go-lucky'? (Rose 110)

The comment summarizes Morton's dilemma, too. In choosing Jackson's life, he was passing through the strait gate of the half-world – but what other choice was open to a footloose Creole boy whose family was sinking into squalid sub-gentility and who, in the Victorian phraseology, had 'no prospects', 'no expectations'? If he rejected Jackson as a sexual model, Morton already felt harsh tension about music and musicians as outside the bounds of middle-class standards – unmanly, effeminate, effete.

But Jackson was a self-advertised homosexual (his greatest hit, 'Pretty Baby', with its original, uncensored and unpopped lyrics [later revised by Gus Kahn for singer-comedienne Fanny Brice, perhaps for her 'Baby Snooks' act], is fairly obviously aimed at a male lover):

You can talk about your jelly roll,

But none of them compare with pretty baby,

With pretty baby of mine.

Slyly, Jackson used to play and sing this passage whenever Morton stopped to visit him on a job (it may be one initial source of the 'Jelly Roll' monicker). So Morton felt the wrenching impact of a love and adulation equally comprised of shame and rejection, which drove him sometimes to hyper-masculine ranting, boasts of heterosexual feats and prowess and a horror of self-revealing tenderness, even though he harboured a deep streak of romantic sentimentality and used it lavishly in his exquisite melodies and lyrics. (Lomax 45)

One source of Morton's combative competitiveness was his conviction that he already knew the only entertainer in the world who was better than F. L. Morton, that any half-hand bigshots he encountered could not compare to Jackson and, by extension, with Jackson's prize pupil, Jelly Roll Morton. His endless bragging about New Orleans musicians was a way of saying 'I have seen and played with the best of the best – what can you possibly offer, either as a competitor or a companion?' Jackson was the touchstone of greatness, the ideal to be striven for but never attained.

The impact of Jackson on a listener was described by Morton's friend, business partner and confidant Roy Carew, recalling his first impression (*c.* 1904) on standing outside the interesting brothel-keeper and female cornettist Madame Gonzales' place and hearing Jackson sing and play:

> *It was a man's voice that had at times a sort of wild earnestness to it. High notes, low notes, the singer executed them perfectly, blending them into a perfect performance with the remarkable piano style. As I stood there, I noticed another listener standing on the edge of the sidewalk a little ways away. I did not know who he was, but afterwards found out that he was another local piano player, Kid Ross, I think. I never got to know the man, but I will never forget our short conversation. 'Who in the world is that?' I asked, indicating the unseen player as I stepped over to him. 'Tony Jackson,' he replied. 'He knows a thousand songs.'* (Rose 113)

He was known by all and vividly recalled for decades after his early death in 1921. Manuel Manetta, the pianist, teacher and multi-instrumentalist mentor of many New Orleans jazzmen, said of Jackson: 'Tony was in charge from the day he went to work. We *all* listened to him. Nobody could match him. He played *anything*! Blues, opera – anything!' (Rose 111)

Jackson went to Chicago (about 1906, Morton said) and was also wildly successful there, in the posh brothels and cafes. It was not long before Morton followed in his wake, but he was a smaller fish in the big pond and had a harder scuffle to make it (he claimed to have bested

Jackson in a battle of music – but only by underhanded trickery). Morton would follow Jackson's trail to fame and glory the rest of his life, striving to reach the heights his idol explored and to impress himself on the national consciousness with a popular hit like 'Pretty Baby'.

What Morton did absorb from his close-up study of Jackson was how to operate safely in The Life – the half-world of prostitution, gambling, drugs, drink and assorted petty crime. It was an uncertain and dangerous life of ups and downs, the wheel of fortune ruling all, and to live it you needed nerve, self-confidence, simple courage and ingenuity. He could go a long way on his music – playing, singing, bandleading, arranging – but he needed other skills to stay alive, fed and happy on the road. For Morton, that meant most often pimping: 'Nowadays we think of Morton primarily as a pianist, composer, and bandleader, and his activities as a pool shark and pimp have receded into the background, if they are in the picture at all. In fact, though, from his early teens until he was about thirty-two, he used his music as a front for his hustling.' (Pastras 18) Morton casually admitted as much on several occasions, and he was wholly familiar with the tough world of the prostitutes and their short, dreary lives.

Modern consciousness of Morton's career sometimes flinches at the squalor and minor criminality revealed here. This squeamishness probably accounts for the skewed and malicious portrait of Morton concocted by black playwright George C Wolfe for *Jelly's Last Jam*, the early 1990s musical sponsored by actor-dancer Gregory Hines (Morton's beautiful and intricate music was oversimplified and mangled for the production by Luther Henderson). Because Morton – purportedly – was a light-skinned Creole racist, he is 'tried' in this musical and found wanting in solidarity toward negritude – but the satire is probably as much prompted by Morton's hyper-masculine boasting and (reckoned by the unctuous political correctness standards of today) misogynistic behaviour towards women (including selling them). The propagandistic tone of the show makes it clear that Morton is a symbolic scapegoat for a bundle of 'correct' views, *c.* 1990, and that lambasting him (while unashamedly appropriating and revamping his music to fit the parameters of hip-hop) is a way to lecture the current audience on 'doing right' and on the Bad Old Days of darkies bereft of modern sociopolitical views. Ironically, had Morton followed Tony Jackson's model all the way and been homosexual, he would have been useless as a hoodoo doll for Wolfe, Hines and Henderson.

The reality of Morton's life was undoubtedly more complex and precarious than we can imagine. When he talks of narrow escapes and carrying that 'hard-hitting .38 Special', it isn't just hyperbole or tall tales. He was on the margins of society in many ways, including being an outlaw (although he had only a minor police record). While he may have 'professionally' mistreated women, he was courtly and charming in his normal relations with them (he was warmly remembered by Mabel Bertrand Morton as a gentle and thoughtful husband) and made no scurrilous remarks about them in the Library of Congress autobiography, aside from the lyrics to some very dirty blues.

The shadow of Tony Jackson as a surrogate family member seems indelible in Morton's life and career. Jackson died when Morton was just beginning to make a mark in the music business, after his initial success in Chicago with 'Original Jelly Roll Blues' (1915) and before the definitive solo piano sessions for Gennett in 1923–24 – a tragic moment in his early career. There is no longer the tug of mixed motives of admiration, rejection (of the homosexuality) and competition in artistry that defined their intricate dance. Morton is thoroughly on his own in a world that rapidly forgets Jackson, except for the echoes of his published music. Even in death, he left a pointed little memento for his most apt pupil: 'Accomplish all you can as quick as you can – they forget you fast!'

The pattern and circumstances of Morton's early life invite psychoanalytical approaches to the man and the artist. Alan Lomax was attracted to these angles in *Mister Jelly Roll* (published in 1950), gleaned from his recorded interviews and research into the family and friends. The motif he follows most consistently is the 'absent father' syndrome many sociologists saw as a basis for root problems in African-American culture. He felt that Morton, surrounded by feminine models – his mother, sister and aunts – and bereft of male role models, developed a pattern of fleeing from relationships and searching for a male figure to help shape his identity. This is facile parlour analysis, but it points to disturbing iterations in Morton's life.

Morton had two absent fathers – two men who had failed his family. Ed Lamothe was an itinerant labourer and a jazz trombonist – a peripatetic figure rather like the feckless Nanki-poo in Gilbert and Sullivan's *The Mikado* (a prince disguised as a footloose minstrel who is also a renegade band trombone player). He wandered out of Louise and Morton's lives, to be replaced by Willie Morton, an illiterate porter for hotels and businesses, who also did not stay long after siring Louise's two daughters. Morton, as a boy, knew that men cut and ran, especially musicians, with their mysterious freedom and talents. Does this account for his rootlessness and restlessness, his inability to find a place in the world beyond New Orleans that he could call home?

He left New Orleans early, around 1907 by his reckoning, and never returned, yet the city and its culture were ingrained in him to the point of obsession. Like James Joyce, again, who fled Dublin as a young man (using 'silence, exile and cunning' as his defenses, he said) yet spent the rest of his life recalling it in microscopic detail and making it his *sole* topic of writing, Morton sang nothing but New Orleans in his music. Like Joyce, Morton was sustained by strong women who could bring order to his life and domesticate him. The first of his may-be, would-be 'wives' was a girl from

Ollie 'Dink' Johnson, Anita Gonzales' half-brother, a Morton piano protégé and a multi-instrumentalist, who also played drums and clarinet.

a family of talented musicians living in Biloxi, who caught Morton's eye and entrapped his heart for the rest of his life.

Bessie Johnson, who used the name Anita Gonzales, was a hustler and scheming entrepreneur at least as skilful and energetic as Morton himself. The half-sister of Bill and Dink Johnson, musicians Morton had known and hired since New Orleans days, Anita was charming and manipulative, and often successful in her money-making efforts. Morton met her as an adolescent and found her again in Los Angeles while she sojourned on the West Coast from 1917–23. She was the woman to whom he returned as he was dying.

Anita was a light-skinned Creole who evidently created the persona of 'Gonzales' as a way to access the whole culture – 'passing for white': 'The ploy of creating some kind of Hispanic origin in order to pass for white – or at least something other than black – was fairly common, especially among those blacks who were a bit too swarthy to pass convincingly as whites of the Anglo-German variety.' (Pastras 37)

It is an odd idea, since she was publicly linked with her half-brothers (Bill had managed the famous Original Creole Band, which Anita had underwritten, and Dink played with them), and they were more obviously black – and *not* named Gonzales!

Morton fell under Anita's spell in several ways – she was sexually alluring, a powerful personality (several years older than Morton) and exotic. The operative word may be 'spell', because Anita is one of the actors in the recurring drama of witchcraft (voodoo or hoodoo), which Morton believed intruded into and somehow controlled his life. Pastras devotes a detailed chapter to Anita's background and the way she supplanted Eulalie Hecaud/Laura Hunter in Morton's life. His 'Lalee' was a self-advertised voodoo witch, a white witch retailing benevolent powers, and Anita was determined to be her equal in Morton's life and career.

Morton's mysterious voodoo godmother, Lalee/Laura Hunter, had moved to Los Angeles before 1920 and died there in 1940, a year before Morton. Anita Gonzales gave the information for Hunter's death certificate, because she was another Eulalie Hecaud godchild. She and Morton were connected by the woman and by early meetings in their youth (a romantic, gothic tale echoing Charles Dickens' *Great Expectations*!). When Morton went to California in 1940, he was returning to an old flame, a woman who had been his lover and 'wife' (in fact if not by law) in the early 1920s, and for whom he wrote two of his more romantic tunes – 'Mamanita', a dark and swirling tango, and 'Sweet Anita

Mine', a cheery pop tune from the late 1920s. She was a constant figure in his life, but one from whom he was mostly estranged through his career.

Anita had enough of a grip on him to entice him from the miseries of late-Depression New York to sunny California. In 1940, as his health collapsed and his business plans with Roy Carew seemed futile and abortive, Morton chained his old Cadillac to the back of his old Lincoln and headed west, to find (one more time) redemption and renewal over the horizon, in the company of a woman who may have fleeced and handled him but who never rejected or forgot him. By her testimony, Morton, the love of her life, died in her arms. But she was as good a mythographer as Mr Jelly Lord, and that's how passionate romances on the fringe of the dark voodoo world – or in Dickens novels – were supposed to end. (Pastras 32—73)

In Morton's mind, he was an exile like an orphan in a Victorian melodrama, a victim of his family's narrowness, prudery and self-inflated gentility. He recalled the drama of his great-grandmother Mimi Pechet's act of banishment:

> My [great-]grandmother gave me that Frenchman look and said to me in French, 'Your mother is gone and can't help her little girls now. She left Amede and Mimi to their only grandmother to raise as good girls. A musician is nothing but a bum and a scalawag. I don't want you round your sisters. I reckon you better move.' (Lomax 25–26)

Morton went to visit in Biloxi, where Anita and the Johnsons lived. He was impelled by grief and self-dramatization:

> The first night after my great-grandmother told me to go, I attended the Grand Theatre and saw a play in which they sang a very sweet song, entitled, Give Me Back My Dead Daughter's Child. I thought about how my mother had died and left me a

motherless child out in this wide world to mourn, and I began
to cry. (Lomax 41)

As this fantasy of self-pity blossomed, young Morton seems to have put himself in both his sisters' place and in his own, and to have begun to see his great-grandmother as an implacable authority like the stage persona. Mainly, he felt like a motherless child, and this orphaning never quite left the man of later years.

The second domestic drama of Morton's later life was with Mabel Bertrand, 'Fussy Mabel' as he called her in the song title, who was in some ways diametric to Anita Gonzales but an equally solid force in stabilizing his life. She was a young and seemingly fragile chorine Morton met in 1927 in a Chicago nightclub. He was struck by her beauty and then fascinated by her story – she was from New Orleans, the daughter of a doctor, from that refined Creole society that Morton's family had emulated, and had been sent to a convent for education. She defined her background as French and Shawnee (the genealogies in the 'high-yaller' world created by racism and segregation are as convention-ridden and predictable as dime novels), but she went to showbiz from the convent, after both her parents died in her adolescence. Her story overlaps Morton's in many ways – two orphans fleeing to The Life and finding each other by the lightning chance of popular fiction.

Morton saw her as a woman malleable to his needs and demands, a refuge from the vacillating fortunes of his life in music. She knew by her own experience the whimsical oscillations of life on the wicked stage (she had travelled the country and the world as a singer and dancer in a vaudeville act with one Billy Arnte, who had mentored her and taught her some sophistication). Morton said he was going to 'kidnap' Mabel, as if they colluded in a Robin Hood fantasy, and take her out of show business for her own good. They married (it is disputed if this was a legal marriage, if he was married previously to Anita Gonzales, as he often claimed, or to Rose Brown), and she became a super-valet, secretary, cook and live-in lover to a slightly older (by perhaps six or eight years), slightly mysterious man she obviously revered. Morton shaped her to his stressful life and showered her with as much security as he could muster while he and the nation went slip-sliding into the Depression. His relationship with her sounds closer to a father-daughter bond than a marriage partnership, and his 'kidnapped' bride seems to have been maintained as an object of romantic fantasy, leaving Mabel on a tottery pedestal and sometimes shut out of his workaday life.

Both Anita and Mabel testified that Morton was obsessively jealous of his women, whom he also wished to show off as emblems of his status and manhood. Both went to jobs with him and sat passively on the stage, like ornaments to his success. Both had show business experience and interests – Anita was also a singer and talented enough to write the lyrics to 'Dead Man Blues' for Morton. But he treated both women as domestic accessories and was determined to keep them from working or exerting much independence. He was still enough of a middle-class Creole to impose conservative standards on his marriages, however fraudulent the relationships might have been.

Mabel was patient, loyal, dependable, and she stood by him for richer or poorer, in health and sickness. His final departure from her in 1940, when he had to leave the cold, wintry East and head back to the land of sunshine and opportunity he remembered out in LA, was a betrayal on his part. He walked out on her – albeit under colossal pressure – as he had learned that men walk out on women, as sliphorn artist Ed Lamothe had done some 40 years ago to Louise. In his illness, poverty and exhaustion, he must have felt a corrosive guilt. He tried to keep up with brief bulletin-like letters (some days with odd sign-offs like 'From a real pal' and 'One to depend on', never quite 'I love you'). His last communiqué to Mabel was a bare pencil scrawl on a money order blank, *will write soon Still sick*.

A stark end to the Ferd and Mabel story, end of all the phantom memories and longings for family and New Orleans, of the haunting by vanished friends and competitors like Tony Jackson; end of the tangled affairs of the man with three 'marriages' and no one true marriage. Morton's arduous cross-country trek was one last attempt to simultaneously go back (to a prosperous, peaceful past) and ahead (to a promising new future), to invent a new life, a new career. But in the end, the unequal struggle with age and bad health led him to the grave.

CHAPTER EIGHT

MYTH vs. REALITY

More than other biographies in jazz, Jelly Roll Morton's story is embedded in geological layers of mythology, both comic and tragic. His devotees, as fervently as his detractors, construct and communicate romantic and baroque clouds of half-truth, opinion and plain fabrication. Given to hyperbole himself, Morton has been the cause of hyperbole in others and often the victim of his own successful boasting, mythologizing and self-promotion.

Myths and allegations of varying kinds dog Morton's story, some dating back to his early years, some elicited later from fellow musicians in interviews, some rising from purely aesthetic differences (Morton became a hallowed icon for the stubbornly conservative jazz musicians and fans called Mouldy Figs in the jazz criticism wars of the 1940s and 1950s and was therefore often a prime target for vituperations by jazz Modernists and their allies). Some tales are as persistent as bad rumours and impossible to attribute, others were stated clearly on the record. The most vivid and common canards are as follows.

1. Morton was a 'weak'/inept pianist. This idea is stated in various ways, but it is a fundamental attempt to deny the ample sonic evidence of Morton's recordings. The bassist George 'Pops' Foster (1892–1969), as opinionated and outspoken as most New Orleans musicians, worked with Morton and testified with a straight face that Morton had a 'weak left

hand' and was forced to hire a second pianist to play left-hand parts on his recordings. In an as-told-to autobiography, Foster opined:

> *He had a good right hand but his left hand was no good ... I don't know this first hand, but some of the guys said that he had to get high-powered guys like Tony Jackson, Albert Calb* [sic – Carroll or Cahill?]*, or Eudell* [Udell] *Wilson to go out and cut the bass parts of a record for him. Jelly would play the right hand and the other guy would play the bass behind what he did.*
> (Stoddard 95)

This is roughly equivalent to alleging that Ted Williams was a weak hitter and always had others bat for him! Morton was renowned for his distinctive and powerful left-hand playing, and *why* Foster would try to pass on this whopper is incomprehensible.

Of the same order were comments by Duke Ellington (an old enemy and the butt of some of Morton's most scathing comments about jazz and non-jazz practices) when Ellington insisted that Morton could not keep a strict beat as a pianist and that his timekeeping wandered and wavered, evidently misunderstanding the supple and subtle beat that Morton created in his tangos and other 'Spanish tinge' numbers. On first hearing, Morton's behind-the-beat rhythms sound ambiguous, but they are as tight as a metronome and highly effective in making the broken Latin rhythms swing. Ellington also offered a gratuitously catty comment on Morton in more general terms: '... Ellington had in earlier years said of Jelly Roll Morton, "He played piano like one of those high-school teachers in Washington; as a matter of fact, high-school teachers played better jazz."' (Jewell 187) This may only be fermented sour grapes from a competitor lavishly praised as a leader, composer and arranger but less often stroked for his piano skills, although Ellington was an excellent stride player.

Morton as Maestro: 'I'm the King!' Victor publicized Morton's Red Hot Peppers
recordings lavishly, and Morton cheerfully hammed it up for the camera.

2. Morton was musically illiterate or at least unable to score or arrange music. The denial of Morton's use of scores is filled with confusion. Most Red Hot Peppers sidemen, when interviewed, said Morton's usual practice was to use the stock arrangements available – the Melrose brothers were publishing them and wanted Morton to promote them via his records. Morton then modified the stocks, adding, deleting and editing, to make a usable recording score. He sometimes sketched simple lead sheets or solo lines on paper. He also coached the band from the piano, playing melody lines and suggesting riffs. They then established an outline or 'routine' for the piece – order of strains, ensembles, solos – then cut a disc. By listening to playbacks from the takes, musicians got their routines firmly in their heads and made changes and improvements to suit themselves. The sidemen uniformly testified that Morton did not tamper with solo spots or demand specific musical lines, except for introductions and endings, when the band was tightly coordinated. His work was a skilled combination of written arrangement and head arranging, and Morton had the special talents necessary to elicit brilliant performances from fine musicians.

Despite this testimony and aural evidence, Morton's enemies alleged he was a phony, a nonreader or a 'faker' in early jazz parlance. Because he could improvise so fluently on the spot, 'making it up as he went along' on themes and ideas others suggested, he seemed only a keyboard-reader – but Bach, Beethoven, Mozart and many others had the same lightning improvisatory talents, often writing pieces down only *after* they had played and refined them without paper. The Library of Congress recordings show this in action on nearly every disc: Morton plucks a theme or tune from the air or is asked by Alan Lomax to play one, and without hesitation or fumbling, he not only plays the theme but constructs a chain of brilliant original variations. Those 1938 recordings give ample, irrefutable evidence of the genius Morton claimed to possess.

In addition to aural evidence, some of Morton's peers testified to his self-schooling in reading and writing music and its results. One of his tutors was Lovie Austin (1887–1972), the superb blues accompanist, bandleader and singer of the 1920s, who was an accomplished and literate arranger and composer. She admired Morton and first met him in Chicago as he came off his vaudeville run with Mack & Mack. She became a friend, a tutor and a musical amanuensis as he assembled his folio of superb piano jazz works, showing him how to annotate and score the music lodged in his head and fingers. Austin described him as a phenomenal player:

> *I heard Jelly play all kinds of music. He could play anything, popular or classical, but he'd learn them. He didn't read them, he'd learn them. If you played something for him, he didn't need to hear it but one time and he'd play it as good as you could play it. He had the most wonderful ear I ever heard in my life. I thought I was good, but Jelly Roll was much better than I was.*

Austin had a close relationship with Morton and served as a gentle female companion for a man notably short of simple, affectionate relationships with women:

> *He used to sit me down and tell me about things that happened to him in New Orleans. And I'd listen; I was a good listener. He'd tell about trying to be a man when he was nothing but a kid. He would try to make the gals, you know, but the gals would call him a kid and run him out.* (Russell 352)

In his travels, Morton's education was more than just musical – he was succeeding in 'becoming a man'. Austin was unusual in accepting Morton as a colleague and not a competitor, while other musicians felt threatened by his dazzling talents and his brash public persona.

As well as admirers, Morton collected legions of enemies in his wake – sometimes jealous rivals, sometimes people who simply disapproved of his life and the world in which he routinely moved (as Earl Hines once backhandedly called him 'the best of the underworld pianists'). One such was Marge Creath Singleton, sister of the nearly legendary Charlie Creath, the powerful and imposing St Louis (and riverboat) trumpeter and bandleader, and wife of New Orleans drummer Zutty Singleton. Interviewed in 1969, she recalled her sour impressions of Morton from his St Louis visit of 1916. Morton himself recalled sojourns in that city as unalloyed triumphs, when he taught the whole school of old-fashioned St Louis ragtimers a thing or two about jazz. Marge Singleton's view was not so sanguine:

> *Yes, I remember Jelly Roll – in East St Louis ... Jelly was a friend of my brother Charlie Creath. They were both alike – a whole lot alike, bragged a lot ... I used to go to the movies every Sunday. It was only a nickel to get in on Sunday afternoons, and Jelly played piano. The piano was right to the side of the screen, a big upright piano. And Jelly was accompanying the movie, sometimes sad music, you know, sometimes fast, and ragtime. It was just nickelodeon piano playing, that's all. Jelly Roll was just another nickelodeon piano player.* (Russell 493–94)

Morton's odd habit of taking on any kind of local work, no matter how menial, here gets him labelled as one forced by incompetence to be a workaday musical hack. Singleton also notes and disapproves of Morton's pimping and gambling, which strike her also as marks of a reprobate and incapable musician. Clearly, she transferred to Morton her disgust with and regret over her brother's moral lapses. She played piano in Creath's band, so she also probably expresses professional envy of Morton's later fame and presumed fortune. There seems to be bitterness that Morton was known as a big shot, while her talented husband Zutty never got his proper due as a jazz great.

Marge Singleton defends the St Louis ragtimers, especially Tom Turpin, as Morton's superiors. The old ragtime men were nearly legendary, while Morton seemed a half-hand bigshot with a line of palaver and little to show for his musical talents:

> ... he was just considered a 'chittlin' piano player'. They used to call them 'chittlin''; if you didn't have a big name you was just a chittlin' piano player. The big man around St Louis was Tom Turpin, and there was another piano player – Louis Chauvin. Now, when you spoke of them you had to speak with a lot of respect.

She won't drop her damnation of Morton as a jumped-up nobody: '... we paid a nickel to get in, and that was for the movie – not to see Jelly Roll. He was just a chittlin' piano player.' (496) Her 50-year-old memories of Morton at least seem vivid and real to the reader – Morton always left a mark, even when it was a black mark in someone's tables of moral credits and debits.

3. Morton was a smalltime 'tune thief' who talked himself into fame and fortune. Much of this legend stems from his onetime agent Harrison Smith's allegations and attempts to cash in on Morton copyrights (he tried much the same thing with Duke Ellington). Morton swam with the sharks, and other publishers and tunesmiths like Clarence and Spencer Williams were also predatory and rapacious. It explains Morton's attitude toward W. C. Handy, who he viewed as another carnivore out to copyright and sell any music not tacked down. Morton's attitude toward 'transforming' music by others adds ambiguity to his practices, and he made the same farfetched personal claims on 'floating folk or blues strains' as did many others. He and Clarence Williams fought a running battle for ownership of the 'Alabama Bound' tune (Morton turns it also into 'Don't

You Leave Me Here'), which probably predated both of them by a generation. The Texas 'ragtime' guitarist Henry Thomas played archaic versions of these and other disputed numbers that must date well back into the nineteenth century.

'Floating' blues and folk themes abounded by the turn of the twentieth century, since most black musicians were: a) not professionals and b) totally outside the culture that controlled and exploited musical productions – copyright, publishing, promotion, etc. Morton was trying to crack the barriers to that culture, but his alliances with semi-piratical hustlers like the Melrose brothers (and to some extent the Spikes brothers of LA) were futile. When he 'transformed' these folk materials, he felt it was the same operation he applied to properly 'owned' music like Joplin's 'Original Rags' or Santo Pecora's 'She's Crying for Me'. So, when he claimed to have 'written' a tune like 'Alabama Bound' or 'If I Was Whiskey and You Were a Duck' (a.k.a. 'Hesitation Blues'), he was not simply inventing a Munchausen tale. To him, the process of finding, learning and renovating primitive materials and creating brilliant variations was an act of 'composition' and assertion of ownership.

Since the whole world of pop music navigated through a maze of legal, quasi-legal and quite illegal processes (by modern standards) of 'ownership', it is difficult to separate sheep from goats and to understand motives of people generations dead. The Melroses left ample statements of their money-making intent and contempt for the sources of their fortunes, but most operators in this world at least tried to wear a cloak of respectability. When Roy Carew helped Morton set up Tempo Music and began untangling all skeins of Morton's long productivity, it was a good-faith effort to put him into the modern corporate music world. Morton was right to mistrust publishers, promoters, record companies and the rest of the industry, given their abysmal Jim Crow attitudes toward African-

American music and its practitioners. But no simple alternative existed.

ʚ⧽ ⧼ɞ

On the other side of the spectrum from Morton detractors are legions of idolaters and hagiographers, who built a legend of Morton as a victim of baseless slander and a 'pure' artist at heart, whose career was undermined by ignorance, racism and music-industry greed. In this view, Morton was blameless and innocent of conniving and borderline theft, a Creole saint more sinned against than sinning. Those mythologers pressing this case fall into categories that may seem mysterious to modern listeners:

1. Dedicated and obsessive record collectors of the 1930s and 1940s: Heading this large international posse of zealous amateurs was William Russell (1905–92), a man whose life altered when he accidentally stumbled across a Red Hot Peppers record. It was a profound epiphany that shaped a long, productive life's work in the service of New Orleans jazz, as Russell understood it. He was a genuinely saintly person, of a kind that you might associate with Eastern religions – self-abnegating, a servant to others, indefatigable in his work and compulsive in collecting and analyzing materials about the music and musicians he loved. He lived as simply as a Trappist monk, except for the mountains of stored 'collections' he maintained – boxes and boxes of sheet music, clippings, correspondence and other memorabilia or data of even remote importance in the history of African-American music and its creators.

In 1929 Russell was a college teacher in New York City, on a trajectory to become a serious composer of modern music (he played violin but was to write some of the most interesting modern music for percussion ensembles). He ran across and listened to Morton's 'Shoeshiner's Drag' (a record only a year old at that date) and had a road-to-Damascus experience – he was instantly converted to this music he had never heard and, by extension, to all forms of early jazz and blues. Russell toured the country during the Depression, playing with a Balinese gamelan orchestra, and learned about absorbing the music of other cultures; he also began collecting jazz records in a serious way. The addicted record collector is an intriguing figure in jazz history, the source of modern historical and analytical interests in the music. No serious academics promoted its study, and while significant modern composers were vitally interested (Darius Milhaud, Igor Stravinsky, Maurice Ravel and many others), jazz was not discussed except by fans (a word we need to remember as deriving from 'fanatic') and the musicians themselves.

As a collector, Russell found himself in a cosmos peopled by other collectors – almost always white, middle-class and often just out of college, where they first met jazz. They founded the first focused and serious jazz history and criticism in America, beginning in magazine and periodical publications and ending with the collective assembly of a fat anthology, *Jazzmen*, edited by Frederic Ramsey, Jr., and Charles Edward Smith, and published in 1939. It tried to tell the story of early jazz up to the Swing Era, and William Russell was an important contributor. As he wrote about jazz and musicians, Russell collected more records, buying them mostly for pennies from junk stores, and began searching out facts and historical information and interviewing anyone pertinent to his interests. At the centre of his collections were reams of material about Jelly Roll Morton. He met Morton in Washington and New York in 1938, which impelled his dedicated collecting and preserving, assembling the giant collection which swelled over the next five decades.

Russell finally arranged his copious but unsorted materials as a fascinating 'scrapbook' just before his death in 1992; this was published in 1999 in a volume large enough to be a footstool and heavy enough to anchor a cabin cruiser (*Oh, Mister Jelly*). It reflects Russell's tireless devotion, but it also is notably 'raw' material – it does not acknowledge later research on Morton's family, ancestry and his self-invention by equally dedicated diggers and scholars such as Lawrence Gushee. It preserves Mortoniana without discrimination or reservation – it is all there, truth and lies, facts and errors. Russell could never bring himself to write a book on Morton, partly because he hoped Roy Carew would take up the task (Carew's important materials are included in the scrapbook) and partly because to stop the collecting and begin the writing would have meant acknowledging Morton was dead, gone and forever beyond the reach of praise or damnation. (Reich and Haines 245–48)

Record collectors did invaluable service by finding and preserving original recordings, along with photos, artifacts and memories, as they turned from shellac discs to surviving musicians as research targets. They also instigated odd 'culture wars' over the old music vs. current jazz in the 1940s and 1950s, which probably obfuscated as much as enlightened the discourse on the music. They literally snatched much material from the trash collectors and scrap drives of the Second World War, in which much of early twentieth-century popular culture went to the inescapable 'war effort'. The collectors also wanted to canonize their music and its heroes, and Morton was often subject to deification in the pages of little jazz magazines and in vociferous arguments across big music trade papers.

2. Converts gathered by Alan Lomax and the backwash of the Library of Congress interviews: the recordings Lomax cut were made available to the public in the 1940s on acetates and finally on 12 large 78 rpm record albums sold by Circle Records. As LP records appeared, the Circle albums were transferred to this new medium. Thereafter, the recordings were edited and reissued a number of times on LPs, cassette tapes and CDs, never staying in print long and in varying formats. None of the issues included every bit of the Library of Congress material. The very obscene blues that Alan Lomax

elicited from Morton, purportedly to document Storyville's culture by a surviving witness, were not generally available, and original acetates that were botched or defective were omitted. The recording quality was always a problem, especially the matter of wobbly recording speed, which was usually not corrected to make the music play at correct pitch.

But the recordings became both famous and notorious, with prurient interest stirred and responses to Morton's musical illustrations ranging from awe to disgust. The dominant feeling, however, was that Morton was simply speaking his mind and recollecting in tranquillity, that he conveyed a spotless picture of the romantic past of jazz. The autobiography was underpinned by a complex agenda, for both Lomax and Morton. The folk music collector wanted Morton to conform to ideas about 'folk' musicians and black artists, while Morton saw the sessions as a prime medium for his views and grievances, a way to get the *real* Jelly Roll story told. It was the ultimate bully pulpit and soapbox for posterity, a series of recordings to join the archive of musical proof of genius Morton had cut for Gennett, OKeh, Victor and others.

Part of the response to the autobiography was to its nearly hypnotic form. As edited, it carries forward an elaborate narrative, peopled by dozens of characters Morton evokes, with music running, background and foreground, as an integral part of the tale. It is different from and more powerful than any conventional memoir, and the control Morton exerted is insidious and spellbinding. We get no documentation from outside the story, no corroboration or contradiction from other sources, so we quickly absorb Morton's worldview and beliefs. It is hard *not* to believe that 'Tiger Rag' evolved in any way other than the one Morton illustrates, hard to be sceptical of his depiction of The District, Louisiana culture, the compelling central role of Ferd Morton in the development and promulgation of jazz. No one ever made more skillful use of the wordless rhetoric of music than Morton, and many were converted who heard the Library of Congress testimony. The recent CD set on Rounder Records brings all the resources of digital sound technology to bear in making the records clear, correctly pitched and crystalline in quality, further enhancing the works' mesmerizing effect.

3. The dismissive Modernists and the reactionary Mouldy Figs. After the scarifying jazz wars of the 1940s, Morton was often denigrated by convinced Modernists as a hidebound musical relic, whose skills as a pianist and composer were exaggerated. He was called a 'one-finger' player by Moderns expecting to hear the basic stride pattern that marked most swing pianists, or the restless experimentation of a proto-Modernist like Earl Hines. His rhythm was faulted as 'corny' (ragtime rhythms and beat) and old-fashioned even when Morton was at his peak. His band records seemed mere generic 'Dixieland' to inattentive listeners, and his bragging was offensively uncool.

The rupture between early jazz and bebop was abrupt and absolute in many ways. Morton, Louis Armstrong and other New Orleans pioneers seemed remote – from the 'old days' and from 'out west' (not New Yorkers) – and disconnected from the minimalist rhythms and outreaching harmonic experiments of the new jazz. Some swing figures were cool and tolerated – Artie Shaw and Lester Young bridged the gap easily, as did Ellington, up to a point – but even that generation was felt to be hoary and superannuated. In the 1940s, jazz was still felt a very young man's music, a 'youth culture' intolerant of ageing and conservatism. Morton was in his early fifties when he died; Armstrong and Ellington were younger men, but to twenty-year-old bopsters like Thelonious Monk, Dizzie Gillespie and Charlie Parker and their cohorts, they were ancients. The tide of the future seemed to be with heedless youth, as in the 1920s, and the old dinosaurs hanging around were embarrassing

Charlie 'Bird' Parker, the master spirit, icon and incarnation of bop and the jazz
revolution of the 1940s.

reminders of jazz's 'primitive' beginnings and its connections with crime and the gutter. The beboppers wore coats and ties, natty berets and Modernist sunglasses, and were the picture of bourgeois bohemianism, part-time students at Julliard, not raggedy old refugees from ratty whorehouses and saloons.

Morton was not well-known enough in the early 1940s to be a major point of contention in the jazz culture wars; he was of little interest to most young Modernists, and the idea of a 'jazz heritage' or any continuity with the past was anathema for most of them. They were the new broom to sweep American clean of the old-timey, square and laughably simple music from New Orleans back in oughty-ought. It took some decades of perspective for the grandchildren of bebop to see that the story of jazz had continuity, and evolution, not revolution, was its chief characteristic. The advent of jazz education, first in colleges and universities, then in public schools and via public radio and TV, advanced the idea of jazz as a continuum and a subject worthy of scholarly and analytical discussion. Something was gained and lost in this process, and by now the heavy, levelling hand of academe may be as oppressive as the fog of ignorance and folklore that surrounded jazz for decades.

The Mouldy Figs who steadfastly battled the Modernists left their own idolatrous vision of Morton. He was an icon for the fans of oldtime jazz, as much for his rowdy ways and romantic biography as for his music. He became the model of the genius neglected by history and thrust aside by the relentless Modernism of the new bebop, who – unlike Louis Armstrong and others – did not live long enough to oppose it in person, leaving his fans to lead a posthumous crusade in his name.

❧❧❧   ❧❧❧

Other kinds of myths and lies circulate about Morton. The most recent canards are listed by Reich and Gaines in their introduction to *Jelly's Blues*:

More than half a century after his death, in 1941, he was termed
a racist by the fanciful Broadway musical Jelly's Last Jam *(1992),*
a cliché by the movie The Legend of 1900 *(1999), and a brute*
and a bully by the Ken Burns TV documentary Jazz *(2001).* (xii)

It is curious how powerful a lightning rod Morton remains, more than a century after his birth. In life at the centre of controversy and argumentation, in death he still seems a figure to fascinate and repel jazz fanatics in equal measure. Even those ignorant of his life and career have 'heard that he –' and there follows a bizarre tale or half-truth wrung from who-knows-what distant source.

One significant source of confusion, half-truth and distortion is the work of his principal biographer, Alan Lomax. With a long and distinguished career as a collector and preserver of African-American music and lore, Lomax is a grey eminence in Morton's story and in a way Morton's saviour. However, he also has a more sinister role in the saga of Mr Jelly Lord. At the end of his life, Lomax published a retrospective summary of his career, *The Land Where the Blues Began* (1993), and since his death details of his career hidden or obfuscated have come to light, including ways in which Lomax shaped, appropriated and revised history in order to suit his own theses and predilections. The case is disturbing and demands attention from anyone pursuing the facts in the career of Ferdinand J. Lamothe, a.k.a. Jelly Roll Morton.

Like many self-taught, field-trained musicologists of his generation, Lomax was something of a buccaneer, taking possession of information and ideas too readily. He knew what he knew, he had an idiosyncratic vision of the South and the omnipresent spectre of race and racism, and he often asked leading questions in interviews and put his own words, ideas and beliefs into his subjects' mouths (as with his tireless pursuit of the lowlife of the brothels and 'dirty blues' with Morton). In another musical autobiography he recorded in 1941 with folksinger Woody Guthrie, prepared as a radio series, he also often bullied and manipulated Guthrie into giving the 'correct' (i.e. Lomax-style) responses to questions and to shaping his own story to suit Lomax's ideas and theories.

Lomax's repeated, large-scale manipulation of research ideas and information is documented in a recent study, *Lost Delta Found*, edited by Robert Gordon and Bruce Nemerov (Vanderbilt University Press, 2005). The book carefully reconstructs the conduct of a field study of Coahoma County, Mississippi, in 1941–42, led by three African-American Fisk University researchers, John W. Work, Lewis Wade Jones and Samuel C. Adams, Jr.. Lomax became involved with this project at its inception and then virtually hijacked it.

Without going into details, it is a case of Lomax throwing his weight around (the great weight of the Library of Congress's reputation), evidently undervaluing the three Fisk workers (all of whom were or would become important scholarly researchers into black music and who pioneered careful study of local social and cultural conditions in the South). The Second World War was a factor in derailing the study, but Lomax's self-important intrusions also undermined it, and it slipped into oblivion in scattered files and archives (some in Lomax's possession).

Gordon and Nemerov note that Lomax mined this aborted study for his own purposes in his late autobiographical study *The Land Where the Blues Began*, which places Alan Lomax squarely in the middle of the history of blues in the Mississippi Delta:

> *When Lomax published his book in 1993, John Work was mentioned three times: in the preface, he was mentioned in association with the musical transcriptions; in the sole text mention, he was present at the recording of Muddy Waters; in the acknowledgements, his name is listed with Jones and Adams.*

Adams is not otherwise mentioned; Jones, who is cited several times, is the only one portrayed as an actual participant in the research. (24)

So Lomax did his best to make the sources of much information in his writing disappear and to erase the details of contributions from the black scholars who set up the study and collected virtually all the data. He was also often cavalier or careless with details and transcriptions, transposing McKinley Morganfield's *nom de guitar* from Muddy Water (singular) to Muddy Waters when he recorded him, leaving him stuck with an unwanted plural for the rest of his illustrious career.

Lomax contributed numerous simple errors, typos and misprints to the Morton tale, and he added a personal spin to events and ideas, in order to justify his vision of Morton as a certain kind of black musician – more of a folk figure than Morton actually was. He did not exactly fit into the category of musicians such as Huddie 'Leadbelly' Ledbetter and other itinerant country bluesmen, which were the archetypes Lomax had recorded and interviewed with his father. To some extent, Lomax was out of his depth with Morton, and when he applied a procrustean logic to the biography he was compiling, it may have distorted or deleted many facets of Morton's complex personality.

Likewise, even positive and well-meaning characters in Morton's life contributed to mysteries and misconstructions – with friends like this, he didn't need enemies! Many elements of Morton's story remain unknown and perhaps unknowable at this late date. Alan Lomax helped save much in regard to Morton's complex life and times, but he also helped to generate the clouds of myths, mistakes and misunderstandings that obscure some of the tale.

Morton also helped to obfuscate his story, sometimes deliberately, sometimes by accident. He habitually used the rowdy frontier humour associated with wild men like Davy Crockett or Mike Fink ('I'm a ring-tailed roarer, half man and half alligator!'), and the ancient African-American comic tradition of 'Signifyin'', which involved the outrageous slanging matches we find in the Dirty Dozens, in blues and in the obscene and satirical rhyming 'toasts' that are ancestors of today's rap music monologues. Those on the receiving end of his comic diatribes often failed to see Morton's humourous, self-parodying intent.

A man described by many who knew him well as kind, funny, energetic and exciting, an individual, gentle and unassuming, is besmirched by tales from rivals or half-acquaintances angered by Morton's sometimes ham-handed ribbing or his outrageous self-advertising (an act as old as early vaudeville, where he grew up). It is difficult to find another example of such a polarizing figure in jazz: most musicians, truth be told, lead lives too pedestrian and dull to merit much acrimony or anger. It may be the romantic, larger-than-life quality to Morton's story that irritates those who believe that the workaday musicians who built the edifice of jazz are cheated by his grandiosity. But America loves heroes, and jazz was always a heroic enterprise.

This is why Morton thought in these categories when he spoke his autobiography to Alan Lomax. He recalled the big, bad, bold characters he had met and seen, and the larger-than-life exploits they represented. It is why a character so shadowy as to be little more than a name – Buddy Bolden, for example – is an endless object of wonder and curiosity: who was the Father of Jazz, and how did that god slip down from Olympus to beget his bastard daughter on the goddess Harmony?

We have many more facts and artifacts from Morton than from Bolden, but Jelly Roll still seems a figure from the Golden Age, not just a hustler and jobbing musician who had to scuffle for nickels and dimes. Some kind of envy, some disdain for greatness, dogs him – perhaps because jazz is the most democratic of musics, the great leveller, where you must show what you can do every time you play a chorus, where everyone has an equal voice and all must work together to make the music live. New Orleans bands were notoriously ensemble groups – 'never take down!' was their motto: *everyone plays all the time*. Morton was both of this collective ethos and somehow above it, a bandsman and a leader and a solo musician, always a little bit lonely, a little bit apart from the band. And fans and musicians since (who know anything at all about him and the old jazz) seem faintly resentful of his size and his swashbuckling egotism. They want cheery old black fellas with big grins or quiet and unassuming professor-like presences – 'respectable' folk, not baggy monsters who brag and laugh raucously and unpredictably.

We are not far away from Mrs Grundy and from Mark Twain's Aunt Polly and Miss Watson, who want to 'sivilize' us (and Morton), make us go to Sunday School, wear stiff Buster Brown collars and behave ourselves. But Huck Finn had the right answer to all that – 'All right, then, I'll go to Hell!'

CHAPTER NINE

THE HEARTLAND

■————————■

Because Ferd Morton early became a wanderer and explorer of the American scene – mainly the backstreet empire of African-American ghettos, vice districts and entertainment centres across the country – he seems detached and homeless, even though memories of New Orleans and its culture permeated everything he thought and did, all his music and lyrics. As he put his feelings in a late pop song (1938) that he hoped might help to revive his collapsed fortunes, 'My Home Is in a Southern Town'; as he pondered much earlier, he named one wordless but potently evocative melody 'New Orleans Joys'.

The city of New Orleans, when Morton was a boy, was a seething, polyglot, multicultural cauldron, mixed over a period of two hundred years and housing people of every heritage, bearing multitudinous and complex cultures. It was Caribbean, deeply Southern, exotic, foreign, homely, composed of immigrants and migrants from everywhere – and therefore profoundly American. But its peculiarities – the sprinkling of Creole French through its dialects, the cosmopolitan gaiety of everyday life, which included in musical terms listening to street vendors and singers, and also going to the French Opera – set it apart from any other US city. As Morton travelled, he learned just how strange his familiar New Orleans was.

It was a place where shopkeepers threw in a little extra something when you made a purchase and called it 'lagniappe'. It was a place which had seen major battles that saved the American Republic, that sheltered romantic pirates with French names, that existed amidst a slave empire but prospered owing to free men and women of colour who had been premier citizens since the beginning of the eighteenth century. It boasted African singing, chanting and dancing at Congo Square, a tradition of militias, marching societies and benevolent orders that sponsored early jazz and made a brass band tradition, once common across America, central to the life and death of the black population. It grew its own odd ceremonies and social orders like the Mardi Gras Indians, virtually a subculture that existed in a parallel universe to the gaudy lunacy of upper-class white Mardi Gras traditions. It carried on daily life down under the shadow of levees holding back the Mississippi and buried its folks above ground, because the city floated on its water table. Its people learned to live through plagues of cholera, typhoid, Yellow Jack and other diseases born of tropical heat and water.

The city was way beyond quaint into downright gothic and strange, like the teeming imaginary medieval world invented by British fantasy writer Mervyn Peake in his Gormenghast trilogy. New Orleans was a little world in which almost anything could happen, and in the 1938 oral biography, Morton recited endless tales of wonder from his youth. One indication of this world's oddity from the very beginning was its way of laying out a city on swampland banking the Mississippi River Delta and then naming the streets and boulevards that defined it. The shrewd journalist and cultural commentator Lafcadio Hearn noted this in his short tenure as a New Orleanian in the 1870s and 1880s:

> At the time of the French revolution there was an outbreak in
> France of Roman and Greek fashions. The modern French tried
> to imitate the ancient classics by assuming the Roman dress and
> Roman names. The Creoles who, although dominated by the

Spaniards, were red republicans in these days, followed the fashion and all the names of antiquity were introduced into Louisiana and survive there to this day. Achille (Achilles), Alcibiade (Alcibiades), Numa, Demosthene (Demosthenes), came into fashion. The streets found a similar fate and the new faubourg Ste. Marie was liberally christened from pagan mythology. The nine Muses, three graces, the twelve greater gods and the twelve lesser ones, and the demi-gods, all stood godparents for streets. The city fathers went beyond this, and there was a Nayades and a Dryades, a Water Work, a Euphrosine street, and beyond without end.

The city fathers also drew on Greek classical traditions and imposed them on the city, first passing them through Creole French spelling and pronunciation:

The classical scholar who visits New Orleans and hears the names of the muses so frightfully distorted may regard it as unfortunate that Greek mythology had been chosen. The explanation of the mispronunciation, however, will relieve the people of New Orleans of any charge of ignorance. The Greek names are simply pronounced in the French style. Thus the street that the scholar would call Melpomene, of four syllables and with the last 'e' sounded, would be in French Melpomene, and is translated by the people of New Orleans into Melpomeen. So Calliope is Callioap; Terpsichore, Terpsikor; Euterpe, Euterp; and others in the same way . . . . even Felicity Street – it is named, by the by, after a woman (Felicite), not happiness – is actually called by many intelligent persons Filly-city. (Hearn 19–21)

Growing up in this place, young Ferd Lamothe's ears were filled with music – even the discordant music of a strange, self-invented language unique to the city and its people. In his transplantings and wanderings, he never forgot this harmony and the variegated culture from which it sprang.

But Morton's productive working life was spent on the West Coast, in and around Chicago and finally in New York. His path of motion is a graph of cultural trends in the US of his era. Morton left New Orleans around 1907, travelling around the South and near Southwest (mainly Texas), playing smalltime vaudeville, finally reaching Chicago around 1913. He headed to the West Coast (the Los Angeles conurbation) around 1917 and made a stand there for six years (1923), when he was very busy with composing and playing but also consumed with schemes that he and Anita Gonzales were cooking up, and (probably) with his 'Pacific Coast Line' of prostitutes. He returned to Chicago and the Midwest in 1923 and began turning his years of compiling original music into jobs and recordings. He stayed in Chicago until 1928, when he followed the centre of gravity of black entertainment to New York, and tried to break into yet another tough market.

In each of the three big places where Morton scratched a toehold, he became a vital force in the jazz and entertainment scene. Working with the Spikes brothers and others around LA, Morton played at amusement parks and other outdoor venues, putting on revues, fronting bands and sponsoring visiting musicians as important as King Oliver and his new Chicago band. He was a local character followed by the local black press and known to everyone in the half-world – The Life. He repeated the same process in Chicago, where the jazz scene boiled and the opportunities for black entertainers were vastly more lucrative and more numerous than on the West Coast. By the time he reached New York, it was much harder to crack into bigtime music and entertainment. He always felt New York was a 'closed shop', with the best jobs and venues sewed up by longtime locals, controlled by gangsters and barred to wandering strangers, no matter how talented and persistent.

The West Coast years were a useful prelude to his return to Chicago, where in 1915 he published 'Original Jelly Roll Blues' and viewed the people of the city of Chicago as friends and compatriots in his jazz creations. In California, he made connections and learned more facets of his trade. His loose partnership with the Spikes brothers let him see the inside of music publishing, booking and recording. His ventures with Anita Gonzales honed his skills as an entrepreneur. He met and renewed ties with New Orleans veterans such as Kid Ory and Mutt Carey (through his 'in-law' connections – Bill and Oliver 'Dink' Johnson, Anita's brothers), and at one point was instrumental in getting King Oliver's Creole Jazz Band out on a tour. Morton was widening his apprenticeship in the whole music business available to African-Americans, from jazz playing and publishing to vaudeville, to the nightclub business and bandleading.

When he returned to Chicago, these skills and interests were vital. He found that prostitution was tightly organized by mobsters in both Chicago and New York, so he turned to his musical talents. The result was a steady flow of hot dance jobs with bands he could front and, more significantly, the recordings for Gennett and Victor that preserved and disseminated his unique version of jazz as it

Papa Mutt Carey, Kid Ory's longtime collaborator and a master of the New Orleans trumpet style.

had grown up in New Orleans and graduated to the wide world in Chicago. While his music always referred back to New Orleans, it was shaped and flavoured by the bigger picture of African-American music in the 1920s. Morton was keenly aware of musical trends and tastes, and while he did not chase chimeras, he was willing to sample, to learn, to appreciate and to adapt what he found in others' work. He is often characterized as a reckless competitor with never a good word for a potential rival, but younger musicians uniformly recall Morton as a patient teacher and mentor who gave much time to helping new jazzmen develop and make the bigtime.

Morton's Chicago – like his Los Angeles and his New York – was limited by the forces of segregation and discrimination that dominated his lifetime. He had grown up in a cosmopolitan city with a very complex attitude toward issues such as ethnic identity, class and caste. New Orleans breathed an air of freedom that may have been illusory, but it was comforting and sustaining for a young man uncertainly facing an adult life. Having learned the mores and sensibility of the culture as a child, Morton could navigate the complex rules of behaviour without much thought. He was a Creole, and he knew where and how Creoles fitted into the ethnic scales, what they could and could not do and think and dream. But America itself – all of it, the huge, indescribable agglomeration of peoples and places – was too hard to understand without experiencing it. This is one force that impelled Morton on his wanderings – an appetite to see, hear, taste, smell the vastness of the US and to fit into its wholeness.

He learned what people of colour quickly learned in the early twentieth century – that they were unknown quantities in many equations – at once 'invisible', as novelist and cultural critic Ralph Ellison explained it, and 'too visible'. In New Orleans, he could blend like a chameleon with his background. Elsewhere, he was not only a stranger but a stranger of a strange colour – and that needed explaining. The literature of the 1890s and 1900s reflected the strains and fears over this issue. Charles Chesnutt, the pioneer African-American novelist, like many others in the 1890s, wrote 'tragic mulatto' tales about people in the years after Reconstruction, caught in the dangerous crevasse between *white and black* – the reductionist way in which Jim Crow and institutionalized American apartheid were defining 'race'. The culture literally wanted the matter to be a black-and-white issue, a binary problem of yes/no, easily identified and easily solved.

But life is not simple, on any level, and living inside the skin of Ferd Lamothe Morton was a damn sight harder than saying 'I am white' or 'I am black' or (even) 'I am Creole'. Some people of colour thought a simple solution was 'passing' – but that is the crux of the 'tragic mulatto' tale: trying to be what you are not is an intolerable denial of the self, of true identity and meaning, bound to end badly. The cultural edict ran: *If you are any colour but true, certified and indisputable WHITE, you are* ipso facto *a second-class citizen or Untouchable. You have no option but to admit who and what you are and take your lumps.* But this is simpler than reality and the inflexible rule of the Law of Colour: what 'colour' is a Gypsy, a Sephardic Jew, a swarthy Italian or Croatian, a Mexican, Cuban, Spaniard, Chinese, Japanese, Polynesian, AmerIndian?

In *Invisible Man*, that supreme summary of black life up to the middle of the twentieth century, Ralph Ellison posed the issue in a frightening, surreal allegory, as his young protagonist reaches New York from the Deep South and takes a job at a paint factory, the place that 'colours' society and covers up its differences. A malicious old black man is teaching the youngster the ropes, and he mentions the company's slogan: 'If It's Optic White, It's the Right White.' The young man thinks, 'I ... suddenly had to repress a laugh as a childhood jingle rang through my mind: "If you're white, you're right," I said.' (Ellison, *Invisible Man*, 218) For his impudence, the young man is blown up in an explosion and treated to a brain operation designed to make him 'think correctly' about such ideas as 'race'.

The puzzle in reality was much more complex and ambiguous than the simple-minded racist creed declared. The burden of proof, therefore, was always on the bearer of a given skin: you must repeatedly and forever 'prove' yourself to be 100 percent Aryan, white, Anglo-Saxon, whatever the nomenclature of the moment might be. You must learn the comportment of a master, a privileged member of the upper orders, a natural aristocrat, a talented climber of the cultural heights: *address, Parnassus, Olympus, Top of the World, Ma!* So the issue of 'passing' might be resolved by claiming marginally acceptable exotic identities: I am a: 1) Cuban, 2) Puerto Rican, 3) Spaniard, 4) Italian – all several self-evident ladder rungs above: 1) 'pure' African-American, 2) AmerIndian, 3) 'mulatto', 'Creole', 'octoroon' or other euphemism. So African-American baseball players not content to languish in their 'place' in the Black Leagues could become 'Cuban' stars imported at great expense (if their skin shades would stand the eyeball test), so a travelling entertainer might casually, indirectly, hint at Mexican aristocratic heredity, or adopt a Filipino name. The race game became an unbearable struggle in detecting and maintaining not just status but personal identity in a society that might on a whim re-jig the rules and invoke draconian punishments for anyone tiptoeing across the Colour Bar.

Morton's strategy was more direct and honest, in an odd way. He simply adopted a joking but challenging attitude of superiority and self-confidence, sublimely ignored the social conventions he was supposed to follow and outfaced everyone around him. It was often described as egoism or braggadocio or conceit, but it was an armor of *amour propre* that sustained him in a tough world of competitive show business. The reaction of the Melrose brothers to his arrival in their Chicago music store is a classic example of Mr Jelly Lord's epiphany: he hit the scene, shot off his

mouth, sat down at the piano, dazzled the rubes and left an indelible impression on everyone in earshot.

Alan Lomax, as he analyzed Morton in *Mister Jelly Roll*, got it subtly wrong, as he often did: 'Jelly Roll's whole life was constructed around his denial of his

Morton takes a break from sidewalk debating to mug for the camera in 1930s Harlem.

Negro status. He was a mulatto, a New Orleans man, a higher-up, a No. 1 recording artist, but not quite a Negro. Of course this is typical of New Orleans Creoles.' (Lomax 218) This is the treacherous germ of a theory that has led to blunt and stupid misreadings of Morton's character. For Morton, no such thing as 'Negro status' existed, and he acted as any decent person should inside the cage of a social tyranny such as 'race'. Lawrence Gushee feels that Lomax's obsessive focus on the idea of Morton's 'Creole' status, while it helped him structure his book, also led to 'the obnoxious notion that Morton was something of a "racist", one of today's most insulting and carelessly employed epithets.' ('Afterword', *Mister Jelly Roll*, 2005 edn.)

Morton's self-concept was not an act of self-denial but of self-assertion. By sheer nerve and bravado, Morton exuded heroic self-confidence and capability, thus by personal example denying the foundation myth that people of colour were shiftless, cowardly, self-denying and incapable. He outfaced Jim Crow America by assuming he could do anything he wished in this world. It was an act of rising above lunatic 'rules' of a culture run by idiots, bigots and self-appointed guardians of 'racial purity'. The seriousness of his effort is masked sometimes by the comedy he used as a tool in wielding his obdurate self-confidence. The strange, symbiotic relationship with the Melrose brothers exemplifies Morton's business relationships. As Lomax retails it, the scene of their first meeting is straight out of low vaudeville comedy:

> ... Jelly Roll made his entrance into the Melrose establishment so dramatic that Lester Melrose still remembered it vividly after twenty-five years. 'A fellow walked into our store with a big red bandana around his neck and a ten gallon cowboy hat on his head and hollored [sic], 'Listen, everybody, I'm Jelly Roll Morton from New Orleans, the originator of jazz!' He talked for an hour without stopping about how good he was and then he sat down at the piano and proved he was every bit as good as he claimed and better. That was when Jelly Roll got his start.'
>
> (Lomax 185)

Note that Melrose, portrayed as a bumpkin, was still a shrewd enough operator to get in his claim for credit at the end: Morton was 'given' his 'start' by the generous and selfless Melrose boys! It is like a scene from a William Faulkner novel: one of the malignant, many-faced Snopes clan gulled by a shrewd, self-sufficient black man (say, Lucas Beauchamp) but still clinging to his genetically imprinted commercial instinct. (The Melroses drew Morton's attention in the first place because they had flown a huge banner advertising his 'Wolverine Blues' in their semi-pirated edition.)

So the heartland that Morton moved through was not just the big, bustling cities of New Orleans, then Los Angeles, then Chicago and finally New York. It was the 'invisible empire', to borrow the Ku Klux Klan's slogan, of institutionalized racism in America early in the twentieth century, a mental and emotional landscape as unyielding as the banquettes and boulevards of New Orleans or the wide avenues of central Los Angeles. He felt alone in the world – cast out by his family, far from his magical godmother and her spells and charms, without an ally in his struggles to make the white musical establishment pay its dues to the black 'originators' of jazz.

The physical landscapes themselves and the way in which the locales presented the racist face of America varied greatly. New Orleans was, to repeat, a complex case, with near-integration in many neighbourhoods but a brooding sense of caste and class over the whole community, with its 'higher-ups' as powerful in the black community as their white counterparts elsewhere. In Los Angeles multi-ethnic tensions raged, too – all rubbed together, old Hispanic settlers and johnny-come-lately eastern white migrants, Asian immigrants, a fairly large black community in the central city, new arrivals of all sorts as the population swelled after the First World War. Chicago was exploding with the massive emigration from the rural South – gone were the days of sharecropping in chattel-slavery-like conditions, King Cotton a presiding monoculture, the ideals of No Surrender flying from every county courthouse flagpole. Chicago was booming, and black migrants found not only work, but choices of work, a near-miracle. Meanwhile New York, by the time Morton arrived, was the capital of African-American culture, with its Harlem Renaissance and the tides of art and entertainment still running strong for black residents. The evil days of the Depression with its mantra of 'Last hired, first fired' would change the conditions, but in the late 1920s hope still glimmered like a tiny light at the end of a very long tunnel.

Morton spent 1914–16 in Chicago with old friends and rivals such as Tony Jackson, and he had a flourishing reputation. It is not clear why he was attracted by the West, except out of a need for new worlds to conquer and his keen radar for developing cultural trends – California was a magnet for many black people in those years. He spent 1917–23 out there, mostly in Los Angeles but also in Washington State in the wilds, following Anita Gonzales, the old sweetheart who had bewitched him as a boy. In Los Angeles he hooked up with the go-getting Spikes brothers, put together bands and became something of a celebrity, but it was not yet a jazz-friendly environment. Morton had to use all the strings to his bow – resurrected vaudeville routines, cabaret-managing, running amusement parks, juggling every opportunity that came his way. He was known to the rich and famous, and at one point his 'Spanish tinge' masterpiece 'The Crave' was taken up as a craze by the movie colony, among luminaries such as the Pickfords, Charlie Chaplin and Roscoe 'Fatty' Arbuckle. (Pastras 80–84)

He and Anita Gonzales also, around 1919, made a foray into San Francisco. They ran a nightclub, The Jupiter, in the notorious Barbary Coast district, operating it as a black and tan club (whites and blacks alike, despite the tacit and overt segregation of the city). This seems to have been Morton's instinctual preference – again, to wish the reality of Jim Crow away by outfacing it. However, the place became a target for heavy duty police harassment (Morton thought mostly because of its black and tan orientation), and jazz-knowledgeable musicians were hard to find in the city.

Herbert Asbury in his survey of the wild San Francisco demimonde, *The Barbary Coast*, mentions The Jupiter in a long catalogue of dives, first-floor and basement galleries on Pacific Street, citing the extravagant amounts of money changing hands in these operations: 'one dive operator paid nine hundred dollars a month on a ten-year lease for a cellar about sixty feet long and thirty feet wide.' The Jupiter was a basement cabaret, among many Asbury lists by name – and such names: the OK Café, the US Café, the So Different, the House of All Nations, Spider Kelly's, the Headlight, the Dragon. Morton and Gonzales faced fierce, long-established competition in a business and a locale that neither of them really understood. (Asbury 288)

The Jupiter was an albatross and a money pit, and Morton and Gonzales had to give up the fight. Gonzales left him and headed north (to Alaska, she told him), and he rushed to find her, winding up with her in remote Tacoma, then Seattle, then Vancouver. After desultory trials and successes in musical jobs and enterprises as various as boxing promotion and bootlegging, Morton and Anita headed back toward Los Angeles in late spring of 1921, after Morton underwent some further solo wandering in areas as remote as Colorado and Wyoming. (Pastras 94–107, Reich and Gaines 62–65)

While in Los Angeles, Morton also jobbed around the region, including work in Tia Juana, the nearby Mexican border town then (as now) known for its wide-open, unregulated and non-stop entertainment. His work there in 1921 produced two of his finest piano pieces – 'Kansas City Stomp' (named for a local bar where he played) and 'The Pearls' (referring to a pretty waitress there who caught Morton's eye). They became superb band numbers for his 1927–28 Red Hot Peppers bands in Chicago and New York. (He also recalled the place in recording the little pop tune 'Tia Juana' as a piano solo.) He must have noted the pervasive racism and casual xenophobia directed at Mexicans, but he found the town and people congenial, and he could not turn down work. It may have been a pleasant reminder of the healthy international culture in New Orleans, which had its long roots in Spanish history, too, as Morton insisted. On the visa Morton took out for his Mexican work, his photo shows a self-assured and businesslike Ferd with a neat suit and natty cap, staring defiantly into the camera. (Pastras 113)

The western venture for Morton was an introduction to pioneering and the ethic of self-sufficiency that still marked the region. Even in a big metroplex like Los Angeles, the culture was still about making do, frugality and unsophisticated simplicity, a great distance from the smooth worldliness and cosmopolitan bonhomie of ancient New Orleans or the raw, on-the-make hustle of Chicago. The movie industry was there to stay, but it was still an unvarnished and naïve venture, only a decade from baggy-pants vaudeville routines and open-air film studios in New Jersey or Manhattan. No one knew it would soon dominate US and world culture and dictate fashion, entertainment and manners. The phrase 'California Culture' would have made little sense to Americans east of the Rockies, and the sense of landing in a backwater recently abandoned by starving pioneers, hardrock miners and old cowhands lingered in the air.

So by 1923, Morton dropped his frustrating pursuit of Anita Gonzales, gathered a fat portfolio of music he had penned and perfected since he left the East and headed back to Chicago. He had sponsored King Oliver's Creole Jazz Band on their California trip of 1922, and he knew they were doing very well. If they could do it – New Orleans veterans no wiser, more hardworking or proficient than Morton – then it was time to take a second bite of the apple, get the town by the tail and make that big black population take notice of the music only he could make. Chicago had a thousand possibilities that the West never showed him. No more cowboy racism and cornball musicians to confront, no more digging at old veins in the goldfields of the meagre entertainment scene there. Chicago was full of musicians, showgirls, clubs and cabarets, dives and dancehalls – and recording studios, music entrepreneurs, publishers and hucksters. His kind of place. He'd blow into town from the Wild West, wearing a red bandanna and a ten gallon hat, and then ...

CHAPTER TEN

PUBLIC vs. PRIVATE

■————————■

After Morton dropped out of active recording in the early 1930s he scrabbled for work around New York, but he was no longer the public figure he had been in the dazzling 1920s. His current wife Mabel Bertrand was still awed by his professional wardrobe – racks of fine suits and overcoats, drawers of bright silk shirts – but the once-gaudy Jelly Roll was reduced to sideman jobs, anything to gather a few shekels. He was still the hustler, entrepreneur and sidewalk rhetorician, he still drove a big Lincoln or (when he chose) a big Cadillac, but he was no longer the young and ebullient Mr Jelly Lord, one of nature's aristocrats.

The Depression frightened him, as it did all Americans, with its intensity and its seeming permanence. The bottom had fallen out of the bright New Age of the 1920s, and who knew what grim future was overtaking it? The news from Europe and the rest of the world was worse, and the happy expatriates of the last decade trickled back to the US – better hard times at home than in a foreign land. Morton, too, felt cornered by history and fortune, the good luck of the pool shark, card sharp and carefree speculator drained by the waves of grey newspaper headlines that appeared day after day.

The public persona Morton had crafted in the 20-odd years since he shook the dust of New Orleans off his feet was of the brash, optimistic, indefatigable hustler, the quicksilver-slippery trickster who cruises close to the wind and succeeds solely by shit, grit and mother wit – Jack the Rabbit

A bread line in Harlem at the nadir of the Depression.

or Peetie Wheatstraw in the black mythology author Ralph Ellison
followed. In the middle of *Invisible Man* (1952), his seminal text on blues
and black culture, his nameless central character encounters an avatar of
this legendary type, who may be Br'er Rabbit at one moment and
something else in the next incarnation. This mysterious stranger gives
advice to the innocent protagonist, who has come to Harlem from the rural
South to find his fortune and – more importantly – to find his identity:

> *'All it takes to get along in this here man's town is a little shit,*
> *grit and mother-wit. And man, I was bawn with all*
> *three. In fact, I'maseventhsonofaseventhsonbawnwitha-*
> *cauloverbotheyesandraisedonblackcatboneshighjohntheconque-*
> *rorandgreasygreens – ' he spieled with twinkling eyes, his lips*

working rapidly. 'You dig me, daddy? . . . .My name is Peter
Wheatstraw, I'm the Devil's only son-in-law, so roll 'em! You're
a southern boy, ain't you?' (Ellison 176)

This wily character could hunker down in hard times and be a long-term
survivor, but Morton was first of all determined to get his due – to recover
what he reckoned as $3 million in fees and royalties owing him from
crooked publishers like the Melroses and sharp promoters like Harrison
Smith – and all the white bandleaders who had 'stolen his stuff' and who
played 'King Porter Stomp' for millions of screaming jitterbugs, or who
lifted his best riffs and turned them into million-selling novelties like 'Flat
Foot Floogie'.

In his darkest hours, Morton felt a helpless victim of a curse, that
hoodoo worked on him, remembering his magic godmother Lalee (Eulalie
Hecaud/Laura Hunter) and various threats people had made. Black magic
was more acceptable to him than sheer bad luck or his inability to cleave
through misfortune one more time and clamber back atop the heap. He
could not accept that musical styles had changed, that popular culture is an
arena of fickleness and discarded loyalties, that today's big hit is tomorrow's
refuse. People had loved 'Original Jelly Roll Blues' in 1915, they had been
crazy for 'Milenberg Joys' and 'Black Bottom Stomp' and 'Jungle Blues' in
the 1920s. Why didn't they listen to him now? He knew he could make
even better music, with his accumulated craft and his knack for listening
and transforming big hits into original arrangements.

When he dropped by Harlem's Rhythm Club to jaw with the other idle
musicians, some young kids treated him like a clown, a superannuated and
sad old man (all of 45), all wind about the old days and self-adoration, who
put down the exciting new music of today. A few, like reedman Russell
Procope, saw that Morton not only knew what he was talking about but
could teach anyone willing to listen. But the men tired of Morton's nonstop

tirades about bad music (Omer Simeon recalled him shouting 'I'm the master!' and 'anything you play on your horn, you're playing *Jelly Roll'* [Lomax 220]) and crooked promoters, and the indolence of slackers who hung around street corners without jobs (although he was right there, with his soapbox and his portmanteau of opinions). He was the prophet without honour, and it was hard to shake that reputation in a depressed culture.

By 1938, the Depression seemed in the reckoning of many observers to be lifting, and people let a little hope seep back into their souls – maybe it would vanish, and we would go back to something like the old America that adults remembered with joy. The tide in Morton's fortunes also turned: he formed an alliance with Roy Carew and seemed on the road to resurrecting his business as a professional musician, he was to begin the epochal Library of Congress recordings with Alan Lomax, which would assure his lasting fame and his niche in the jazz pantheon, so he took matters into his own hands and reached the national media with his story and his complaints.

Like many turning points in Morton's improbable odyssey, it came about by accident or fortuity. Morton was a faithful listener to the radio programme by Robert Ripley (*Believe It or Not*), the widely syndicated cartoonist and retailer of purportedly 'amazing' facts, notions and what we now call *factoids* – statistical artifacts and odd ideas such as Q: 'How far would all the sausage manufactured annually in the US stretch?' A: 'To and from the moon three times (X million miles)', etc. It was a mine of exotic and useless data that Jelly Roll loved and could quote in argument. In March of 1938, Ripley's national broadcast included a vignette on W. C. Handy, pioneer blues-finder, bandleader and publisher. Handy, in Morton's mind, was one of the gang of tune pirates and glory-hogs who had suppressed his fortunes, clouded his own reputation and generally lied and connived about their roles in the rise of African-American music.

W. C. Handy in his publishing office, New York City, 1949.

Ripley's program was an innocent enough encomium to Handy, on the order of a 'Where Are They Now?' feature, but Ripley introduced Handy as the 'originator of jazz and blues'. The idea of his radio hero presenting a man Morton considered a charlatan and poseur as the 'factual' inventor of jazz goaded him to write Ripley a letter, with a copy to *Down Beat* magazine (then only four years old but already a respected showbiz gospel). Morton complimented Ripley by calling his broadcast 'a great contribution to natural science' but begged to set the historical record straight.

Morton told Ripley that with his broadcast he had 'done me a great injustice and you have almost misled many of your fans'. He went on ingenuously to ridicule Handy for being called 'professor' (a common enough racist way of acknowledging any black teacher in the south, and the way piano 'ticklers' in vice districts were habitually addressed) and said Handy had 'taken advantage of some unprotected material that floats around' (pretty much true but also common practice for everyone in the business, including Morton, as with his appropriation of the ancient 'Buddy Bolden's Blues' theme). Here he put in print his famous assertion that 'New Orleans is the cradle of jazz, and I, myself, happened to be the creator in the year 1902.'

The letter concluded with a bald indication of its intention, 'I only give you the facts that you may force your pal to his rightful position in fair life.' That is straight from Morton's heart: a powerful media factotum like Ripley might help beat back the tides of ill fortune and maliciously contrived hoodoo to help Morton get his 'rightful position in fair life'. Morton felt that he was waging a war against injustice and unfairness, as if he finally began to comprehend the implacable forces of class and caste that hampered and hindered him like – like little devils, or the malignant actions of witchcraft!

In many ways, Jelly Roll Morton was an archetypal American – optimistic, cheerful, hardworking, self-reliant and self-confident, convinced that life in the Republic is fair and just, as advertised and promised in those grand documents written by the Founders. He had ignored the factuality of ever-tightening Jim Crow rule and discrimination, ever-worsening socio-economic conditions for people of colour and (especially in the Depression) the ruination of the working class and its bagful of once-bright promises. Morton's letter to Ripley closes with his awareness of the darkening world situation: 'Lord protect us from more

Hitlers and Mussolinis.' As if he were now bereft of innocence and might be a target himself of those sinister, un-American and evil empires far across the seas. (Lomax 236–37)

Morton's outburst was the prelude to his last period of intense productivity and good luck. He made headlines, the letter was printed by *Down Beat*, Handy sent in a response, and people began to wonder what the history of jazz and blues might actually be. Hitherto, this had all dwelt in peoples minds as 'new music', as novelties and ephemera, the detritus of the entertainment industry and popular culture, nothing to be taken seriously or remembered. Morton wanted to force a little history on them, make them pay attention, like Arthur Miller's archetypal tragic hero of the twentieth century, Willie Loman.

The music America had loved and mindlessly embraced was made by real men and women, by complex intelligences, and it was receding into the past. The day's hepcats and jive artists weren't interested in the past, nor were the jitterbugs and rug-cutters, but as Morton always preached, the past was there in everything they played and heard. *His* music was out there, uncredited and unacknowledged (and, of course, unbought), and this was just not the way America worked, where inventiveness and creativity and ingenuity were equivalent to virtue, where our national prophet was Ben Franklin, the inventor, businessman, trader and purveyor of intensely practical wisdom – how to create yourself, how to better that creation, how to control nature by science, labour by efficiency and wealth by prudence and foresight.

As Morton knew too well, in showbiz *fame* and *notoriety* were always interchangeable terms. He was scorned for the attack on so venerable a figure as W. C. Handy (who looked a lot like the caricature of Uncle Tom), he was laughed at as an arrant braggart, but he was also remembered and reconsidered. The Library of Congress stint enlarged this new fame, and

Tempo Music Co. gave him a solid platform on which to stand while he developed a new career. That came in the form of his last recordings. He returned to Victor, who on the strength of his new fame was willing to record the music – people were beginning to think and wonder about the 'old' jazz and the grand, romantic mythology of New Orleans Morton had spun in his autobiography.

Victor wanted Morton to put together a band to revisit music from the turn of the century, the era of the fabled Buddy Bolden. Other companies were also aware of this niche market for early jazz; Decca recorded Louis Armstrong and Sidney Bechet in an only partially successful retrieval of the Clarence Williams Blue Five days of 1925. Victor recorded Bechet and Tommy Ladnier extensively, in the classic repertory. French critic and enthusiast Hugues Panassie was instrumental in goading Victor to pay attention to the old jazz again. Bob Crosby's young Bobcats band made a living and hit the pop charts replaying the jazz classics of the early 1920s – tunes by King Oliver, blues, standards played in a style that was part standard Dixieland and part pure homage to black jazz masters such as Morton. When asked about living pianists he admired, Morton singled out Crosby's Bob Zurke as one who had found the true path to real jazz. A big jazz revival was underway and was under the general public's radar but in the 1940s, shortly after Morton's death, it would become a worldwide phenomenon.

Now the persona Morton had cultivated and that was widely known among musicians emerged on the national popular culture scene. He was not in the league of Louis Armstrong or Fats Waller as beloved icons, but people who had missed him in the 1920s ('race' records were just that – sold to black people only) were discovering him through record collecting. 'Collecting hot' was the catchphrase for this obsessive hobby, first a college-kid phenomenon but then spreading to a lot of serious and dedicated adults. The big labels were about to embark on reissue programmes, which would dig those old masters out of the vaults, make pressings available in fancy albums and create a small growth industry in early jazz and blues *redux*.

As he completed the large Library of Congress project with Alan Lomax, Morton was primed to record material he had dredged from memory. In Washington, during December, 1938, he recorded four piano solo sides released on the new, small Jazzman label: his astounding 'Finger Buster', a blazing up-tempo cutting-contest specialty number; 'Creepy Feeling', one of his most effective blue tangos; 'Windin' Boy Blues'; and 'Honky Tonk Music', a clever elaboration of blues and boogie-woogie piano tricks. The discs grew directly from work recorded on Lomax's acetate recorder. They show Morton playing very accurately and confidently, in surprisingly good form, considering that he had been stabbed in the neck by a drunken patron while working at the Jungle Inn a few months earlier and had a slow recovery from the wounding.

Next, in New York he turned to the Victor contract, assembling the best group he could round up: Sidney De Paris (trumpet), Claude Jones (trombone), Albert Nicholas (clarinet) and Sidney Bechet (soprano sax), Happy Caldwell (tenor sax), Lawrence Lucie (guitar), Wellman Braud (bass) and Zutty Singleton (drums). Several were staunch veterans of Red Hot Peppers sessions (Nicholas, Singleton), others were Morton's choice for best on their instruments (Bechet, Caldwell); Braud was a veteran New Orleanian who had been at home with Duke Ellington for a decade, Lucie was a young protégé and De Paris the brother of a Morton-favoured trombonist, Wilbur De Paris. The sound that the group achieved was a blend of modern Swing-Era jive (especially De Paris) and solidly traditional playing (especially Morton, Nicholas and Bechet). This synthesis seems sometimes unstable in the playing.

On 14 September 1939 the band cut four sides: 'Oh, Didn't He

Ramble?', staged as an old-time New Orleans funeral and parade; 'High Society', featuring both reeds on the so-called 'Alphonse Picou' clarinet solo; 'I Thought I Heard Buddy Bolden Say', an homage with extensive lyrics to recreate the dawn of jazz; 'Windin' Boy Blues', to celebrate the equally legendary Jelly Roll in his first incarnation as kid whorehouse tickler Windin' Boy. Morton coaxed and cajoled performances out of the heterogeneous group, and jazz critic Frederic Ramsey, about to publish the groundbreaking anthology *Jazzmen* along with Charles Edward Smith, was an observer at the session, took extensive notes and wrote it up. (Lomax 313–16)

While the session was not wholly smooth, Victor went on to a second one, on 28 September 1939, cutting another four sides, using the same group with a couple of emendations – Sidney Bechet was out and Fred Robinson replaced Claude Jones on trombone. They cut 'Climax Rag', a James Scott classic piano rag (1914), also a favourite with New Orleans bandsmen; 'Don't You Leave Me Here', the archaic blues whose copyright Morton and Clarence Williams tussled over and a variant of the 'Alabama Bound' theme; 'West End Blues', the Clarence Williams number made famous by King Oliver and then elevated to celestial status by Louis Armstrong's version with the Hot Five (1928); and 'Ballin' the Jack', Chris Smith's sturdy old dance-routine standard, which Morton turned into a tricky and wiggly meditation for Albert Nicholas, and which Morton sang with obvious enthusiasm.

In some ways, this session worked better. 'Climax Rag' was a difficult number in Morton's version, and he pressed the group to get it right. The other numbers are simpler and looser, but they demanded precision and concentration that Morton sweated out of the band. From the two sessions 'Oh, Didn't He Ramble?' was a hit, because for once the semi-vaudeville patter worked to evoke an atmosphere and to 'explicate' the music and the funeral routine (which Morton had discussed at length in his last Library of Congress sessions). 'High Society' was successful from the sheer weight and quality of the two veteran reedmen. Bechet and Nicholas worked well in tandem, and the old march evoked the heyday of street bands and freewheeling parades, second-liners and festivities in the style only New Orleans could imagine. The highly personal versions of 'I Thought I Heard Buddy Bolden Say' and 'Windin' Boy Blues' were basically Morton showpieces, and he carried them off by charisma alone. The other pieces were what musicians of an earlier era called 'characteristic', i.e. typical or traditional in style and feeling.

The whole sequence of sides made what today would be called a 'concept album', an interlinked set or suite that makes a substantive point or creates an overarching theme. Morton in this, as in most of his work, was years ahead of the supposedly modern and progressive music industry with its technologies and promotion gimmicks. The chance to explore his treasure trove of memories and experiences gave Morton the insight to use his musical past and imprint it on the cold, indifferent and (he would say) *cruel* present. How the world chose to receive his gift of memory was not his business – he made and delivered it, the rest was up to posterity.

Before leaving the wintry East forever, Morton made two more sets of recordings, again stemming from the Library of Congress memories. On 14 December 1939 he went into Reeves' Sound Studio and cut eight sides of solo piano, all from his classic repertory and bearing on his reconstruction of jazz history for Lomax and the world: 'Sporting House Rag', to illustrate his best Windin' Boy style; 'Original Rags', one of his most successful transformations, from Scott Joplin's 1899 score; 'The Crave', a dark, sensuous and haunting 'Spanish tinge' number; 'The Naked Dance', a fingerbusting and lightning-fast, can-can-like number, illustrating the upper technical limits of bawdy house piano; 'Mister Joe', a medium-tempo stomp with a lot of swing and an old Morton favourite, also known as 'Buffalo Rag'; 'King Porter Stomp', Morton's signature swing-and-stomp tune, played definitively here, as if to sign off on one of the basic theme songs of the Swing Era; 'Windin' Boy Blues', another, slower and bluesy version of the song; and 'The Animule Ball', a slightly creepy and sardonic commentary on the animal kingdom, by analogy and inference including human beings in its census.

Two days later, on 16 December Morton returned to the studio and recorded five more sides: 'Buddy Bolden's Blues', another version of the Bolden saga and the little 'funky butt' theme (aka. 'St Louis Tickle', as published in 1904 by Theron Bennett; a second (and better) crack at 'The Naked Dance', which was chosen for release; 'Don't You Leave Me Here' again – it was a big hit in the mid-1920s, whether Morton or Williams 'wrote' it; 'Mamie's Blues', a version of the old standard '219 Blues', and the single track which justified the whole set of recordings; this was an absolutely haunting and mesmerizing rendition, channelling an old-time New Orleans player and singer (Mamie Desdoume) of the rock-bottom elemental blues – as simple and inexhaustible as a haiku; and 'Michigan Water Blues', an ancient blues that Morton and Williams had claimed as an original composition, memorable for the couplet 'Michigan water tastes like sherry wine, / Mississippi water tastes like turpentine.'

These sessions were a loving and extended postscript to the Library of Congress project. They revealed Morton in a relaxed and confident mood, playing simply and affectingly. No show-off stuff or fireworks other than 'The Naked Dance' (which stopped traffic in record stores, along with 'Mamie's Blues'). This was the best a tired and chronically ill Morton, suffering from pneumonia and the beginnings of congestive heart failure in the wake of his stabbing, could muster. The records were issued by a small label, General Records, as an album, *New Orleans Memories*. It has rarely been out of print in the last 65 years.

The final band project began a few weeks later, on 4 January 1940. Morton gathered another recording group, not for Victor but for little General Records again. The band was made up of Henry 'Red' Allen (trumpet), Joe Britton (trombone), Albert Nicholas (clarinet), Eddie Williams (alto sax), Wellman Braud (bass) and Zutty Singleton (drums). This is even closer to a 'New Orleans' band than the Victor bunch, with Britton and Williams the odd men out. Red Allen was one of the premier New Orleans trumpet men, right at Louis Armstrong's elbow (literally and figuratively) in the 1930s, as a sideman in Armstrong's big band and a frequent competitor with his own groups. The three-square rhythm section of Morton, Braud and Singleton was about as basic New Orleans as could be assembled, and Morton was always happy with Nicholas' light and brilliant clarinet sound.

If there was a problem it was with the material. Morton was determined now not to be trapped in the gulch of nostalgia but to mine his present and recent productivity, too. As he and Carew put Tempo Music Co. together, Morton had begun composing numbers he hoped to be competitive in the bigtime pop music game. All his life he had chased the brass ring of gigantic fame, the fame that arrived through pure pop music blockbuster hits, the sort that Cole Porter, George Gershwin and Irving Berlin rolled out on production lines, that drove all the engines of Tin Pan Alley, that underpinned Broadway and made the big bands *big*. One mega-hit could mean a lifetime of security, comfort and everlasting fame.

So Morton was as anxious to get these new and contemporary tunes on wax as to mine the lodes of memory and unique experience. The first session (Jelly Roll Morton Seven) was devoted to 'Sweet Substitute', a very pretty and quite workable pop tune exactly in the vein of 'Someday

Sweetheart', the great number that never quite paid off in the middle 1920s; 'Panama', a William H. Tyers tango long ago converted by New Orleans jazzmen into a driving, swinging march; 'Good Old New York', a negligible jump tune that tries to tap some 'hometown' market of sentimental bonhomie as probable in New York City as a frozen daiquiri in central Hell; and 'Big Lip Blues', a semi-pop blues and one of Morton's attempts at humour best left unexamined (his lyrics at one point say 'Two and two make three', which may be premature New Math). While the sidemen play well, they often exhibit less than convincing interest.

A second band session was for the Morton Sextet (same group less trombone), on 23 January 1940. They cut on this day 'Why', another lightweight Morton pop tune but very well sung and 'sold' by Morton; 'Get the Bucket', a much better stab at a jolly riff number by Morton, with a lot of swing and hypnotically simple-minded lyrics ('Get the bucket, get the bucket', etc.); 'If You Knew', another sentimental pop number that sounds like faded vaudeville but features a fetching Morton vocal; 'Shake It', an up-tempo dance number evidently aimed at the crazed rug-cutters and jitterbugs that followed the big swing bands. The session works smoothly and shows Morton still firmly in command of his professional methods and leadership.

The last segment of this project was on 30 January 1940, with the band again a Morton Seven – the same group as the Sextet, now with Claude Jones' trombone dealt in. They cut four more sides: 'Dirty, Dirty, Dirty', a Morton number that might have anticipated sales by title alone but is a fairly fetching jump blues that would have interested the Savoy Sultans or John Kirby, of big-little band fame; a smooth swing number, 'Swinging the Elks', part of Morton's long-standing campaign to get the fraternal order singing (and buying) his songs – a.k.a. 'We Are Elks', this little march failed to dent the market at a national Benevolent and Protective Order of

Elks convention; 'Mama's Got a Baby', Morton's lively transformation and rearrangement of an ancient Mardi Gras number, associated with the Indians and appearing in a strain of Robert Hoffman's 'Dixie Queen' rag of 1906, sometimes called 'Tee-nah-nah' or 'If You Don't Shake (You Get No Cake)'; 'My Home Is in a Southern Town', naked nostalgia and homesickness from Morton, aimed at the endless market for 'Dixie' tunes and ravings about cornbread, grits, cotton fields, darkies and everything else associated with the Good Old South That Never Existed. Again, Morton paces the band through the tunes, and they are played at a level somewhat above demo-record standards, although they were meant by Morton to be his tickets to another level of songwriting and popular appeal.

He was actually fairly close to this ideal, as utopian as it seems. He appeared on popular national radio network broadcasts (*We the People* and *The Chamber Music Society of Lower Basin Street*), and if his life had followed the route one of those popular showbiz B-movies of the day, he would somehow have been discovered, have written a smash-hit song, married the radio network executive's beautiful (and fair) daughter and vanished in an apotheosis of white-robed jazz musicians playing golden horns and harps and ushering Mr Jelly Roll straight into the Valhalla of Great Musicians, where he could converse with Tony Jackson, Porter King and Mozart for eternity.

These last recording sessions are mixed in quality, but they reveal how he thought he could use the base of Tempo Music as a launching pad for a post-Depression career. He reached for the golden prize of the pop music market, but he continued to draw on the experiences and materials of his past, as he had recited it to Alan Lomax. This split vision – of oldtime Jelly Roll and up-to-date Mr Jelly – might have paid off in both ways, if fate had allowed him more years. He was in his fifties and, with the right breaks, he might have had a decade of productivity in him. He seemed to own an inexhaustible mine of musical ideas and resources, even when beat, broke and down.

Some of his last intuitions were right on the money, even prescient. 'Mama's Got a Baby' is the sort of novelty tune that might have caught on, not too different from some of the Slim (Galliard) and Slam (Stewart) numbers of the 1940s. The catchy 'Get the Bucket' is a riff tune like 'Flat Foot Floogie', and a good jump number. 'Why' is an engaging and sentimental ballad, which some good singer could have delivered like air mail. He was better at the cardboard-South material than (say) Phil Harris, who made a fortune as the vaudeville-shouting cracker ('That's What I Like about the South'). And Morton was skillful enough to pitch a tender ballad and croon, not as suavely as Nat King Cole but not far off the mark. With any useful guidance or even a sliver of opportunity to get onto national radio (like Fats Waller in Cincinnati), the denouement of his tale might have been domestic comedy, not tragic melodrama.

For NBC's quirky *Chamber Music Society of Lower Basin Street* broadcast, Morton cut two tunes surviving on air-checks – 'Windin' Boy Blues' with the studio 'Dixieland' band led by Henry 'Hot Lips' Levine and, with drummer Nat Levine, 'King Porter Stomp'. The programme was by no means at the zenith of radio popularity, but the appearance hints at what could have happened to Morton if he had ever cracked the impermeable and invisible barriers that kept a veteran African-American musician of the era from getting up out of the back of the bus.

He was in the bigtime ballpark with numbers such as 'Sweet Substitute', but he had no one to mentor him into the real Tin Pan Alley. While sometimes virtue is rewarded in popular culture, more often than not it takes guile, grease and cunning to make the jump from 'well known' to 'famous'. That a Creole with a street/ghetto education would make this leap is unlikely, and Morton constitutionally was resistant to taking good advice, no matter the source. He had little good experience from leaning on others, and it was long decades since Tony Jackson disappeared from his life.

After his stint of recording in New York, Morton had reached the end of his long, lonesome road. Tired to the bone and intermittently ill with high blood pressure, pneumonia and other after-effects of the knifing at the Jungle Inn (which may have nicked a lung), he set out like a pioneer, driving for the West Coast, his Garden of Eden 20 years before. At least the sun would shine out there and thaw the everlastingly bitter New York City chill from his bones. Once there, he dug out his new scores and started assembling and rehearsing a big band with New Orleans veterans in the area, determined to struggle on and reach that Gold Mine in the Sky. Instead, he died in Los Angeles on 10 July 1941.

In recent years, many of Morton's papers and memorabilia have surfaced, the story related in detail by Phil Pastras in his excellent *Dead Man Blues*, which plumbs Morton's West Coast history, in the teens and early 1920s and again in 1941. One trove among all the papers and materials unearthed were music manuscripts and scores, including arrangements for big band that show Morton privately writing music decades in advance of his time in their sonorities and scoring. All the old boasts about how he knew all about this modern stuff and how he'd messed around with crazy chords in his time and the rest seem borne out by the music. He left one complete big band arrangement in a wholly contemporary style – 'Oh! Baby!', described by one critic as 'Luncefordian' and like a Sy Oliver score (Pastras 183) – and another remarkable piece even more advanced, well ahead of the jazz composers and arrangers of 1941. This was 'Gan-Jam', which Reich and Gaines say was 'pointing toward the next generation's avant-garde' (249) Critic Barry McRae said the exotic number 'suggested a touch of Eastern promise rather than a Spanish tinge[,] and it used a brass and reed mix that owed nothing to the accepted patterns of 1940 big band fare. If anything, it looked forward to *Pithecanthropus* Mingus but with breaks rather than all-ins and with a decidedly off-center relationship between melody and rhythm.' (Pastras 183)

So the revelations Morton promised in his vision of jazz were true after all, packages set aside while he made a last unsuccessful try at success on New York City's terms, but opened when he reached the promised land of California. If his health had improved, if he had got his hands on even a derisory sum of money, if any agent, promoter, record executive, agent or visionary musician had paid a moment's attention to Morton's grandiose plans and promises, if ... if ... if ...

CHAPTER ELEVEN

THE CRITICS

■————————■

Jelly Roll Morton's career was over before modern jazz criticism and history were properly founded. The reportage on Morton during his early working life was almost entirely in black newspapers' entertainment pages, which chronicled his comings and goings and gave brief puff statements about his ventures, the comments provided about any sufficiently well-known African-American performer. Aside from some correspondence and journalism in *Down Beat* magazine in the late 1930s, significant commentary on Morton as a major jazz figure is post mortem, written with the hindsight of history, not a sense of immediacy.

During his lifetime, especially in the last five years, when he became a lightning rod for controversy over the 'invention' of jazz, his peers chose sides and attacked or defended him but rarely in detailed or organized ways. It was purely personal and generally poisonous, forecasting the wars of Mouldy Figs vs. Modernists in the mid-1940s. Morton was often ironic or half-serious in his rhetoric, but many younger eastern musicians had no ear for nuances of Creole comedy and were offended by what seemed colossal arrogance and ignorance. They did not recognize the trickster/jokester mask that Morton wore and took his aggressive teasing for abuse and mockery. Most of his New Orleans peers understood Morton's jokes, while African-Americans from the North and East had no ear for his routines of self-mockery and comic exaggeration.

Morton penseroso – another of the 1926 Victor publicity studies

Recognition of Morton's status as a central figure in 1920s jazz came slowly. He was still very much alive when Frederic Ramsey, Jr., Charles Edward Smith and their colleagues were assembling *Jazzmen*, the pioneering collection of critical-historical essays (1939). He was in touch with William Russell, a key figure in the group, but he is mentioned only peripherally. There is a chapter on King Oliver's Creole Jazz Band, one on Louis Armstrong, one on Bix Beiderbecke, others on white jazz but nothing significant on Morton. Russell felt so bad about the omission that he wanted to dedicate the book to Morton as a gesture of goodwill but was prevented by 'technical reasons'. Morton was not pleased and let Russell know he thought the book just another link in the conspiracy of silence and ignorance about him and his contributions to the music.

Within a few years, record reissue programmes made Morton's music widely available, and little jazz magazines and anthologies of criticism amended the *Jazzmen* lacuna. In the 1940s Alan Lomax laboured on a book about Morton, as did Roy Carew, with a large collection of Morton material, including the letters and files of Tempo Music. But nothing of magnitude appeared until Lomax's *Mister Jelly Roll* in 1950, a major jazz publishing event. Only a few books on individual jazzmen had appeared, mostly popular biographies, and this was a monumental study for the era. It made widely accessible the Library of Congress material in transcribed form. The recordings had been available on 78 rpm record albums – a large set available in a limited edition from Rudi Blesh's Circle Records, but expensive and bulky. The release of the series by Circle (also in 1950) on the new LP ('long playing' – 33⅓ rpm, 12-inch vinyl discs) format made the recordings more accessible (and Riverside Records re-released the LP version a few years later), but for every person who heard the records, scores read Lomax's book.

This was a mixed blessing, as jazz fans slowly realized. Lomax presented Morton in a vivid, racy narrative, much of it in his own words from the recordings but bridged by Lomax's editorial and social comments – a stab at the sociology of New Orleans jazz and a good bit of interpretative gloss on why Morton said certain things and what his statements implied. It was not a strict chronological biography but skipped around through various themes and topics – Morton as a solo artist and his uneven relationship with his sidemen and peers, his travels and vivid adventures, Morton's love life, his ups and downs as a successful professional. The book was less history than *his story*.

Lomax did extensive auxiliary research and interviewing, to develop and corroborate Morton's narrative, much very valuable and timely, catching veteran New Orleans musicians just before they vanished and making clear useful links in Morton's tale. On the other hand, Lomax introduced swarms of small but confusing errors, misreadings and mishearings into the work, some leaving critics and researchers baffled for decades. The largest problem was his understanding (or *mis*understanding) of Morton's soft Creole accent, which was not problematic on most words but which became crucial in deciphering names of obscure people, places and things. This extended to Morton's story of his family: Eulalie Hecaud's surname became 'Echo', Morton's own chosen surname may often have been pronounced and spelt 'Mouton', and 'Lamothe' was consistently written as 'LaMenthe'. (In newspaper accounts of his vaudeville itinerary, the last name even turns up as 'Moten', so others also misheard the sounds.) Piano players Morton described came out with mangled names – Albert Carroll was printed as 'Cahill' and Artie Matthews as 'Audie' – and many other names, central and peripheral, were skewed.

Lomax's ambivalent role in shaping Morton's heritage is hard to assess. On the one hand, he often interrupted Morton's narration in the recording sessions to pose trivial questions that fitted his own agenda – the description of African-American musicians as victims of political and social oppression who triumphed despite their limitations, illiteracy and ignorance. This was a possible model for 'folk' musicians of the sort he and his father John had followed, interviewed and recorded for years – itinerant workers, cowboys, prison inmates, down-and-outers. It hardly suited a sophisticated professional musical creator like Morton, with years of work on subtle, individualistic and complex music and a wealth of experience in and around bigtime show business and popular music. Also, Lomax's prurient coaxing of Morton to play the 'dirty blues' – after-hours pornography demanded for private parties – was disruptive and confusing. Morton complied (Lomax kept his whiskey glass full as a lagniappe) but unenthusiastically. For him, the lowdown music recalled the sty of nastiness and vulgarity he had waded through as young man without enough leverage to set his own standards. It was an unpacking of dirty laundry for a worldwide audience (potentially) and for the long, harsh judgment of posterity.

And Morton's hesitation was well-founded – one common critical reaction to Morton was that he was a dirty-minded, lowdown whorehouse tickler and gutter habitué trying to get above himself with preposterous claims about his contributions to America's only wholly original music. Even though the most graphic indecent passages of the Library of Congress discs were omitted from the Circle issues and were not in Lomax's text, jazz hounds who went to the Library itself could hear the originals, transcribe the naughty bits and pass them around as titillating evidence of Morton's depravity. Few thought to blame the staid, white interviewer with the official credentials for distorting the interviews.

Nevertheless, in writing *Mister Jelly Roll*, Lomax did a signal service to jazz criticism and history. The book was revisionist history, putting Morton back into the big picture that *Jazzmen* had tried to paint and making connections between him and his contemporaries. It contained a full discography and other editorial matter that set readers on a path to finding and hearing Morton's music. It also gave the rambling tale Morton had dictated with such impromptu brilliance important context and continuity. It was sympathetic and at times heroic in characterizing him, and Lomax was especially effective in tracing an emotional map of Morton and his relationships with women, his family and colleagues. For a man most often a somewhat mysterious loner in life, a surprising number of people were at least wellwishers and some felt they were his friends. Lomax transmitted their warmth and affection clearly and arrived at a genuinely moving conclusion as he wrote of Morton's last dire weeks and months on earth.

During and after the publication of *Mister Jelly Roll*, fans and jazz critics had written small and large articles on Morton and his music for the flocks of little magazines for record collectors and hot music aficionados. One of the first important ones was a thorough musicological analysis by William Russell of Morton's solo piano recording of 'Froggie Moore' (or 'Frog-i-More'), one of his early ragtime-to-jazz works. The short essay showed how a musician educated to Russell's level, and with his keen ear for nuances of the music, could show jazz piano as a keyboard music as serious and subtle as Bach's *Well-Tempered Clavier*. Russell's essay was published in 1944 in a record collector's magazine called *The Needle*, and it is an unmatched model for jazz historical and analytical thinking.

It is part detective story, part detailed history and part sympathetic listening and musical charting. A single record of 'Froggie Moore', a 'test pressing' made in a studio and not intended for release, was found by collector John Steiner. It was dubbed and released as a jazz reissue, and Russell reviewed it. With his huge stockpile of Morton materials and his close knowledge of Morton's career, Russell could explain its background and make an educated guess as to its date. He compared this version to King Oliver's 1923 band recording of the tune and a later version of similar themes, which Morton released as 'Sweetheart o' Mine' for Vocalion in 1926. He guessed at the title's significance and quoted Harrison Smith on what others would later confirm as the right answer –

it was a piece written to accompany a vaudeville contortionist who was called 'Moore, the Frog Man' and who dressed up in a frog outfit. (Morton seemed to be drawn mystically to contortionists – the eccentric 'gaspipe' clarinettist Wilton Crawley, who recorded with him in 1930, was also an astonishing rubber man – see Chapter 2.)

Russell then devoted pages to a meticulous analysis of 'Froggie Moore's' structure, harmonic patterns and the characteristics of Morton's piano playing. It was the first in-depth appreciation of Morton as a major artist and musical craftsman, convincing in its details and in Russell's measured conclusions. It was far removed from the usual encomia-or-brickbats arguments about Morton and his music, and it demanded that others accept him – and other jazz figures – as 'serious' musicians who developed and diffused a major form of American music, which should be known and understood by culturally literate Americans. Most fan and collector magazines were still in a stage of zealous advocacy of any and all jazz, regardless of quality or durability. Russell's insights into the music as an abstract structure and the musician as the transmitter of emotion through that structure are important and brilliantly written: 'Somehow Jelly Roll had the *touch* to transmit the warmth of his rich personality into piano tone. He was the master of those devices that gave a feeling of blueness to his harmony, the illusion of smear and roughness to his tone, and the characteristic turns of melodic pattern peculiar to Negro music. Most important of all, however, was his feeling for a joyful, raggy, and stompy rhythm – a beat that really moved, a swing that "rocked the joint".' (Williams, *Art of Jazz* 26)

Unfortunately, Russell gave us far too little of his wisdom. He wrote an equally insightful and brilliant essay on three major boogie woogie pianists for the *Hot Record Society Rag* in 1939, at the height of the craze for that blues piano school, and for the rest of his long life he added to and organized the huge 'scrapbook' of Morton information, published finally in 1999 as *'Oh, Mister Jelly'*, but he was almost silent in his own hand about the music he so loved and admired. Instead, he devoted himself with monk-like rigour to finding and recording veteran musicians for his important American Music label, to steadfast research and interview work with assorted musicians and bystanders on the New Orleans scene and to aiding and succoring musicians down and out, ill or just in need of simple kindness. (Williams, *Art of Jazz*, 95–108)

Other forums than small, obscure fan journals and ephemeral music magazines joined in the gathering criticism and history of Ferdinand Lamothe Morton. In the mid-1940s *Esquire* magazine, one of the premier glossies in the great epoch of magazines, took a special interest in jazz and its contemporary culture. Arnold Gingrich, the flamboyant editor (and the model for the magazine's popeyed logo 'Eskie'), promoted the music and the growing subculture of serious fans, who fitted into *Esquire*'s target audience of men who were well-off and sophisticated (or those who wished to be thought such). Its glossy, airbrushed girly art was thought daring at the time and became famous through adoption by the Air Force as nose art on Second World War bombers and fighter planes. *Esquire* published a distinguished list of current authors, mainly of the hairy-chested school but including a pantheon of cherished literary greats, including F. Scott Fitzgerald and Ernest Hemingway, from the 1920s and 1930s. It also was an arbiter of fashion for sophisticates and trend-watchers, competing with *The New Yorker* in terms of literary standards and taste.

The magazine sponsored forums and polls to assemble 'all-star' jazz groups and to rank by readers' votes favoured musicians, then presented concerts and all-star recording sessions to promote winners (and *Esquire*, by extension). This was not a new process – music magazines *Down Beat* and *Metronome* had established the fashion of polling readers, and *Metronome* had then begun sponsoring concerts and recordings by all-star groups of poll winners. But jazz had hit the bigtime when it was also touted and displayed in the broad, glossy pages of *Esquire*. Fortunately or unfortunately, depending on how to think about whether there is or isn't such a thing as 'bad publicity', the polls and all-star gimmicks ignited controversy over choices and over the whole issue of 'old-time' vs. 'Modernistic' jazz. Morton was often a central figure in heated debates – viewed as a heroic ancestor-figure by traditionalists and as an over-rated, self-obsessed braggart and illiterate by Modernists. Other jazzmen were swept into the civil warfare, but Morton was a potent example, owing to his flamboyance and the apocryphal folklore accruing to him (see Chapter 8).

Annual *Esquire Jazz Books* were published, 1944–47, delving back into the magazine's files for earlier articles and with commissioned new historical surveys of jazz. They included poll results for each year in detail, with photographs and bio-discographical information on musicians elected. While they included discussion of major early jazz figures, Morton is only included in brief notes or asides. It would be five years before readers saw *Mister Jelly Roll*, and he seemed a remote figure to wartime and postwar swing audiences. Some interesting passages in the yearbooks are worth noting.

In the 1944 *Jazz Book*, the presiding writer Paul Eduard Miller wrote an editorial introductory chapter called 'Hot Jazz: Prophet without Honor', giving a cultural context for the book. In it, he summarized the state of serious jazz writing to date:

> *In 1930 a feature article by Charles Edward Smith appeared in* Symposium. *Two years later Robert Goffin, a Belgian lawyer, brought out his* Aux Frontiers du Jazz in Brussels, *and in 1934 Roger Pryor Dodge contributed* Harpsichords and Jazz Trumpets *to the once famous* Hound and Horn. *The same*

year Hugues Panassie wrote his French edition of Hot Jazz. *Hot clubs began to spring up in Europe and America, and by 1934, also, the collecting of characteristic music was recognized by a general magazine with publication in* Esquire *of Charles Edward Smith's* Collecting Hot. (8)

This volume reprinted Smith's seminal essay along with four other important jazz pieces printed by *Esquire* since 1934.

Elsewhere in the 1944 *Jazz Book*, Jelly Roll Morton was listed by black writer-cartoonist E. Sims Campbell with others: 'Tom Turpin of St Louis, Scott Joplin, Jelly Roll Morton were the great swing pianists [in early years], and by great I mean their pieces were as intricate as Bach.' It is amusing to see the generic pop term 'swing' used here, but it would have connected better with young readers than 'jazz' or 'ragtime'. And Paul Eduard Miller wrote a summary piece on 'Jazz Greats: Musicians and Bands' to create a dream all-star group, listing Morton with other pianists (most still living) – Teddy Wilson, Johnny Guarneri, Fats Waller, Earl Hines, Bob Zurke, Mary Lou Williams and Art Tatum. Miller felt impelled to defend his inclusion of Morton:

Of this group, Morton is the only one who did not perform in what might be labeled a 'modern' style. To many listeners his recordings will sound dated, what the swing fans call 'corny'. Perhaps his playing does catch the flavor of ragtime; nevertheless, his was one of the most original talents in all jazz: both his piano execution and his melodic writing easily are distinguishable as wholly his own. Melodies flowed from his fingers, and in his long series of Victor recordings during the twenties these have been set down for all of us to hear. (96)

This is as clear and respectful a brief encomium as anyone in a general magazine would write about Morton for years.

In the 1946 *Jazz Book*, an odd (and undoubtedly erroneous) report occurred in a compendious 'Chicago Jazz History' by Paul Eduard Miller and jazz journalist George Hoefer, gathering from an unnamed source the following item:

> *One unusual orchestra of this period ... remained intact barely long enough for any recording company to set down its music in wax. This was the Morton-Handy Band, headed by both Jelly Roll Morton and William Christopher Handy. The personnel included, besides pianist Morton and cornetist Handy, cornetist Tig Gray, trombonist Roy Palmer, bassist Baby Williams, banjoist Walter Dixon, drummer Johnny Bell; the clarinet posts were held by Jimmie O'Bryant, Horace Euabanks [sic] and one who is remembered by his contemporaries only as 'Balls'. The date of the band is about 1923; the place, Chicago, where it was organized for tours throughout the Midwest. As might be expected, disputes soon arose over the 'rights', position and billing of the two leaders. That they were temperamentally incompatible soon became evident; the venture collapsed after, at the most, two months.* (21)

This is one of those plausible fictions with enough factual detail to seem correct, but it was probably prompted by the Morton-Handy feud of 1938 and its notoriety. This seems a way to explain it, as the result of ancient bandstand grudges. Morton did use clarinettist Horace Eubanks on early (1923) band sides for OKeh, and one 'Balls' Ball is listed as clarinettist on four Morton band sides cut in 1924 for the little Autograph label. Jimmie O'Bryant was a busy Chicago reedman who worked with many washboard and hokum bands, and 'Tig' Gray must be a misprint (or mishearing) for Thomas 'Tick' Gray, a cornettist known for his work with King Oliver's Dixie Syncopators. No one else seems to think Morton worked with W. C. Handy, and his recollections in *Mister Jelly Roll* are of Handy in Memphis years earlier.

Before listeners properly understood the range and value of his music, Morton was a missile in the jazz wars and a byword for genius or for phony braggadocio. Some invoking Morton, positively or negatively, knew little about his music beyond random encounters. It was like those who could recognize Dizzy Gillespie's photograph – goatee, glasses, beret, bent trumpet – and draw farfetched conclusions from that image alone.

One of the best summaries of this jazz war was written by Canadian Ernest Borneman, an anthropologist with a deep interest in jazz, caught in the crossfire as an editor of *The Record Changer*, the most solid and respected of the pro-traditional magazines. Borneman wrote a two-part memoir for *Harper's* magazine in 1947 to detail the contention in an even-handed way (as befitted a scientific anthropologist). He encountered what he called the 'cult' of jazz fandom as a student in Germany and England in the 1920s and 1930s, and he describes the genus *recordus collecticus* and his folkways, mores and religious beliefs, as Borneman met and observed him.

Borneman did not maintain his objectivity when initiated by collectors and fanatics of American jazz he met in Europe, but was converted himself as a dedicated record-hunter and collector, trawling markets and junk stores, his head crammed full of names, dates, serial numbers and other arcana of the true devotee. He stayed in Britain during the Second World War and worked for the Ministry of Information. While doing this, he was asked to write for *The Record Changer* and contributed a popular column, 'The Anthropologist Looks at Jazz'. Then he found himself sucked into the vortex of controversy over new and old jazz, 'purity' and 'progress'.

The second part of Borneman's *Harper's* article details arguments in the jazz wars, especially the scurrilous exchanges between pianist-writer Art

Hodes (Mouldy Fig) and pianist-writer Leonard Feather (Modernist). As a side note, Borneman told the famous story of critic-impresario John Hammond's resurrection of the piano blues style soon called 'boogie woogie', and the rediscovery of its main practitioners in the 1930s. He also detailed the story of William Russell, Eugene Williams and Rudi Blesh and their efforts to resuscitate William Geary 'Bunk' Johnson as a trumpet player and standard-bearer for the oldest of old jazz – the next best thing to unearthing Buddy Bolden and putting a cornet to his lips. Borneman was fascinated with the sound of jazz when a German professor played for him one of the phenomenally rare Kid Ory Sunshine/Nordskog records from 1921 – 'Ory's Creole Trombone'. So he entered the scene to pursue the pure jazz. By the mid-1940s, at the apex of the jazz wars, he was mellowed and ironic in viewing the expenditure of bile and earnestness in the exchanges.

He quotes one of Leonard Feather's diatribes, shortly after the derisive name 'Mouldy Figs' was first hurled by the Modernists:

> 'The Moldy Figs are to music what [racist Mississippi Congressman John] Rankin and [racist Mississippi Senator Theodore] Bilbo are to politics and [combative right-wing columnist Westbrook] Pegler to the press. They are the extreme right-wingers of jazz, the voice of reaction in music. Just as the fascists tend to divide group against group and distinguish between Negroes, Jews, Italians, and 'Real Americans', so do the Moldy Figs try to categorize New Orleans, Chicago, swing music, and 'the real jazz'. Just as the fascists have tried to foist their views on the public through the vermin press of Social Justice, The Broom, and X-Ray, so have the Figs yapped their heads off in The Jazz Record, Jazz Session, and Record Changer.' (Borneman 269)

And so on – *serious stuff*! Feather's hysterical ranting makes Borneman's case that fans are 'fanatics' and argue with the burning fervour of True

Believers, regardless of positions and points. Feather was a convinced and dedicated anti-Mortonist who rarely missed a chance to denigrate the music, personality and opinions of Ferd Morton.

Borneman demonstrates how political the argument became (evidenced by the Leonard Feather piece above), identified with right- and left-wing political arguments at the end of the Second World War and before the dismal sunrise of the Cold War. It does not touch on Jelly Roll Morton, but it illustrates the stage in jazz historical and journalistic writing a few years after his death. As the centrality of jazz in African-American music and a force in all modern American popular culture became clear to the general public, the inner circle of fans, collectors and self-anointed illuminati were the main sources of information and misinformation on the music. Innocent listeners and readers had no gazette to list the sides of the conflict and explain who was aligned with whom in the melee.

Lomax's 1950 book helped to create a whole picture of Morton and his accomplishments, and the reissue programmes that flourished on the new LP records in the 1950s made accessible examples of all his music. Music publishers holding Melrose sheet-music versions of Morton's piano scores reprinted in folio form most of his solo music. Jazz magazines and the first jazz reference works listed Morton's work in detail, and his name became familiar to fans and at least a faint echo to the general public. The process yielded mixed results. As Morton became known as a reference point in jazz history, he was both praised and damned.

Duke Ellington, in a well-known gratuitous swipe, dragged Morton's name into an otherwise gracious 1959 introduction commissioned for Leonard Feather's pioneering *Encyclopedia of Jazz*:

> *The piano players were very important in the early days, and the great piano players were always on the East Coast; there never was anybody in the West who could play two notes. (By 'West'*

Duke Ellington, master pianist, composer and bandleader, exuding his own patented charm and self-assurance.

> *I mean New Orleans; in those days there was no other West to speak of.) Jelly Roll Morton, who was mainly a writer and had more music published than anyone else, played piano like one of those high school teachers in Washington; as a matter of fact, high school teachers played better jazz. Among other things, his rhythm was unsteady; but that's the kind of piano the West was geared up to.* (Feather 14)

This jibe is puzzling in its 'sectionalism' (why alienate *everyone* west of New York or Washington?) and its reductionist dismissal of 'anybody' (i.e.

everybody) in the West being unable to play 'two notes'. It almost makes Morton's characteristic sweeping condemnations seem moderate and thoughtful. Ellington never understood Morton's subtle and complex manipulation of the beat in the 'Spanish tinge' and other passages, which seem to some listeners to lose the strict 4/4 pulse of jazz – although modern pianist Dave Brubeck got it quite clearly right in a 1957 *Down Beat* magazine interview: 'I've never heard anybody [but Morton] play that far behind the beat, never since or before. And I think it's very important for me and for all people to have a thorough understanding of the pioneers.' (Russell 541) It is curious, because *this* is what you might expect Ellington to write for a reference book about jazz old and new.

In 1950, when Lomax published *Mister Jelly Roll*, another momentous event occurred – the publication of *They All Played Ragtime*, a big social history of the pre-jazz scene by designer-art historian Rudi Blesh and his partner Harriet Janis. It bore directly on the emerging reputation of Jelly Roll Morton, because Blesh and Janis made his story central in their narrative. Blesh had issued the commercial Circle albums of the Library of Congress material and was both familiar and fascinated with Morton as an artist and as an authoritative voice on ragtime, jazz and their intersections. Selections from Morton's narrative appeared throughout the ragtime book, and he was useful as a 'missing link' in an evolutionary scheme: '... Jelly Roll is the true connecting link between ragtime and jazz. No one need ever speculate again on how the Negro in America transformed white music into black ...' (176)

In 1946, Blesh had published *Shining Trumpets*, a general history of early jazz written in lush purple prose and resolutely, defiantly, pure Mouldy Fig in ideology. The book contained many passages on Morton as a pianist-bandleader-composer, most of them ecstatic in their praises. It met with considerable ire and derision, but *They All Played Ragtime* seemed more temperate and reasoned. It was compiled from materials gathered by Blesh and Janis but also by a number of other field researchers and reporters, who may have moderated Blesh's decided opinions. The book was invaluable for its interviews and correspondence with veterans of the ragtime era, a cadre of musicians about to disappear forever. Blesh and Janis emphasized the centrality of the musicians whose works were published by Missourian John S. Stark, the pioneer ragtime promoter, including as foremost the 'big three' of classic ragtime, Scott Joplin, James Scott and Joseph Lamb. Blesh and Janis had the extreme good fortune of tracking down and interviewing Joe Lamb, still alive and hale in his New Jersey home, getting him to record and appear as a player despite years of bodily rust and failing hearing. Their work laid the foundations for a worldwide ragtime revival that would blossom twenty years after they sent *They All Played Ragtime* into the world – too late for Harriet Janis, who died young, but in time to be much enjoyed and appreciated by Rudi Blesh.

Their book was popular, sold well and was revised and reprinted over the years. At its publication, it spread the gospel of Jelly Roll almost as well as Lomax's book, with extensive quotes from the oral autobiography and a solid context of other music into which they meshed. They brought to the attention of incipient ragtime fans the existence and significance of piano jazz parallel to the earlier music. While most fans were pianists who loved ragtime because it was clearly notated and could be learned and mastered just like little pieces by Muzio Clementi, Domenico Scarlatti or Mozart, the book also lauded difficult improvised 'ear music' and the jazz tradition of developing, extending and decorating scores, of swinging the printed notes in an intuitive way. John Stark and Scott Joplin sternly admonished musicians to follow the printed score, not to rush the music and not to muddle it with freewheeling adaptations, while Morton opened another way – the road to his 'transformation' that like alchemy changed the inert written score into the gold of intuition and imagination.

The deep partisanship for early jazz by Blesh appeared in *They All Played Ragtime*'s summary of Morton's career (again, in 1950 not widely known to readers):

> *Morton's phonograph records run into many hundreds and preserve the keyboard mastery, both individual and brilliant, that few could match. Today's generation of pianists, with a few notable exceptions, laugh Jelly Roll off as corny and old-fashioned. His recorded playing remains a challenge, however, that not many care to meet as they dazzle a gullible public with wiggling scale work and a few cheap and easy tricks.* (182–83)

Skirmishes in the jazz wars continued through the 1950s, until modern jazz itself mutated and took multiple directions, some raising questions and arguments among the Modernists' own ranks. The battle over the oldtimers seemed ancient history, something out of Plutarch, by the time rock'n'roll and soul music of the 1960s ousted any kind of jazz from the general public consciousness. Too many big internecine wars raged, over civil rights, Vietnam, women's roles, to leave room for such small-scale cultural bickering of the 1940s and 1950s. By the 1960s, a magisterial modern jazz critic like Martin Williams could put Morton firmly into context as a major figure in jazz history, while an impressionistic jazz journalist like Whitney Balliett could disagree sharply on Morton's status without igniting a new war of words. Either way, Morton was permanently resident in his niche in history.

One problem with criticism and commentary on Morton is the great dilemma that encompasses all jazz criticism and history – the supreme difficulty of writing about music, especially music depending on a conglomeration of factors at a given instant of history, the moment of creation. A widely known gnomic saying attributed to many, including rock guru Frank Zappa and eccentric modern jazz pianist-composer-philosopher Thelonious Monk, states the problem succinctly: 'Writing about music is like dancing about architecture'. The best meditation on this issue was written by Orrin Keepnews, for years co-proprietor of Riverside Records, in the 1950s and 1960s the best American jazz reissue company, and a writer of inspired liner notes. In a diatribe aptly called 'A Bad Idea, Poorly Executed ...', Keepnews undercuts the rationale of jazz writers, educators and self-appointed critics:

> *Among the things I am most certain about is that jazz cannot be perceived in any abstract way. I suppose you can enjoy it by simply sitting and letting it wash over you. But to have any chance at understanding it well enough to be qualified to comment on the music, you somehow have to make the effort to get inside. No one can draw you a map, and I don't believe you can achieve it by taking courses. Jazz insists on belief, but just being an adoring fan isn't enough. Experience alone doesn't do it; I'm afraid that in my opinion there are writers who have been at it (and making a living thereby) almost forever without actually understanding it at all.* (in Gottlieb 1060)

The insight and empathy jazz criticism and commentary require are more demanding than many forms of criticism, but because the high-cultural hauteur about jazz and popular culture still lingers, many assume that writing about jazz is a trivial chore for either half-witted hipsters or overstuffed academics – and the prophecy is self-fulfilling.

By a vote of cultural acclamation, Jelly Roll Morton became a central and esteemed figure in jazz history. Reissues made his music readily available to anyone with an interest, academic programmes in teaching jazz techniques and history flourished, and Morton was good for a number of lectures in any introductory course. From the 1960s onward, younger performer-historians such as Bob Greene, James Dapogny and Richard 'Butch' Thompson made records, performed regularly in public, transcribed recorded performances and clarified published scores of Morton's best works. His music was routinely in the basic band books for revival groups from Japan to Australia to Buenos Aires to Britain, France and Italy and every other place with a yen for US culture. Over 50 years of earnest work by revivalists meant that Morton was, by the 1990s, back in approximately the position he had occupied *c*. 1926 – at the centre of a canon of hot jazz and one of its most significant arbiters.

In the twenty-first century, the Internet Age, Morton's name on a major search engine calls up a list of over 841,000 citations on the web (as of April 2007). While his is not a household name, it is one recognized by most listeners to jazz and blues, and his music is available on dozens of CDs. His basic recordings, especially the classic Red Hot Peppers sides, have never been unavailable since the 1940s and show no signs of disappearing, despite innumerable tidal changes in musical culture and taste since Morton's death. Some basic qualities in those pretty little tunes, with their ragtime structure and jazz sensibility, seem ageless. The music's range – from deep blue meditation to red-hot joy – expresses an emotional spectrum genuinely American and still shared by generations born long after Morton's death. His subtle influences in the way that jazz was shaped, transmitted and recreated have left traces, like fingerprints or DNA, on the musical fashions and styles that succeeded him. Likely Morton's shade, up yonder in a place with a Greek name familiar from the street signs of his boyhood New Orleans – Parnassus or Olympus, maybe – is uttering some version of his most famous boast: 'Man, whatever you're listenin' to, it's Jelly Roll style!'

CHAPTER TWELVE

THE LEGACY

■——————■

The lasting influence on American music and culture by Jelly Roll Morton as a composer, leader and, above all, as a solo jazz pianist, is profound and complex. During his lifetime he left a trail of students, disciples and converts to 'Jelly Roll style' piano, many prominent and themselves influential on other pianists. Then he became a keystone in the worldwide jazz revival movement of the 1940s and 1950s, when his music was rediscovered and played in many forms. As his history and legend spread, so did his music, the entire recorded legacy reissued and played, discussed and argued over by new generations and (more importantly) by a vast audience beyond the 'race' market at which his original records were aimed. By the mid-1940s, he was one of a half-dozen major figures always named in the history of jazz, as people then understood it. At a time when many peers in the jazz world were still alive and active, Morton became a golden myth and representative heroic image of early jazz.

What attracted novice hot-music fans to Morton at first was his 'colourful' persona – the Windin' Boy/Jelly Roll figure Morton recreated when he spoke into Lomax's recorders in Coolidge Auditorium in 1938. Then the reality of his music struck people through reissues overseen by the ever-swelling ranks of obsessive record collectors and fans. Buddy Bolden was a dim presence in the story of jazz – no recordings, no documentation, only a single photograph and only words of ancient musicians to flesh out his epic tale. Morton was there – his voice on disc, his music on disc and piano roll, his music republished or found in those heaps of sheet music on sale in junk stores everywhere. He was a figure more alive and three-dimensional in death than he had been in life, and in Morton's case that is saying much. His legend swelled in the retelling, and old-timers in interviews eagerly dredged up racy memories of Morton, real or invented. They pressed forward to say, 'Sure, I played with good old Jelly back in oughty-eight at Tintype Hall!'

Watching the process of Morton's canonization in the 1940s and 1950s was probably like watching Christianity emerge in the first centuries after 33 AD. Disciples and converts popped up everywhere, new bits of doctrine emerged from research; the gospel according to Morton was compiled, winnowed, collated and edited into an agreed Revised Standard Version (complete with credos and prayers), disseminated around the world. And the image and example of Morton became the touchstone for jazz purity, for the truth and efficacy of belief in that old-time authentic New Orleans music, forever and ever, amen!

But to think about his influence on musicians first, we must think how the piano orthodoxy of Morton was transmitted. It came in waves, like a leisurely invasion of America by apostles sharing the Good News of New Orleans Joys:

1. Apostles and Disciples: the First Wave

We have much primary material on Morton as a forceful missionary for his version of piano jazz, the new music he carried on the road with him after he left New Orleans in 1907, which claimed national attention by 1915 along with the publication of 'Original Jelly Roll Blues'. Among musicians who left memories of Morton as a teacher and proselytizer for the new music were Lil Hardin (1898–1971) and Mary Lou Williams (1910–81), who met him and were informal 'students' of his. Neither was permanently shaped by the contact with Morton but both learned and used more than superficial tricks of technique.

Mary Lou Williams, pianist and composer, a sometime protégé of Jelly Roll Morton, and the emdoiment of sheer elagance and joy, at New York City's Cafe Society Downtown, 1949.

Probably the most famous Morton disciple, however, and a tragic figure, was Frank Melrose (1907–41), the youngest Melrose brother and (as in a fairytale or cautionary melodrama), the 'good' brother, as opposed to Walter and Lester, the insatiable rascals who thoroughly fleeced and exploited Morton as publishers and agents. Frank wanted nothing from Morton but his knowledge – how to play the piano with the drive, *joie de vivre* and precision that was intuitive to the Creole. He learned from Morton, absorbed his stomp style and, more importantly, learned to play the deep-down blues. He made only a handful of recordings before he was mysteriously killed on a street after a job in northern Indiana in 1941, but his playing is astonishing for a white player of the day – brooding and urgent, an archaic piano blues that the boogie woogie revival of the 1930s uncovered in dozens of untutored but brilliant pianists, mostly from the Deep South and outside the realm of jazz and blues, as the 1920s had known them.

Morton knew and mentored three pianists working on the West Coast – his brother-in-law Oliver 'Dink' Johnson (1892–1954), a skilful multi-instrumentalist (he played drums with the semi-legendary Original Creole Orchestra in 1913 and recorded in 1921 on clarinet with Kid Ory's Sunshine Orchestra) who left ample recordings of his own highly original music as shaped by Morton; Albert Wesley 'Buster' Wilson (1897–1949), a mainstay of Kid Ory's rebuilt band in the 1940s and 1950s; and Bertha Gonsoulin (dates unknown), who played with King Oliver's Creole Jazz Band during its West Coast stint in the early 1920s. All were distinctive stylists despite the obvious Morton influence, and all had careers in music well after Morton's death, keeping his piano legacy alive and available. Dink Johnson exhibited a boisterous personality rather like Morton's and loved to work as a solo pianist-singer in the bars he ran. Wilson was a superb band pianist, putting a very strong and kinetic drive under the already four-square Ory rhythm section. Gonsoulin, in performances with revival-era New Orleans musicians in California (including revealing duets with Bunk Johnson), showed she had not forgotten either the Master's lessons or the legendary New Orleans beat.

Other pianists of the day heard and absorbed Morton's revolutionary style, and traces appear in the playing of Bob Zurke (1912–44) of Bob Crosby's Bobcats. It also fundamentally shaped Paul Lingle (1902–62), the eccentric and reclusive white West Coast ragtime and blues pianist, who met and learned from Morton in the 1920s. Lingle persistently refused to record, but when he did (for Good Time Jazz in 1952), four of the eight sides released were Morton numbers. Another West Coast revivalist, Burt Bales (1916– 89), was band pianist with Lu Watters' Yerba Buena Jazz Band and with Bob Scobey and Turk Murphy later. His playing was heavily influenced by Morton, as he freely admitted.

Bennie Moten's (1894–1935) work as a pianist, composer and bandleader was shaped by early influences of Morton in the flourishing Midwest of the 'territory' bands (Moten's popular Kansas City band caught the Morton fever and tried to shape itself as a Mortonian big group). Traces of Morton's distinctive style turn up in stride and blues pianists who brushed against him early in cutting contests and jam sessions, such as Willie 'The Lion' Smith and James P. Johnson. Eubie Blake could, if pressed, render accurate versions of Jelly Roll style from memory, a tribute to the impression it made on the stride players.

2. Apostles and Disciples: the Second Wave

When young fans and collectors educated the public (and record companies) about Morton's legacy, a cadre of younger musicians were immediate converts to his style. Most were white and fairly callow converts to this music by African-Americans old enough to have been contemporaries of their fathers or grandfathers. But they made up for wisdom with zeal, learning everything about their heroes and emulating them obsessively.

Among the emergent Morton followers was Don Ewell (1916–83), a brilliant player in the forefront of the emerging jazz revival. He had, by the mid-1940s, learned Morton's style, along with those of Fats Waller, James P. Johnson and other brilliant stride and blues players, and he worked with New Orleans musicians resuscitated by William Russell and others who had encouraged them to return to music. He played with Baby Dodds, Albert Nicholas and others and was pianist with Bunk Johnson's band during its successful New York stand in 1945–46. Ewell went on to influence another generation of players. Unlike Lingle, Ewell was not shy of recording and left a large legacy of accomplished and original playing over four decades – solo, in small Morton-like groups and with revival musicians and younger players' bands.

Other fervent Morton flag-wavers in the decade after his death included Johnny Wittwer, a capable ragtime player, and New Orleanian Armand Hug (1910–77) who was interested in Morton in a scholarly way but also reproduced his keyboard style with accuracy. Another touched by the Morton style was Dick Wellstood (1938–87), who began with Bechet disciple Bob Wilber in a Scarsdale, New York, 'kid band' that was a brief sensation in the late 1940s and went on to a long career as a solo and band pianist. Into the 1950s, more young players of the jazz revival joined the Morton parade, and few pianists working with early jazz were untouched by his example. His vigorous, two-handed approach was especially useful as a model of early jazz band piano style, a glue to hold an ensemble together.

3. Other Influences – the Bigger Picture
Aside from acolytes of the jazz revival intent on absorbing and reproducing Morton's piano style in detail, ever-extending ripples radiated from his example. While the jazz wars of 1940s criticism flared and

waned, Morton was recognized as a pioneer even by committed and avowed Modernists. Charles Mingus (1922–79), a premier modern jazz bassist, composer and bandleader, was fascinated with Morton as a composer and arranger of instrumental colour. In the 1950s, when modern jazz was streaking like a rocket ship into an uncharted future, Mingus turned to Morton and Ellington (for whom he had worked in a brief, stormy period) for models helpful to the 'new' jazz composer.

Mingus heard something in Morton that his contemporaries failed to notice or disdained because it was all 'old stuff' by musicians they presumed to be musically illiterate and 'sloppy' (a favourite slur by conservatory-educated and technically sharp sight-readers). Among Mingus' conscious tributes to early jazzmen were 'Goodbye Pork Pie Hat', a valediction to tenor sax master Lester Young, 'Open Letter to Duke', an Ellington homage, and 'Jelly Roll', a musical allusion to Morton's blues band recordings.

More recently, African-American piano prodigy and self-avowed retriever of ragtime and early jazz and ragtime into the modern idiom Marcus Roberts (b. 1963) has worked with classic ragtime – especially Scott Joplin's – and with early jazz models like Morton and James P. Johnson. His playing and composing strives to fuse idioms and feelings of early jazz with Modernist techniques and harmonies, in the path of work by the individualistic piano genius Thelonious Monk (1917–82), who made a conscious effort to absorb and extend the work of Duke Ellington and to pay homage to earlier music. Roberts' work is very personal, not a direct imitation of Morton, but he repeats and expands the basic musical knowledge that Morton valued and taught. Roberts is the sole major African-American jazz pianist to devote a significant effort to resuscitating Morton's music in today's context.

Morton's influence as a songwriter and cultural legend also influenced musical theatre in the 1980s and 1990s. In contrast to the ignorant and tendentious attack in the Wolfe-Henderson *Jelly's Last Jam* (see Chapter 7), Creole singer-dancer Vernel Bagneris (b. 1949) has made a career of impersonating Morton in revues and speaking, singing and dancing to his music, recreated by the longstanding jazz revival Swedish-American team of clarinettist Orange Kellin and pianist Lars Edegran. They began their musical theatre work in New Orleans with Bagneris in *One Mo' Time* (1979), a highly successful recreation of black music and vaudeville routines from the early twentieth century, featuring veteran singers, dancers and pit musicians (notably elderly trumpet wizard Cladys 'Jabbo' Smith). Bagneris, a writer and actor, has crafted a representation of Morton that is subtle, sensitive and biographically and musically accurate. The most recent incarnation of his show was *Jelly Roll* (1996), an authentic survey of Morton's life and music. Bagneris' work is the sincerest form of flattery and reveals a three-dimensional portrait of the complex man and artist.

In general terms, Morton influenced many contemporaries through his recordings, scores and appearances. With the Gennett piano solos and the first Red Hot Peppers recordings, he demonstrated what jazz on disc could mean. In the first years of jazz recording, the medium was of little import to working musicians. Records were made casually, in mysterious and hectic procedures, and the finished products were used as promotional gimmicks. They sold as advance samples of what the musician or band would provide in live performance. Almost no musician thought of recordings as anything but a means of selling themselves and their work – ephemeral, crude and aesthetically ugly advertising, which somehow made money for record companies, and perhaps for managers or agents, but usually meant only a flat fee – chicken feed – for anyone recording. Royalties were not negotiated or never reached the artists, and few musicians bothered to listen to the records when they were produced.

Morton began to change this attitude. In his usual imperious manner, Morton took charge of recording sessions as peremptorily as he co-opted performances, jam sessions, etc. He had a vision of recordings as a tool for levering himself to national attention and the elusive bigtime. And his sense of craft drove him to record as skillfully as possible. When critic Martin Williams titled an early essay on Morton 'Three-Minute Form' (1959), he made a powerful observation on how Morton learned (and taught) the art of making music to fit the severe limitations of the recording apparatus, using it to full advantage. Because he had such a strong sense of musical architectonics, Morton could shape his little compositions into perfect miniatures, like the exquisite Japanese sash ornaments called *netsuke*, which although small are not fragile but monumental in feeling, residing in a perfect world exactly like our own except for scale.

For Morton, recordings were a vital chance to get things right and leave a document for posterity more persuasive than his scores – an aural picture with the subtle details insusceptible of notation in place. Alone in major 1920s jazz figures, Morton treasured the idea that he was a 'recording artist' in the illustrious Victor Talking Machine Co.'s catalogue. The idea of 'race' records seems not to have discomfited him as narrow or exclusionary, and he may have expunged it from his consciousness. Like much else in the America of his lifetime that was troubling, threatening or limiting in the overbearing culture of segregation and discrimination, Morton ignored imputed barriers to his activities and success. If no one physically stopped him, he sat in with the NORK, used Volly de Faut on records and otherwise worked as if both colour-blind and deaf to the incessant shouts and rage of institutional racism around him. His preference for managing or working in black-and-tan clubs seems to grow from the same impulse to find an unsegregated audience or medium.

4. Morton and the Jazz Revival

One of the saddest ironies in a life shaped by sad ironies was that Ferd Morton died on the eve of a huge renaissance of music he had created and promoted for nearly 40 years. The stirrings of a revival of older jazz began amidst the Depression that put most of musicians out of work – there is the initial irony. Bands like Bob Crosby's Bobcats in the late 1930s self-consciously turned to the immediate past for inspiration, looking as much to African-American as white jazz models for their materials, especially music from the Oliver-Armstrong songbook. At the same time, budding jazz critics, historians and record collectors entered the scene. Hugues Panassie, an energetic French commentator, wrote several books (generally inaccurate, since he got his material second- or third-hand and at transatlantic distance), including the well-known *Le Jazz Hot*, and came to the US in 1938 at invitation from Victor Records to round up and record jazz heroes, including Sidney Bechet, Mezz Mezzrow and Tommy Ladnier.

Musicians like the respected Chicago cornettist Muggsy Spanier made self-conscious attempts to revive music played in the 1920s. Spanier formed a highly praised 'Ragtime Band' in 1939 but could not sustain it, for economic reasons. Decca Records, which weathered the slump by selling popular records at reduced prices, in 1940 began putting out music from 1920s jazz stars such as Armstrong and Bechet, brought to the studio to recapitulate their early styles. Columbia Records commissioned an eager college student and jazz buff, George Avakian, to reissue in album in 1941 from Armstrong's greatest OKeh work of the 1920s (Columbia acquired OKeh and its catalogue when General Phonograph Co. folded just before the Depression), initiating the whole tide of jazz reissues by major labels.

Stirring under and behind these trends were young white musicians who had tired of big band work and scuffling on the fringes of the swing craze. They started listening to old records, imagining playing in the styles of their heroes – Armstrong, Oliver, Morton and other giants. Again, the irony is that many musicians they viewed as semi-mythical were still alive, some still in music, others riding out the Depression in any way they could. Joe Oliver died destitute in Savannah in 1938 and Morton in Los Angeles in 1941. Johnny Dodds succumbed to general wear and high blood pressure in 1940. Others were alive and kicking – Armstrong at the peak of his career in many ways, Bechet plotting yet another comeback, others scattered across the US like refugees from an apocalyptic battle.

When trumpeter Lu Watters and a group of like-minded friends in San Francisco assembled what they eventually called the Yerba Buena Jazz Band in the late 1930s, they aimed to call the country's attention to a jazz heritage submerged by the big band era and the dominance of swing as the jazz-pop music of the decade. Six months after Jelly Roll Morton

The youngsters of Lu Watters' Yerba Buena Jazz Band launching a worldwide jazz counter-revolution in the 1940s. L–R: Turk Murphy, Bill Dart, Lu Watters, Bob Scobey, Wallie Rose, Bob Helm.

died in Los Angeles, the novice jazz band recorded in San Francisco, releasing a series of records that were both homages and reworkings of original music from the dawn of jazz. Their first discs included Morton's 'London Café Blues' and 'Milenberg Joys'. Who knows if he would have been pleased by how they were played, but it might have lifted Morton's heart to know that his music rolled on into the future, as he had predicted.

The jazz revival was spurred when enthusiasts discovered and rehabilitated New Orleans jazz pioneers such as William Geary 'Bunk' Johnson (1879–149), Edward 'Kid' Ory (1886–1973), his trumpet sidekick Thomas 'Papa Mutt' Carey (1881–1948), ace clarinettist Jimmie Noone (1895–1944) and others, some on the West Coast and looming large in Morton's last dreams of self-rehabilitation in 1941. What he had tried to start was underway, mostly via the medium of phonograph records made in America and shipped around the world. Young musicians in Britain (Humphrey Lyttelton and many others), France (Claude Luter and Co.), even down in Australia (Graeme Bell, his brother Roger and others) assembled bands, recorded, and carried the banners of the old African-American music everywhere. Within decades there was even a powerful Revivalist band, La Portena, in Buenos Aires, playing Morton's music with an ingrained 'Latin tinge'. The astonishing international phenomenon gathered headway in the 1940s, extended through the 1950s and 1960s, and is alive and thriving in variant shapes and avatars in the twenty-first century.

In all versions of the jazz revival, Morton's music was central. His piano and band numbers were rearranged and translated for musicians of widely varying skills and taste. What was obvious was how sturdy, adaptable and undated his music remained. The beautiful melody lines, harmonies and structures proved timeless and indestructible. In the early 1950s, West Coast Revivalist trombonist Turk Murphy (literally Lu Watters' right-hand man) formed a band and recorded Morton's instrumental classics in rather literal arrangements. Issued as an LP by Columbia, they created controversy, when modern jazz musicians and commentators reviled them as retrograde and primitive renderings of jazz classics, and a diversion from the enterprise of modern jazz as a developing avant-garde music. The Mouldy Figs vs. Modernists civil wars of the mid-1940s threatened to reignite.

Other Revivalist bands went on to revisit Morton's music, and younger pianists such as Bob Greene, James Dapogny, Morten Gunnar Larsen and Richard 'Butch' Thompson became known as Morton specialists through convincing recreations of the Morton piano library. They and others researched the music and unearthed scores and materials (including close transcriptions from recordings) better than the often oversimplified, garbled sheet music published long ago by the Melrose brothers.

Thompson has toured widely over the past 40 years, played regularly on national radio and issued many CDs of Morton performances marked by their adherence to Morton's style and sensibility and by free and fitting improvisations within that frame. The Norwegian pianist Morten Gunnar Larsen has been a staunch advocate of Morton's style and a recreator of rags and ragtime songs, at the keyboard and with a skilled orchestra. Greene in 1974 assembled, toured with and recorded a modern version of the Red Hot Peppers of 1926–27, successfully recreating their challenging arrangements after nearly 50 years. In 1982 Dapogny researched and published a definitive collection of Morton's piano scores, with clear and useful notes throughout, making Morton's music as available to amateur players as republished editions of ragtime printed since the 1970s.

The ragtime revival of the early 1970s, sparked by the hit Paul Newman-Robert Redford movie *The Sting*, its soundtrack score and recordings of ragtime piano and orchestra scores by academy-trained musicians, such as pianists Joshua Rifkin and William Bolcom and the New England Conservatory ragtime ensemble helmed by composer-educator Gunther Schuller, at first adhered to the classic ragtime published and championed by John S. Stark by Scott Joplin, James Scott, Joseph Lamb and a number of others. But in the decades after the revival began, players and listeners moved to other versions of ragtime and other African-American-inflected piano music – piano blues, stride, the honky tonk and barrelhouse styles usually lumped together as 'boogie woogie' since the mid-1930s, and to premier jazz piano stylists such as Jelly Roll Morton, Earl Hines, Fats Waller, James P. Johnson and their legions of descendants.

While his name was never the household word Joplin's became (the ragtime revival was misidentified with Joplin, as if he alone embodied the world of ragtime), Morton became known to a wider audience. Listeners who a decade before would have recoiled at the name 'Jelly Roll' Anybody seemed unfazed by the oddness of the elder African-American guys and probably thought the moniker had something to do with the 'bakery shop', as Morton once explained. His music was transcribed for bands, wind chamber groups, string quartets – any combination of instruments, domestic or exotic. Again, he might have been delighted that his music is so easily translatable and pliable to treatment. Like Mozart's music, it is inherently tough as well as tender, and it retains its core identity no matter how thoroughly you abuse it and alter its superficial shape.

The long-term legacy of Morton's music was as an example of brilliant form and structure, along with Duke Ellington's and music by a few other influential composer-arranger-leaders from early jazz. While the example of ragtime as a composed and notated music was in the background of jazz, it was countered by another stream in the music – the current of improvisation, casual invention and spontaneous utterance. Playing the blues meant using only the slenderest skeleton of chord progressions and plunging into the unknown, discovering melodic or lyrical lines as they came up. Morton first, then Ellington and others saw that by fusing the elegance of ragtime form, with its multiple strains repeated in conventional order, and adding the looseness of blues improvisation, a new world of music opened.

A dilemma that emerged early in the 1920s, as big dance bands took shape and arranging for them became standardized, was how to include score-reading and improvised passages in a seamless whole. Ellington's solution was to create a 'laboratory' band whose personnel was fixed, to use the individual characteristics of musicians in his compositions and scores, and rather literally to 'build in' the idiosyncratic styles of his soloists. It was a beautiful and ingenious 'repertory band' process but one hardly applicable to average jazz or dance bands, whose personnel shifted constantly. Morton's solution was different: he used a mix of stock arrangements, special scoring and 'head' passages for solos and some ensembles, so that his pieces were glued together by written scores, often using a ragtime-like format, but fuelled by the energy of spontaneous improvisation and his own brilliant example.

The Ellington and Morton approaches are more similar than they appear, and despite the mutual animosity they held for each other, the two men were enormously talented creators with similar musical profiles. In a perfect world, they would have recognized and acknowledged this. It is intriguing to imagine a Morton-Ellington collaboration (Morton did use Ellington trumpet sidemen Bubber Miley and Freddie Jenkins on recording dates in 1929–30), as far-fetched as the idea might seem. Morton's last, unplayed experimental big band scores (especially 'Gan-Jam') show him on a Modernist track that would have fascinated Ellington, with his sharp ear for exotic tone colours and textures, and his sense of monumental scale.

The heritage of Morton's mid-1920s work seems swamped by the onset of swing in the next decade, and Ellington strove to keep his work abreast (more often ahead) of such trends. But even Ellington was regarded as quaint or slightly out of step by emergent Modernists of the late 1930s and early 1940s. He diligently rescored and revised earlier masterworks, and he wrote a catalogue of major swing tunes, many becoming standard pop vocal numbers. Morton's plunge off the stage at the depth of the Depression kept him from similar work, except in the quiet of his study. But his shadow loomed behind the big swing parade – 'King Porter Stomp' was the decade's anthem, and unacknowledged Morton passages (as he often protested) appeared everywhere, in the call-and-response riffs of the big bands, in simple riff tunes such as 'Flat Foot Floogie', in revivals of other Morton tunes – Bunny Berigan recorded the ubiquitous 'King Porter Stomp' in 1935 [with Gene Gifford's Orchestra] and an elegant version of 'Jelly Roll Blues' in 1937 – and in the process of arranging and scoring which was standard operating procedure for swing bands.

By tracing over the decades the many recorded versions of Morton's best-known single work, 'King Porter Stomp', a mini-history of jazz could be compiled. Morton recorded a definitive solo piano version of the number in 1926 for Vocalion, after he had cut a brilliant piano roll for Vocalstyle in 1923 and a duet with Joe Oliver's cornet for the obscure Autograph label in 1924. He then revisited the number for a powerful rendition on the 1938 Library of Congress discs, brilliantly recapitulated for the General Records 'New Orleans Memories' album in 1939. But this Morton composition is remembered for the many big band versions of the Swing Era (and later) and became a favourite with musicians and dancers because of its inherent orchestral qualities – its call-and-response figures, strong dance rhythms and interlocking riffs that seem to predict and define the whole footloose swing phenomenon in just three and a half minutes of manic energy.

Fletcher Henderson arranged Morton's tune and recorded it in 1928, and Goodman bought and adapted this arrangement when he assembled his prototypical swing band in 1934–35. It became a standard in every aspiring swing band's basic book and persisted as a tune especially congenial to improvisation. Something in the shape of its three ragtime-like strains and its simple melodies made 'King Porter Stomp' a durable classic.

It was recorded by Glenn Miller's wildly successful swing dance band in the middle of its career. Claude Hopkins, an archetypal black big band leader working the great New York dance halls, recorded it in 1934. The eccentric Modernist Sun Ra recorded it with his Arkestra in 1977. As late as the 1980s, avant-garde composer-arranger Gil Evans could score 'King Porter Stomp' for a big band with electronic passages and conga drums to ram home the 'Spanish tinge' elements. Perhaps Morton was right in the 1930s to anguish so much over all the unpaid royalties from this one indelible composition.

In the late 1920s Morton had tried to organize and maintain a big band, to exploit resources basic in swing. He was unable to cope with the logistics and economics of the process. Ellington had Owney Madden (the mob-connected boss of the Cotton Club) backing him, who gave him the breathing space and the showcase to see how big band scoring worked, how it could be expanded and contracted, how it could be commercially viable and still musically satisfying. Morton's best shots were a few days in recording studios with bands picked up and organized on the spur of the moment. But both men moved on the same trajectory from classic small-band jazz toward a more formalized, larger version of the music. Scores and recordings they made were trail markers for hordes of jazz and pop musicians in the next decade.

When Morton repeated the apparently outrageous notion that he 'invented' jazz, at least some of his idea referred to organizing and arranging a music he found in chaos, existing only in the memories and ideas of musicians (it is what 'traditional' means in the phrase 'traditional jazz', a music passed on by remembered idioms and conventions, the musical equivalent of oral literature), and he tried to notate it, preserve it, connect it and regularize it. His penchant for inventing dance names – 'hunch', 'bump', etc. – is part of this urge, as if he asked himself, 'What is this piece of music *for?*' With his acute sensitivity to rhythm and rhythmic nuances, he categorized musical structures in fine detail (as did Ellington, with dance names such as 'toodle-oo' [todalo] or 'mooche' or 'wobble' filling the same function).

The drive toward formal structure worked for Morton and helped to establish conventions for later jazz. Like ragtime pianists, he held compositions in his memory because they had a memorable form, and he repeated them more or less verbatim. He then notated these compositions when they were complete or polished. This movement from improvisation to notation is a very old one for keyboard composers, and it works very well for virtuosic players (as Handel, Bach, Mozart, Beethoven, etc. showed) who invent as they play and pause to preserve the best of their inventions. The process describes the history of ragtime concisely, which moved from improvised to composed to notated to published to sight-read music in a generation or so. It also describes the particular current of jazz that Morton followed (or, in his terms, 'invented') and that became the mainstream of the music after 1930.

Other musicians such as Louis Armstrong or Sidney Bechet followed another path, that of the improvising virtuoso, undertaking only incidental composing or arranging. Morton, for whatever psychological or emotional reason, needed to organize and preserve his music – on paper, on punched piano rolls, on shellac discs, by whatever medium was accessible. For several decades he developed, polished and deepened his work, returning to music he had begun very early in his career, putting it on piano rolls, then on records as piano solos, then arranging it for band and recording in this format. He never tired of reinventing his music and putting it into new contexts. It is a textbook pattern for a certain kind of jazz genius, which recurs over the history of the music, from Morton and Ellington through Thelonious Monk and Bill Evans to other Moderns. Morton's music is not all of jazz, but it may be the deepest current that still impels the music.

CHRONOLOGY

c. 1890. Born in New Orleans, Louisiana; christened Ferdinand Joseph Lamothe (later adding Mouton [or Morton]).

Lives in Frenchman Street home with mother Louise Monette and father Ed Lamothe, who soon exits. Louise then marries Willie Mouton, a porter. Half-sisters Amedie Eugenie and Frances born in next few years. Is brought up also by Uncle August, Aunt Elena and godmother voodoo queen Eulalie Hecaud/Laura Hunter.

1900–05. Works at a cooperage; begins learning piano both formally (with Professor Nickerson, well-known teacher) and informally from blues pianists and ticklers from The District. At odds with older generation in his family, he leaves home, travels to Gulf Coast, visits Bessie Johnson (a.k.a. Anita Gonzales) in Biloxi, returns to New Orleans to stay with godmother Eulalie Hecaud.

1905–09. Begins itinerant touring with small vaudeville or tent shows, as a bar and bordello pianist (and probably as a pimp) across Gulf Coast. Known in New Orleans as 'Windin' Boy', he now becomes 'Jelly Roll'. Travels to Chicago and (possibly) New York.

c. 1909. Enters vaudeville circuit with Morton & Morton, the Jelly Rolls, playing the Gulf Coast and Southwest. Encounters Spike brothers in Oklahoma *c*. 1912. By 1914, Morton & Morton crossing the Midwest.

1914. Goes to Chicago, working Elite No. 2 nightclub. Sells 'Original Jelly Roll Blues' to Rossiter Music, published in 1915 as both piano and band score; is a big hit nationwide. Stays around Chicago until 1917, then leaves for the West Coast. In Los Angeles, hooks up with Spike brothers again, operates bands, meets Anita Gonzales, works with her on cabarets, runs 'West Coast Line' of girls in off seasons.

1919. Travels to San Francisco to run The Jupiter, fails and follows Gonzales north to Tacoma and Seattle. Goes to Wyoming and Colorado, returns to Los Angeles in 1921, fronts bands, reunites with Gonzales. In 1922 works in Tia

Juana, Mexico, writing 'The Pearls' and 'Kansas City Stomp' during the gig. Works with Spike brothers on their new publishing business.

1923. Returns to Chicago, meets Melrose brothers, travels to Richmond, Indiana, and records for Gennett with the New Orleans Rhythm Kings and on a series of piano solos – all the music he has written in the past decade of rambling. Goes to Cincinnati and cuts 13 piano rolls of his piano solos for the Vocalstyle Piano Roll Company. Continues to set up small recording dates – solo and with pickup bands – and works with bands around Chicago. Melrose brothers publish many Morton piano scores.

September 1926. Begins recording for Victor with his Red Hot Peppers band. Second series of Red Hot Peppers discs recorded in 1927. In 1928, records for Vocalion, Gennett and Columbia with assorted pickup groups. Meets Mabel Bertrand and marries her in Gary, Indiana, in November 1928.

1928. Goes to New York, begins recording with a new version of the Red Hot Peppers for Victor in summer. Records solos, various small-band and big-band numbers for Victor in late 1928 and 1929. Returns to Red Hot Peppers format in 1930, ends Victor recording stint.

1934. Jobs in New York; makes semi-anonymous recordings with Wingy Manone. Endures the Depression through pickup jobs; ends up in Washington, D.C., back at the game of pianist-manager-bouncer in a rough dive called The Jungle Inn.

1938. Meets Alan Lomax, records musical autobiography through summer. Is contacted by Roy Carew, who had heard Morton play in The District as early as 1904. Carew helps Morton set up Tempo Music Publishing Co. to manage his assets. Morton embroiled in W. C. Handy controversy, regains some national attention, goes to New York in late 1938.

1939–40. Records piano solo and band albums for Victor and for General Records. Ill from wounds inflicted during a fracas at The Jungle Inn, Morton decides to return to the West Coast (and Anita Gonzales), while Mabel stays in New York. Makes the trip west in early winter with his two big cars, losing one in a mountain blizzard. Ill in Los Angeles, he tries to organize a band to play his new arrangements, but succumbs to congestive heart failure, dying on 10 July 1941.

DISCOGRAPHY
JELLY ROLL MORTON REISSUES ON CD

Because CDs go in and out of print frequently, consult the Internet or other recent discographical data for availability of these suggested recordings.

Birth of the Hot, RCA Records 63899
Fifteen of the major Red Hot Peppers recordings from the mid-1920s with a few other later sides.

Chicago Years, Louisiana Red Hot Records 623
Twenty major sides from the 1926–28 Red Hot Peppers sessions.

Complete 1926–30 Recordings, JSP Records 903
The best reissue (on 5 CDs) of the Morton band and solo piano recordings, with copious notes and commentary. Brilliant digital-transfer sound.

Complete New Orleans Rhythm Kings, (1922–25). Challenge Records 79031
All the early records by the NORK, including those featuring Morton at the piano. On two CDs.

Complete Victor Recordings, RCA/Bluebird 2361
The complete recordings on Victor, 1926–39, band and piano (5 CDs). Sound sometimes inferior to the JPS set. Extensive notes.

Doctor Jazz, ASV Records 5125
A large (25-track) sample across Morton's recording career, from the Gennett piano solos of 1923 to the General piano solo and band sides of 1940.

Jelly Roll Morton, 1939–40, Chronological Classics 668
The General Records piano and band recordings: the last sessions Morton completed before his death.

Jelly Roll Morton, 1923–24, Milestone Records 69449
A comprehensive collection of the early piano solo recordings (and some band titles) that prepared Morton for his later career. See also the piano roll numbers below.

New Orleans Rhythm Kings, 1922–23, Chronological Classics 1129
Many NORK sides, including all those featuring Morton at the piano.

New Orleans Rhythm Kings with Jelly Roll Morton, Milestone Records 47020
A basic collection of early NORK sides, including all with Morton.

Piano Rolls, Nonesuch Records 79363
Twelve restored rolls (cut in 1924) played and recorded with modern techniques to give lifelike sound. Should be compared with the solo piano records.

Pearls, The, RCA Records 8588
Another sampler, mostly from the Red Hot Peppers' Chicago and New York sessions but with a few 1939 tracks added.

BIBLIOGRAPHY

Asbury, H., *The Barbary Coast*, New York: Knopf, 1933

Blesh, R., *Shining Trumpets*, New York: Knopf, 1946

Blesh, R. & Janis H., *They All Played Ragtime*, New York: Oak Publications, 1971

Borneman, E., 'The Jazz Cult', Part I, *Harper's*, February 1947, 141–47; Part II, *Harper's*, March 1947, 261–73

Carter, W., *Preservation Hall*, New York: W. W. Norton, 1991

Charters, S. B. & Kunstadt, L., *Jazz: A History of the New York Scene*, New York: Da Capo, 1981

Dapogny, J., *Ferdinand 'Jelly Roll' Morton, The Collected Piano Music*, Washington, D.C.: Smithsonian Institution Press, 1982

Davis, J. & Gray Clarke, G. F., 'Eldorado – An Informal History of the Gennett Co.', *Jazz Forum*, V, Autumn 1947, pp. 1–10

Ellison, R., *Invisible Man*, New York: Vintage, 1990

Foreman. R.C., Jr., 'Jazz and Race Records. 1920–32', Ph.D. dissertation, University of Illinois, 1968

Gelatt, R., *The Fabulous Phonograph*, Philadelphia: Lippincott, 1955

Gottlieb, R., ed., *Reading Jazz*, New York: Pantheon, 1996

Gracyk, T. & Hoffman, F., *Popular American Recording Pioneers 1895–1925*, New York: Haworth, 2000

Hearn, L., *Inventing New Orleans*, ed. Starr, F. S., Jackson, Miss.: University Press of Mississippi, 2001

Hodes, A. & Hansen, C., eds., *Selections from the Gutter*, Berkeley, CA.: University of California Press, 1977

Jasen, D. A. & Jones, G., *Black Bottom Stomp*, New York: Routledge, 2002

Jewell, D., *Duke: A Portrait of Duke Ellington*, New York: Norton, 1977

Kay, G. W., 'Those Fabulous Gennetts!' rpt., *Record Changer*, June 1953

Kennedy, R., *Jelly Roll, Bix, and Hoagy*, Bloomington, Ind.: Indiana University Press, 1994

Kenney, W. H., *Chicago Jazz: A Cultural History, 1904–1930*, New York: Oxford University Press, 1993

Levin, F., *Classic Jazz*, Berkeley, CA.: University of California Press, 2000

Lomax, A., *Mister Jelly Roll*, New York: Duell, Sloan and Pearce, 1950

Lomax, J. A., *Adventures of a Ballad Hunter*, New York: Macmillan, 1947

Marquis, D. M., *In Search of Buddy Bolden, First Man of Jazz*, Baton Rouge: Louisiana State University Press, 1978

Miller, P. E., ed., *Esquire's 1944 Jazz Book*, New York: Da Capo, 1971

Miller, P. E., ed., *Esquire's 1945 Jazz Book*, New York: Da Capo, 1971

Miller, P. E., ed., *Esquire's 1946 Jazz Book*, New York: Da Capo, 1971

Monrovia Sound Studio, 'Ferd 'Jelly Roll' Morton, 1890–1941.' www.doctorjazz.freeserve.co.uk.

Murray, A., *The Omni-Americans*, New York: Avon Books, 1970

Pastras, P., *Dead Man Blues – Jelly Roll Morton Way Out West*. Berkley, CA.: University of California Press, 2001

Reich, H. & Gaines, W., *Jelly's Blues*, New York: Da Capo, 2003

Reid, O., and Welch, W. L., *From Tin Foil to Stereo*, Indianapolis: Sams, 1977

Rose, A., *Storyville, New Orleans*, University, Ala.: University of Alabama Press, 1974

Rose, A. & Souchon, E.,. *New Orleans Jazz: A Family Album*, Baton Rouge: Louisiana State University Press, 1967

Russell, W., '*Oh, Mr. Jelly*', Copenhagen: JazzMedia, 1999

Shapiro, N. & Hentoff, N., *Hear Me Talkin' to Ya*, New York: Dover, 1955

Stoddard, T., *Pops Foster*, Berkeley, CA.: University of California Press, 1971

Wright, L., *Mr. Jelly Lord*, Chigwell, Essex: Storyville, 1980

Williams, M., *The Art of Jazz*, New York: Oxford University Press, 1971

Williams, M., *The Jazz Tradition*, New York: New American Library, 1971

INDEX